PAUL SAMUELSON
Massachusetts Institute of Technology

THE SAMUELSON SAMPLER

THOMAS HORTON AND COMPANY
Glen Ridge, New Jersey

Organization and Unity material for Chapters III, VIII and XIV by Portia D Carmichael, Plainfield, New Jersey

Unity Material for Chapters I, II, IV, V, VI, VII, IX, X, XI, XIII, XV and XVI by Rey
Roulston, Fort Lauderdale, Florida

Library of Congress Cataloging Data
Samuelson, Paul Anthony, 1915–
The Samuelson sampler.
CONTENTS: Economic policy.—Fiscal policy and taxation.—Inflation: the evolving
solutions.—
International trade and finance. [etc.]
   1.   United States—Economic conditions—1961–
—Addresses, essays, lectures.   2.   United States—
Economic policy—1971–   —Addresses, essays,
lectures.   3.   Economics—Addresses, essays, lectures.
I.   Title.
HC106.6.S17 GL 300′.8   73-6739

Manufactured in the United States of America

Published by Thomas Horton and Company, 22 Appleton Place, Glen
Ridge, New Jersey 07028

15   14   13   12   11   10   9   8   7   6   5   4   3   2   1

CONTENTS

Chapter Eight SOME REFLECTIONS ON EQUITY   145

Chapter Nine ANY ROOM FOR LOVE?   157

Chapter Ten A LOOK BACK, A LOOK AHEAD, A LOOK AROUND   162

**Chapter Eleven THE ECONOMICS OF POLITICS/THE POLITICS OF   183
ECONOMICS**

PREFACE

When Thomas Horton proposed to publish companion volumes containing the economic columns of Professor Milton Friedman and of mine, I had to agree that this might serve a useful educational purpose. Professor Friedman is an able scholar and a forceful spokesman for the libertarian form of conservative economics. He is also an old friend. Yet my liberal mind is not persuaded by a considerable number of conservative arguments. And I had to agree that learners of economics of all political leanings—right, center, left and new left—might be expected to get a better-rounded view of the debate if exposed to more than one of its sides.

Still, I hesitated to agree to this publication. These analyses of the passing economic scene were *deliberately* written so as not to present a debater's view. Conversion of the reader was farthest from my mind. Instead of trying to press reality into the distorting confines of simple sermons, I wanted to bring out the interesting variety of economic problems.

I've never believed in Economics in One Lesson. And that is why I hesitated. But in the end I acquiesced. With this proviso—no afterthoughts, no prettying up forecasts after the fact, no tampering with commas. Indeed, the publisher agreed to take full responsibility in choosing which of my many contemporary writings to include in the present volume. I take responsibility for the birth of these brain children, but not for their reincarnation in present form.

Economics used to be a dry subject that told you what you couldn't do. From a scholar's viewpoint that was never very good political economy in the first place. Readers of this generation are luckier than we used to be in my time. *You* can go beyond the quantity of economic life to its quality—beyond Gross National

Product to Net Economic Welfare. You can examine unflinchingly the flaws in the system as well as its merits. You can discover where conventional wisdoms need to be junked and, best of all, where new research can add to our knowledge.

I hope these writings add to your interest and enjoyment in political economy.

Paul A. Samuelson
Massachusetts Institute of Technology
March 1973

INTRODUCTORY REMARKS

Casting this series of columns into meaningful chapters was truly engaging. The range of economic, social and political issues with which they deal is broad. Yet, the quality of treatment of each issue gave me a profound respect for Paul A. Samuelson. The experience was further enriched by my writing introductions to three of the chapters. My husband, Bill, provided poignant suggestions, and I express my gratitude to him.

Portia D. Carmichael
Plainfield, New Jersey

I first encountered Professor Paul Samuelson's introductory economics textbook, published by McGraw-Hill, while a student at the University of Minnesota. This was the second edition, of 1951. The first version from which I taught was the 1955 third edition, at the University of Minnesota Duluth. Now involved in a teaching experience with the ninth edition, I can cheerfully admit to moderate seniority in the Paul Samuelson fan club. He is always a pleasure to read and re-read.

Samuelson never lets you down. No matter what the topic, he is in continuous spirited communication with the reader. This is certainly true of the selections presented here.

It is indeed a pleasure and privilege to have participated in this book. I am grateful to Professor Samuelson and publisher Thomas Horton for the opportunity, although I hasten to absolve them of responsibility for the result. I can only hope that I have come through in the spirit intended, and have not gotten in the way too much.

Reyburn R. Roulston
Fort Lauderdale, Florida

Chapter 1

ECONOMIC POLICY

This challenging, sometimes frustrating, but always fascinating area of economic policy can also be rather satisfying on occasion, or when viewed in the perspective of a longer period. The selections that follow certainly bring out these four aspects of economic policy, and include the enjoyable experience of seeing the "proper" policy in action and working as it should.

It is perhaps good to begin on a positive note, and the first reading does just that. There has to be assurance to an otherwise fearful or skeptical reader, in having the ominous Marxian predictions of capitalistic doom properly appraised, or noting that the spectre of a repetition of the depression of the 1930s has been reduced to a negligible probability.

Experience has shown that managed macroeconomics, better known as "the new economics," can accomplish much in reconciling the conflicting goals of a modern, mixed economy. When the twentieth birthday of the Employment Act of 1946 was observed at a Washington gathering, it was not a gloomy wake but a time of moderate rejoicing.

But experience has also demonstrated the significance of the modifier "managed" in front of macroeconomics. This is indicated by the final selection of this chapter, "Economic Policy is an Art." Here it is said that this art consists of "proper priorities and quantitative dosages," referring to proper priorities with respect to economic goals and the correct dosage of specific policy tools.

Blending brevity with clarity, the observations made on the practice of the art indicate the extensive nature of the goals toward which economic policy might be directed. These range from the ever-present dilemma of the full employment versus price stability trade-off to the "battle for men's minds" in the emerging and uncommitted nations. They are impressed by performance, and we want good marks on the scorecard they are keeping. Policy goals can also range from meeting an immediate challenge at home, such as reallocating economic resources after our withdrawal from Vietnam, to seeking the greater global efficiency and total welfare promised by unrestricted trade among nations. The challenge faced by the Nixon Administration is pointed up in these terms, and their performance in the fine art of economic policy is evaluated.

Between the first and the last, the readings deal with both specific developments and general aspects of economic policy. Where it has been suggested that it is a fascinating subject, no comment could improve upon the ability of the selections themselves to convey this spirit.

If it is argued that economic policy can also be frustrating, there is ample testimony here to prove the point. Economic events do not have to follow the specific paths charted for them by even a strong consensus of the economics fraternity. Nor are they forced to adhere to the results anticipated by a specific group of policy-makers. This can be, and most often is, the result of "other things not staying equal." But a significantly different outcome than that predicted can also be due to inadequacies of analysis or, in some instances, of the policy tools themselves. To be honest with itself, economics must chalk all of them up as failures or mistakes. There is no lack of such acknowledgement in this chapter, even though the selection "Lessons of the 1960s" suggests that we have more to be proud of than to apologize for.

Policy actions that do not produce the desired results every time can be remedied by a change of policy. More frustrating than this is to observe disastrous developments that result from economic policy being administered by those hostile to, or neglectful of, the best distilled wisdom of economic analysis.

Any administration has access to the tools provided by modern macroeconomic analysis. In less sympathetic hands, if not less skillful ones, their potential for the accomplishment of good deeds might not be realized. Some notes of such concern are sounded in readings two and three, relative to the Presidential election of 1968. But the following article, on "The New Economics," indicates that the shotgun-like pervasiveness of this body of knowledge can, in general, overwhelm a variety of single-minded rifle-shot theories and objectives. Apparently the New Economics is an idea whose time has come and is here to stay.

The recent past has not been without its dismal moments, and we find here both analysis and policy recommendations as the economy headed toward the 1970 downturn in real output. See "Recession Fears," "Bleak Outlook," and "Fighting Recession."

The practice of economic policy is peopled with lively and interesting personalities. This is suggested in more than one place in the readings of this chapter, and this book, and is found in the selection titled "Bill Martin."

A generation of American economists has grown up while William McChesney Martin, Jr. served as Chairman of the Board of Governors of the Federal Reserve System. A third and older group retired with him. Another generation, in the middle and perhaps more influential, experienced the pangs and pleasures of working most actively with him. To all of them, "William McChesney Martin, Jr." was as much a household expression as "guns and butter," "marginal cost equals marginal revenue," or "equilibrium at full employment." All would join in the sprit of this selection, which not only salutes him on his retirement but also provides some broad perspective on twenty years of monetary policy.

REQUIEM FOR A SCOURGE
October, 1966

There is a specter that haunts Marxian economics—the fear that capitalism can after all be made to work by the methods of the new economics.

Were all those years Karl Marx spent proving that capitalism would end in a great slump years spent in vain? Was that 1917 trip by Lenin to Russia in a sealed freight car really necessary, if capitalism turns out *not* to be dependent upon imperialistic ventures and wars?

I used to count us somewhat fortunate that Marxian economics is indeed the opiate of the Marxists. For if what Oscar Wilde said be true—"These days to be understood is to be found out"—the blinders of the Marxian concepts of "surplus value" and "immiserization of the worker" helped keep our secrets safe from the Russian experts.

But even dope is subject to the law of diminishing returns. The realization is spreading, beyond the Urals but not yet to China, that Sewell Avery of Montgomery Ward might have been dead wrong about the inevitability of a postwar slump.

DIALOGUE IN MOSCOW

To illustrate the way we live now, let me recount an incident. Prof. Franklyn Holzman of Tufts University, an expert on the theory of inflation, had learned Russian in the Army. When talking to some important economists in Moscow during a fellowship tour, he found that they insisted on talking English. It was during the second Eisenhower recession, and Russian experts were gloating over our mounting unemployment.

"How will America solve the problem of technological unemployment due to automation?" they chided him. "Or solve the unemployment that will come when the cold war ends? Or prevent a slump as affluent people oversave?"

Nixon is not the only one who can debate Russians in the kitchen. Holzman, drawing a check on a not-yet-established line of credit, namely the activist Kennedy-Johnson administrations, replied bravely:

"We will spend public funds to rebuild our cities, schools and roads. We will increase social-security payments. We will spend to purify our rivers and skies. And if that's not enough, we will cut tax rates."

Like any Chamber of Commerce vice president, one Russian said: "But all that would cost billions. Your budget could never stand it."

"So much the worse for the budget. If we have to have an antideflationary deficit, we'll have it," said Holzman.

Perplexed, the Russian said, "What are you? A Keynesian or something?"

Jokingly, Holzman retorted in the immortal words, "We're all Keynesians now."

And at this point, the Russians, forgetting their guest's linguistic accomplishments, muttered to themselves: «... в том смысле, что мы все марксисты.» ("Da, they are all Keynesians the way we are all Marxists.")

THE SIMPLE TRUTH

Who is right? Wishing aside, are we in a New Era? Is depression, like polio and the passenger pigeon, extinct? Has the new economics

banned recession in favor of perpetual boom? For brevity I must be
dogmatic.

1. *Great depressions*—cumulative slumps that feed on themselves,
such as our system suffered in the 1930s, 1890s and 1830s—*are indeed
extinct.*

Nothing is impossible in an inexact science like economics. Still,
when a probability becomes negligible, the prudent man should ignore it.

2. *Some recessions we shall probably still have with us, but with much
reduced frequency and virulence.*

The mixed economy of Germany has not had a true recession in
twenty years. Neither has Sweden. What is now called a setback in
Japan, Italy or France would have been thought very heavenly in 1939.
America's postwar record beats anything in capitalism's history.

Whom the gods would destroy they first made mad. Is this more
New Era malarky, 1929 vintage? Here is why I think not.

The big change is democracy. If printing bits of green can save
banks and business from ruin, modern governments *have the power* to
act. And today's electorate will ensure that either party in power *will*
act.

We have eaten of the fruit of the Tree of Knowledge and there
is no going back. For better or for worse.

NEEDED ECONOMIC POLICY
September, 1968

During the war I worked with a mathematician who told me that he
and Harvard University had an understanding. "Any time they ask
me to come, I will go." In the same spirit I am willing to proffer
economic advice to candidate Nixon.

This being so, it would be churlish of me to discriminate against
Governor Agnew. According to calculations of actuarial and election
odds, he has an appreciable chance of being President of the United
States. So let this be in the form of a memorandum to him. If Vice
President Humphrey should chance to eavesdrop on my monologue,
so much the better.

Although the first half of 1968 has been a period of slightly
overexuberant business expansion, the full 10 per cent tax surcharge

plus the full Congressionally planned expenditure cut seem likely to bring on a slowdown in the economy. According to the currently fashionable forecast, real economic growth will be down to a snail's pace by year's end; the unemployment rate will be rising above 4 per cent; profits, both before and after taxes, will be limping.

All this is likely, but of course not inevitable. Nothing ever is in economics. Actually I find myself a bit less pessimistic than the mode; still more bullish than I are those economists who attach primary importance to the recent rapid growth in the money supply. In any case the victor in November will know more then than anyone can know now.

NO SHORTAGE OF CHEFS

The new President will be besieged by contradictory advice. I know a New York banker who will tell him that the only way to defend the dollar will be to encourage as much growth in unemployment as is needed to "break the back" of inflation. Don't listen to that man. He could not be elected dog-catcher in the modern age.

Still he does have a point. And there will be cooler heads—men like Arthur F. Burns, Henry C. Wallich and Paul W. McCracken— who have given advice in the past to both Republicans and Democrats in favor of going easy on the relentless pursuit of the fullest of full employment.

By all means ponder their counsel. But never forget that you are President of all the people:

- of the Negro youths whose unemployment moves 2 percentage points every time the over-all average moves one point;
- of the entrepreneurs whose profits and capital gains droop when the GNP slows down.

Remember too the elderly, who are the major class clearly hurt by the impact of inflation. (Remember this particularly when the level of social-security benefits moves up to the agenda.)

Now that the New Economics has demonstrated the ability of a mixed economy to thwart stagnation, we need a still newer wisdom to determine the golden mean between restraint and stimulus. If, as one econometrician has said, it takes one and a half recessions in this country to reverse inflation, can you afford the cost of such a program?

At this point, Governor Agnew, you may do well to listen to the counsel of Prof. Milton Friedman, who believes that extremism in deflating an economy *in order to maintain a pegged parity of the dollar-exchange rate* is indeed extremism.

FEDERAL CONTINENCE IMPOSSIBLE

Though the same economic theorizing will serve for a Republican or Democrat, philosophical goals do differ between parties. How large should be the role of Washington in trying to solve our urban and racial problems? Should the states and localities take over? Can private corporate enterprise be relied on to carry the ball of ghetto reconstruction?

It is a cliché that opinions on such matters must differ whenever value judgments differ. But let me state a truth for all seasons and parties:

- Unless government motivates business by tax-and-expenditure programs, business cannot be expected to make even a dent in our urban problems. The business of business is business. Its customers are always right. And the consumer who is king is the electorate.

- It is the Federal government which must supply the funds. There is no other place the money can come from. And he who pays the piper must call the tune. Let's not have a military-industrial-urban complex exercising unilateral power in our economy. Hence, private enterprise is no substitute for government planning in dealing with ghettos and poverty.

- Under *laissez faire,* everybody's business is nobody's business. In the good society, everybody's business is everybody's business.

THE END OF AN ERA?
November, 1968

"It was the best of times, it was the worst of times. . . ." What Dickens said of the *ancien régime* can be said of our own day.

On the one hand there are the unpopular and costly Vietnam war and the social unrest that goes with transition from Jim Crow to an open society. But, on the other hand, there is our economic system whose performance in the 1960s has far surpassed the prophecies of even the most optimistic experts.

The New Economics really does work. Wall Street knows it. Main Street, which has been enjoying 92 months of advancing sales, knows it. The accountants who chalk up record corporate profits know it. The children of the workingmen do not know it: but their mothers do, and so do the school nurses who measure the heights and weights of this generation and remember the bony structure of the last. You can bet that the statisticians in the Kremlin know it—down to the last hundred million of GNP.

Who does not know it? Of course, the exponents of orthodox finance deny the obvious. To pick a name not at random, Maurice Stans, who was Eisenhower's Budget Director and who is rumored to be Nixon's choice for Secretary of Treasury, does not know it, as his writings attest.

Like the Bourbons, who were supposed to have learned nothing and forgotten nothing, the Old Right still chants dirges about the Washington octopus and sings the praises of the grass-roots midden. And how could the New Left forget what it has never learned, or wanted to know?

THE CONTINUING TASK

I say the New Economics does work. But it will not work by itself. It is not a perpetual-motion machine.

We have enjoyed unprecedented sustained economic growth because framers of budget, tax and monetary policy have pushed for vigorous growth.

President Eisenhower served no longer in the White House than have Kennedy and Johnson. But he managed to have three historic recessions—those of 1953–54, 1957–58 and 1960–61–to their none.

Why the difference? New discoveries in econometrics since then? New religion on the part of corporate planners? Of course not. Put George M. Humphrey, Robert B. Anderson, Maurice H. Stans and Charles E. Wilson back in the saddle and America can easily sink back into 45th place in the growth sweepstakes, just as was the case in the 1950s.

Even John F. Kennedy had to learn that you cannot get the country moving again just by talking about that goal. And that you certainly cannot keep up the momentum of growth by adhering to what passed for economic wisdom in the past. I have seen letters in the Kennedy files from men who now advise Mr. Nixon, advising the new President that already in 1962 the fourteen-month-old recovery was being pushed too fast!

According to The Wall Street Journal, businessmen and their economists were recently urging at the Hot Springs meeting of the Business Council that the government should deliberately engineer unemployment of "5½ or even 6 per cent . . . for a year or even two years."

BY ONE'S OWN HAND

History records many instances where economic prosperity has been killed by the reverses of nature: destruction of the dikes; salting of the soil; encroachment of the desert. It records cases where economic well-being has perished at the sword of the invader.

All these are sad. But how sad is the spectacle of a democracy that votes out its own economic well-being.

In 1952 the Democrats campaigned on the slogan: "Don't let them take it away." Though this did not beat Eisenhower—indeed, nothing could, then or now—the record shows that the high employment of the early 1950s was allowed to ebb away. Nor will it do to say that only the Korean War could have prolonged the Truman kind of prosperity. What war dollars can do, so can any dollars: in 1968 you don't have to have a Ph.D. in economics to grasp that bit of common sense.

For every mixed economy around the globe, inflation is indeed a problem. Vigorous real growth does not come cheap. And there is some scientific merit to the view that higher unemployment can do something to moderate inflationary expectations.

Right there is the danger. Let every voter—and the new President, whoever he may be—brood over the risk that we repeat the disastrous policies of the stagnant '50s.

THE NEW ECONOMICS
November, 1968

A mule, it is said, has neither pride of ancestry nor hope of posterity. Of the New Economics, it can at least be said that it has a glorious past. Last time out, in a prophetic eulogy entitled "The End of An Era?" I recounted the solid accomplishments of the New Economics, of which certainly the most important has been our unprecedented pace of sustained growth.

But does the New Economics have a future? In years to come, will our children sit around the fire and recount the legends of the days when giants walked the earth, slide rule in hand so to speak, until driven from the citadel by the rude barbarian?

Or, like Early Christianity, will the New Economics have to go underground, kept alive by word-of-mouth communications from one assistant professor to another, waiting upon a more propitious change in the environment? I have read somewhere that wheat grains, buried thousands of years ago in the pyramids of the Pharaohs, can be brought to germinate again. So it is with a good idea whose time has come, has gone by, but will come again.

PIPE DREAMS

But of course I jest. President-elect Nixon is going to find himself doing pretty much what his two predecessors were doing. This is guaranteed by the closeness of the election if by nothing else.

Were the Old Nixon to whisper to the New Nixon, "Keep that budget in balance," he would be sent packing as an impractical extremist.

In the same way, examining the list of Nixon advisers, we can make the following predictions with the confidence that comes from experience with the checks and balances of politics in a Modern, mixed economy:

- Alan Greenspan cannot possibly sell his chief on the merits of Ayn Rand's absurd religion of the selfish.
- Henry Wallich cannot possibly persuade the new President to invest in that "recession and a half" that may be the price of pricking the bubble of inflationary expectations.
- Dr. Friedman's geometric proofs of the merits of free trade—with which I heartily concur—will fall on the deaf ears of a Republican President, who will in all probability not be able to resist the pressures of the lobby for import quotas on steel. And the smart money in Vegas is giving 10-1 odds that floating exchange rates will *not* be adopted by deliberate policy within this decade.

- Martin Anderson's denunciations of the Federal bulldozer—which do contain an ounce of the vermouth of truth, diluted by a gallon of the gin of hysterical exaggeration—will not provide a practical alternative in which private business will be led, "as if by an invisible hand," to solve the frightening problems of our cities.

- Neither Prof. Don Paarlberg nor anyone else has a politically feasible plan for liquidating our ridiculous farm programs. Only an urban, Democratic landslide could recall old Ezra Benson back to perform that labor of Hercules.

- Not all the wisdom of Arthur F. Burns can serve to convert an overvalued dollar into one that enjoys fundamental equilibrium. Dismantling capital controls is easier to promise than to perform. Ending the Vietnam war, with or without honor, is the sole policy action within the grasp of the President that can make an appreciable dent in our large, *basic* international deficit.

- Mr. Nixon, as his own economic adviser, has come out against the negative income tax, favoring instead jobs for all able-bodied workers. Art Buchwald, who never had a course in Economics 1 at Whittier College, thinks this a funny proposal. I do too. If the overheating of the Vietnam war could not create enough jobs to make our frightful welfare system unnecessary, how is an inflation-fighting President to pull off this rope trick?

REALITIES

Next year Richard Nixon is going to be President of the United States. He will not face the economic system of the McKinley era, but rather that of a modern, mixed economy. President Nixon will not be confronted by the electorate of the Calvin Coolidge era, but by an activist, almost hypochondriacal voting population, which, like voters in all the mixed economies of the world, gets very restive and even vicious when unemployment grows by what used to be regarded as modest amounts.

I am not an economic determinist. But I can predict with confidence that Richard Nixon will be using the New Economics if only for the reason that new times make it inescapable.

LESSONS OF THE 1960s
July, 1969

We are on the homestretch of the 1960s. What economic lessons has the decade taught us?

In answering such a question, I am torn two ways. On the one hand, to insist that I have learned nothing is to mark myself as an inflexible Bourbon. On the other hand, to admit that events of the 1960s have revolutionized our understanding of economic principles is to confess that economics is a soft and protean science.

Today I shall eschew the spurious sagacity resident in the golden mean. Objectivity obliges one, I think, to interpret economic experience of the 1960s as broadly confirmatory to the conventional wisdom—particularly to the avant-garde version of it that characterized the new economists on New Year's Eve 1959.

In one of the more quotable idiocies of history, Lincoln Steffens —after a few weeks' trip to Lenin's Russia—said, "I have seen the future. And it works!" Now that the data for the 1960s are virtually in, I can say, "I have seen the past. And it works."

Wisdom is easy after the fact. So let's recall some popular beliefs about economics, held by respectable authorities ten years ago, that have been proved false by history.

BEFORE AND AFTER

1.   Arthur Burns, Herbert Stein, W. Allen Wallis and other economists close to Richard Nixon thought that the John F. Kennedy debate about stagnant American growth was all an elaborate numbers game. When such New Frontiersmen as Walter Heller, Arthur Okun and James Tobin calculated a quantitative "gap" of underemployed resources for the nation and projected growth of our real potential at 4-plus per cent a year, they were hooted at from both the right and left. (Leon Keyserling thought them pikers in their estimates.)

History has awarded the palm of victory to the new economists. Real growth has been pleasantly on target.

2.   Charles Killingsworth, Norbert Wiener, Michael Harrington and other prophets of an automation revolution were sure ten years ago that "structural unemployment" was America's main problem. Rob-

ert Solow and other Kennedy advisers made econometric estimates to show that expansionary fiscal and monetary policies would melt the hard core of unemployment and that little of the excess unemployment that prevailed in 1961 was structural and new.

Again, events proved that macroeconomics can, black youths aside, achieve full employment.

3. In 1960, when I prepared for President-elect Kennedy a Report on the State of the American Economy, I had to express pessimism concerning the ability of any mixed economy to achieve *price stability along with full employment and free markets.* From 1960 to 1964, my fears were agreeably refuted by the moderation in wholesale and other prices.

After the 1965 Vietnam escalation, alas, one's worst fears concerning a "Phillips Curve" problem of creeping inflation were fulfilled. Presidential wage-price guideposts proved no substitute for adequate macroeconomic limitations on demand.

THE SOMETHING NEW

Before leaving the confrontation of expectation with fact, I must call attention to the surprising vitality of mixed economies all over the world in the 1960s. When I was preparing the 1961 edition of my textbook, the growth race with Russia and China was the popular theme of the day. Partly through the bad luck of unfavorable harvests, but mostly through the effectiveness of that new thing under the sun—the mixed economy the advanced nations of the Western world have gained on the Soviet Union and mainland China during the 1960s, both absolutely and relatively.

Perhaps we are already jaded with the Japanese and Common Market miracles. But who would have thought that countries like Austria and Greece, Thailand and Formosa, to say nothing of such "old" economies as Canada and the U.S., would as a group average higher rates of real growth than the Eastern Europe centrally planned bloc? And who could have prophesied the disastrous effects of Maoist ideology on Chinese growth?

Have economists no errors to confess? Plenty. Econometric estimates of GNP have generally been in error on the low side. Few multiplier-and-accelerator models known to me predicted the exuberance of the 1969 investment boom. And still to be argued out within the guild is the proper quantitative potency of monetary versus fiscal policies.

Nonetheless, it's been a good decade. May the next be as good!

RECESSION FEARS
August, 1969

Before Jean Jacques Rousseau, people generally made the mistake of regarding children as little adults. Since Sigmund Freud, there has been no excuse for failing to recognize adults as merely grown-tall children.

One expects to see this common-place verified on the sport pages of the newspaper. But it is on the financial pages, I submit, that Homo sapiens reveals how little progress he has made since Neanderthal times. Sapiens indeed! We flatter ourselves.

Let me introduce in evidence the wild gyrations of financial opinion in the year just past.

1.   In the months following the mid-1968 tax surcharge, both peasants and pundits of Wall Street convinced themselves that fiscal and monetary policies are impotent to brake the economic expansion and dampen inflation.

2.   Now, suddenly, the mob has decided to cut its losses, and has taken up the cry that Washington is contriving an inevitable recession.

- At a recent business-economists' lunch, 15 out of 25 raised their hands in predicting a recession in 1970.
- Mr. Nixon's campaign advisers—Pierre Rinfret and Milton Friedman—have criticized the shape of present Washington policies.
- Even soothsayers who do not rely on killing a goose to see how its entrails and the supply of money have been behaving are joining the ranks of the pessimists.

MADE BY HAND

In my view neither of these hysterical positions is well taken.

Fiscal and monetary policies together—I repeat, *together*—have succeeded in bringing the U.S. *real* growth rate down to half the rate of just before the tax surcharge. That is the primary fact to remember, and not the secondary fact that most analysts somewhat underestimated the momentum of inflationary expectations.

Experience with earlier slow-ups shows that their effects in moderating price and wage hikes will not come at once but only after several months. Hence the 6 per cent plus price inflation of recent months appears likely to move down toward—say—a 4 per cent annual rate by year's end.

If this seems disappointing, well, life is not a nursery parable with a guaranteed happy ending. But neither is it a horror tale or Greek tragedy.

If there should be a recession next year, its swaddling clothes will carry the label "Made in Washington." Those are the kinds of recessions that are easiest to cure, and for that matter to avoid. For what man can do, he can also undo.

"But," it may be argued, "there are lags between the time the Federal Reserve acts and when the effects of those actions show up in the system. Trouble is now on the way from *past* restrictive actions. If monetary and fiscal policies do not ease up soon, it will be too late to avoid a serious recession—e.g., a drop in real growth of 4 per cent per annum with a consequent massive jump in unemployment."

MINI OR MAXI?

Of course there are economic lags. And I admit the scenario *could* work out in this dark way. And in the Eisenhower years, the recessions of 1953–54, 1957–58, and 1960 were allowed to develop without preventive measures being taken. But we have, I keep telling myself, learned something since those times.

The stock market crashed in 1962 and all the leading indicators looked bad. Vigorous action gave the expansion eight times longer to run. Again, in 1966, monetary and fiscal policies contrived to produce a pause. The money bugs assured us a recession was inevitable. When it was averted, they took refuge in insisting that it had been at least a mini-recession.

What then is the shouting all about? To predict that we shall have by 1970 a mini-recession is a joke. If by that is meant simply a significant pause, then, of course, 25 out of 25 economists should agree that we are *already* in a period of stagnation. By the end of the year, real growth stands to be very weak indeed.

But that is precisely what the Nixon Administration has been aiming for. Chairman Paul McCracken, chairman William McChesney Martin, and all the choruses in Troika and Quadriad would sing hosanna and hallelujah if only they could bring off the 1967 cooling-off period once again.

Why get involved in childish games of words, in which you threaten the economy with wolf only to mean a cocker spaniel?

What worries me is not so much that the system will be throttled into a significant decline. What I fear is chronic emphysema from a sustained attack on inflation.

CHANGING OF THE GUARD
February, 1969

How is the new team doing? "Better than expected," is my usual cryptic reply. Interpreting this as expressing a favorable view, my dear old mother recently declared: "Nixon is just pretending to be a good man."

To a behaviorist, a man is what he does. Let the Devil behave himself all week and on Sunday I will pronounce him blessed; others may judge his sincerity. And if Mr. Nixon can keep up the bluff of virtue throughout his whole term, that is all the country asks.

Economics, not theology, is my beat. Just as one cannot pass final judgment on a son-in-law from his behavior at the wedding reception, it is much too soon to form a judgment on the economics of the new Administration. Perhaps no news may be good news.

The pre-November talk about a little bloodletting at the expense of the unemployed in order to end inflation has been soft-pedaled. Irresponsible promises to terminate capital controls quickly have not recently been heard; and, in view of the trouble that Britain got into repeatedly in recent decades as a result of premature "dashes for convertibility," let us hope that the question will be studied carefully before a decision is made.

NEW FACES

Since it is too soon to talk much about the substance of Nixon economic policy, let me say something about his style. His Council of Economic Advisers is a good one, better all for all than any in Eisenhower's time. Having Arthur Burns in the White House as economic counselor and gray eminence may understandably create some uneasiness for the CEA staff, but it is the country's gain to have expert advice from so canny an economist.

Although finding good people to fill the jobs of undersecretaries and assistant secretaries has not been easy, notoriously bad appointments have been avoided. The punch cards have turned up a token liberal in the form of Patrick Moynihan; and Secretary of Labor George Shultz has managed to bag both a woman and a Negro in the one inspired appointment of Mrs. Elizabeth Duncan Koontz, Director of the Women's Bureau in the Labor Department.

When Mr. Nixon visited the Washington ghetto in person, this made the headlines. And properly so. A few slumming tours will not buy off the proletariat; but the first rule of courtship is that you must demonstrate that you do want to be loved.

What has not been sufficiently commented on, in my view, is even more significant. I mean Mr. Nixon's trips in person to talk to the assembled civil servants in the State, Defense and Justice departments.

This is in glaring contrast to the attitudes of the Eisenhower team when it took over. No nineteenth-century Van Buren or Jackson more joyfully worked to turn out the rascals from office than did the new men of 1952. In those dark days of Joseph McCarthy, the existing civil service was looked upon as Commsymps—or worse, as confirmed New Dealers.

OLD FACES

The Marshall plan staff was summarily sacked. If your wife had sold cookies for Spanish refugee relief, your twenty years of seniority in the Fishes and Oysters Division went down the drain. Without any legal cause, highest-ranking civil servants were simply told to fold their tents and go.

I recall one top man in the Treasury, of no partisan bent but guilty of having done good work in the field of tax research, who was told by his new Assistant Secretary that he was through. "Oh, no I'm not,' he said, "I've been here since Herbert Hoover's time, and I have tenure. Moreover, I am a veteran. You just try to remove me."

Now, as every sophisticate knows, civil-service tenure offers no true job protection. It protects one only from being fired for moderate incompetence. If your boss really wants you out, he can usually contrive to abolish your job. But in this case there was the possibility of adverse publicity. The man's wife had never sold cookies for Spanish relief. And after all, he was a veteran.

So they proceeded merely to give him absolutely no work to do. Few able men are willing to go on living in Coventry; and after six months the man in question did resign. The cream of the jest is that the tax code of 1954 was notoriously full of technical errors, which this man's skills might have helped avoid.

Since you can't run a railroad without trained hands, Nixon's initial acts have gone far to make a two-party system in this country really viable.

BILL MARTIN
February, 1970

After nineteen of the longest years, chairman William McChesney Martin Jr. retires from the board of governors of the Federal Reserve System and enters the Valhalla of American central bankers. Let Benjamin Strong, Marriner Eccles, and Allan Sproul give him a hero's welcome.

If asked what he did at the Fed, Martin could reply, "I lasted." And there is a double truth in this: for, at the lengthy meetings of the Open Market Committee, the chairman was known as a man of an iron bottom, able patiently to outsit the most voluble speakers and in the end bless the vote of the majority—a majority that he both formed and reflected.

It is said that in this country only the very rich or the very poor can afford proper medical care. Joined to this half-truth is the related fact that, to have a permanent career in our public service, you must be either rich or poor. Fortunately, Martin could afford to serve the nation.

ON DUTY
Still the public dollar is indeed a hard dollar. There has to be a more pleasant way of spending a lifetime than being castigated by Congressman Wright Patman winter, spring, summer and fall.

The Lord sent Job boils. To Martin and the Reserve Board He has meted out economists. When William McChesney Martin Sr., Bill's father, was president of the Federal Reserve Bank of St. Louis, he did not have to understand the interactions of the accelerator and the multiplier. For the most part he had merely to be able to recognize a 90-day promissory note extended for the furtherance of agriculture, industry and trade—and rediscount it promptly upon presentation. That and counting the vault cash at night was pretty much all.

Montagu Norman, the shadowy Bond-like character who ran the Bank of England at the time of the great crash, used to say that the central bank must yield in the end to the legitimate government in power. But nonetheless, the central bank has the right—nay, the sacred duty—to *nag* the powers that be.

Bill Martin has enjoyed his duty to nag. No commencement day dawns but what he knocks a few points off the Dow Jones averages with a warning against our lax financial practices.

If central bankers can nag, they can also be nagged. It is hard enough to walk a line that will simultaneously please George Meany at the AFL-CIO and George Champion at the American Bankers Association. But what are such mere conflicts of substantive interest compared with the conflicts of economic theorizers? If this season Martin and the board please me, that automatically earns them the vituperation of Milton Friedman!

At a farewell ceremony you do not present the departing guest of honor with a gold watch and an audited report card of merits and demerits. So this is not the place for me to give my balanced evaluation of William Martin. And indeed there have been at least three different Martins.

First there was the Martin of 1951 to 1953, the President Truman appointee who was the architect of the accord that freed the Federal Reserve from the chariot of Secretaries of the Treasury hell-bent on floating bonds at lowest interest rates.

Then there was the Martin of the Eisenhower years who was obsessed by the problem of inflation even at the expense of healthy growth and the unemployed. That Martin, let me confess, was not *my* Martin. (Once, lecturing at Stanford, I was asked by a student what I thought of chairman Martin; and I heard myself, after an awkward pause, replying: "Anyone who likes tennis cannot be all bad.")

VINTAGE YEARS

Finally there was the new Martin—the one who contributed so much to making the decade of the 1960s one of our longest periods of *real* prosperity.

When I write my Monetary History of the United States, I shall no doubt find warts and blemishes even in this golden age. But I shall have to laud the Fed for being tight in 1966, when fiscal policy was abrogated by the President and Congress. And I shall award them an extra honor for having been more-than-average expansionary in the spring of 1967.

Being a fair man, I shall criticize them for paying too little attention to *monetary aggregates as targets* and too much attention to stabilizing interest rates—but I shall do so not from the conviction that a stable trend of money is the *ultima Thule*, but rather from the Keynesian conviction that nature created the central bank so that it might lean successfully against the winds of cyclical disturbance.

BLEAK OUTLOOK
March, 1970

You go to the clinic and the radiologist reports that the shadow on the film was a camera imperfection and nothing to worry about. Suddenly the hospital is a beautiful place, filled with sunshine.

You go to the hospital and learn that there are still ills that science cannot cure. Now you see around you a grim abattoir, from which many will never return.

Economics is like that. Thomas Carlyle called it the "dismal science." But this was because his ulcer was acting up and he and Jane had just had a quarrel. Yet he was listened to: and that was because intelligent people were frightened by the bogey of Malthusian overpopulation, with wages condemned to be forever at the bare minimum of subsistence.

The technological revolution forestalled the curse of Malthus. Economics became the cheerful study of progress. Hostesses began to notice how much more amusing the professor of economics had become.

But then came depression—unnecessary poverty in the midst of plenty. Here for once, the Ph.D.'s came forth with diagnosis and cure.

The insulin of budgetary deficits plus the penicillin of Federal Reserve policy increased the life expectancy of economic expansions by much more than medicine has been able to improve the life expectancy of man.

Even Keynes could not guarantee that mankind would live happily ever after. He left us with an unsolved problem: *How can we have full employment and also price stability?*

FACT

The truth is, we can't. The only way President Nixon, Dr. McCracken, and chairman Burns know to reduce a 4½ per cent inflation to a 3½ per cent inflation is to engineer unemployment and stagnation. To achieve healthy price stability at full employment seems to be beyond the powers of all the king's horses and all the king's men in any present-day mixed economy.

Coming from a liberal, is this an indictment of liberal economics? Of course not. You don't sue the physician for malpractice every time he has a patient die. If that made sense, we should all be immortal.

This is not a finding of one kind of economics. The more conservative columnists in the NEWSWEEK academy claim, in one case, that it takes a recession-and-a-half to cure inflation; and, in the other, that there is a "natural rate of unemployment," which we have managed to avoid only at the cost of accelerating inflation. In plain words, he condemns us to the Hobson's choice—do you want the unemployment now or do you want it later? And in the same plain words, even a recession-and-a-half is not a once-and-for-all cure; it is more the case that it takes an appie every day to keep the doctor away.

FICTION

What about the unsilent minority on the other side? J. K. Galbraith, realizing that economics is too important to leave to economists and also realizing that modesty is an overrated virtue, has a simple prescription. Wage and price controls. In "The New Industrial State," he cuts the Gordian knot with the simple syllogism: in World War II wage and price controls worked well; peace is no different from war; ergo, legislate price stability. One looks forward to a revised and corrected second edition in which he will analyze in detail the universal failures in the mixed economies of Sweden, the Netherlands, France, Britain, Italy and Australia of prolonged price-wage controls.

Make no mistake. Wage and price controls are a powerful weapon in emergency situations. But with the passage of time, experience shows they develop leaks and inequities. Most experts think they should be husbanded for serious crises and not frittered away on creeping inflation.

What about the New Left? They agree that the present rotten system cannot cope with the problem of full employment without inflation. Their prescription is a simple and logical one. If thy myopic eye offends you, pluck it out and replace it with a good one. Exercising it, resting it, giving it the crutch of corrective lenses is tokenism and playing with palliatives. Even if you do not agree, you must admit that these critics are pointing their fingers at what is indeed a flaw in the present order.

My own inference is that we shall find ourselves living with some inflation and some unemployment. It is said that dermatologists are the luckiest of medical men: they never cure their patients but they also never kill them. Prescribers to the mixed economy are in somewhat the same position.

FIGHTING RECESSION
June, 1970

A specter haunts the American economy. It is the threat of a decline more serious than a midi-recession.

No matter what the Nixon economists say in their public speeches and press releases, when they meet in private behind closed doors, they ask each other anxiously: "What's going wrong? Does the stock market know something we don't know? Will unemployment be at 6 per cent by the November elections? Will the corporate backers of the Republican Party find their profits in a tailspin? If Penn Central has been kept from going bankrupt, what other giant corporation are we going to have to bail out tomorrow?"

I think they should be worried. The latest unemployment number shot up to 5 per cent of the labor force. The unemployment rate has risen from the December 3½ per cent level to 5 per cent. That is one of our steepest rises in a five-month period.

Now the official survey of businessmen's intentions to invest in plant and equipment has been cut back from the 10½ per cent increase over last year reported in March to the recent 7½ per cent. And no one believes that these are firm numbers.

Businessmen had been living in a dream world as far as their own prospects were concerned. They were reporting to McGraw-Hill just a little while back that, although profits for the economy as a whole were going to be down, each of them was going to get a rise in profits. Now the cash register is telling those optimists where reality lies. An agonizing reappraisal of inventories and investment plans is therefore taking place.

As more and more workers in manufacturing get laid off—and the May figures were real shockers—the consumer becomes apprehensive and less eager to buy durable goods or housing.

ECONOMIC CROSS FIRES

Usually when business drops, there are some offsetting crumbs of comfort. At least inflation has been licked. Trade unions are being taught a lesson. Workers will be more grateful for their jobs. The stage is being set for sustained future expansion. Such crumbs are now hard to find.

Now as the ills of deflation beset the economy, it finds itself simultaneously being plagued by the ills of inflation. Prices still rise, with few signs of letting up. Wage costs continue to soar, with considerable likelihood we shall have an auto strike this fall that will be serious enough to have macroeconomic implications.

It is not that we can blame the Federal Reserve for the recent worsening in the economy. Since December, the Fed has been engineering growth in the money supply. Indeed in the last three months, in order to prevent an old-fashioned panic in the money market, it has had to increase money far faster than the 2-to-6 per cent annual rate range that so many monetarists advocate. If in the face of this, long-term interest rates have been rising and Wall Street prices generally collapsing, what will these be doing should the Federal Reserve return to a more normal policy?

WHAT TO DO

First, President Nixon should not put off making his speech on the economy out of fear that he has no good news to report. Let him go on TV and, in that convincing Nixon manner, assure the people that until the specter of serious recession has been exorcised, the fight against inflation must take second place.

Second, he should take his cue from Arthur Burns and initiate a strong Presidential campaign against undue price and wage rises. Where some steel company boosts charges excessively or where some construction trade holds out for an indefensible wage increase, the President must be prepared to do more than raise an eyebrow or wag his jaw. He must pillory them before public opinion.

Now that demand is weak, an incomes policy can have real effects and can free the government to introduce programs that keep demand from becoming weaker still but which might otherwise be deemed inflationary.

Third, macroeconomic deeds and not words are what succeed in strengthening business. Federal money should be pumped into the mortgage and housing market when resources are going idle. The budget is not sacrosanct, and a deficit in good cause is good business. Likewise, the Federal Reserve, freed from any shibboleths of numbers, should lean against the wind until a change in the wind is clearly indicated.

I can see many elements of strength in the economy. But this is not the time for taking chances or for laissez faire. It is a time for prudent action.

ECONOMIC POLICY IS AN ART
October, 1970

Item. The Prime Minister of Singapore, Lee Kuan Yew, when passing through Cambridge recently, asked me why an advanced technology like America's should insist on producing low-productivity textiles and common shoes. I touched a nerve of a New England radio audience when I quoted my answer. "We should move our resources to more efficient uses and turn over to the developing countries primitive activities that any emerging economy can do with low-wage labor."

Item. The single question I am most asked when lecturing abroad is this: "Professor Samuelson, doesn't America's prosperity depend upon Cold War expenditures and imperialistic ventures like that in Vietnam?"

Since I keep but one set of books, I give the same answer that I use in the advanced graduate seminar: "When Lenin and Rosa Luxemburg advanced the thesis of capitalism's dependence on outside markets for its prosperity, William Howard Taft was President and Maynard Keynes still a dilettante undergraduate at Cambridge. In the old-fashioned laissez-faire economy, prosperity was indeed a fragile blossom. But for a modern 'mixed economy' in the post-Keynesian era, fiscal and monetary policies can definitely prevent chronic slumps, can offset automation or under-consumption, can insure that resources find paying work opportunities. The two fastest-growing mixed economies have been Germany and Japan—both stripped of their colonies and forbidden to have armies—which is empirical proof of Keynes' theoretical refutation of the imperialism thesis."

I want later, as they say in court, to connect up these items with the barrage of criticisms that economists generally levy against the Administration's current economic policies. I concur in these indictments but wish to state fairly the defenses that the Nixon team can claim.

1.   President Nixon did inherit the inflation resulting from his predecessor's stealthy acceleration of the Vietnam war.

2.   Under the guise of gradualism, the new team eschewed a policy of sharp deflation involving heavy and prolonged unemployment in a doctrinaire attack on inflation.

3.   The trade-off between full employment and price stability does constitute a cruel dilemma for any Administration, Democratic or Republican. No mixed economy has been able yet to find a satisfactory "incomes policy."

Here the defense must rest and the prosecutor take over.

1.   By last spring it became obvious to all post-Keynesians, monetarists and practical men that the Washington game plan had gone awry. Inflation had bene more stubborn than realized, less quenchable by modest once-and-for-all rises in unemployment. Unemployment is worse than expected by everyone's calculations including those of the Administration itself, unemployment will continue to grow well into 1971.

2.   The Federal Reserve deserves high marks for moving all year long toward easier money. It helped avert a liquidity crisis in the wake of the Penn Central failure and Wall Street decline. Chairman Burns explicitly disavowed any monetarist straight jacket on the rate of growth of the money supply.

3.   Congress, ever respondent to voter distress, shifted toward a more expansionary budget policy. Again and again, over the President's veto and in the face of this legislative opposition, Congress voted public programs which—if they had not been passed—would have left us and the President in a far worse situation than that that now prevails.

It is the turn of the judge and jury. What is to be done?

The President is making the tactical error of fighting three economic battles at the same time: The battle against inflation, the battle against further unemployment, the battle of winding down the economic resources going into Vietnam, aerospace, and the Cold War generally.

The art of economic policy is that of proper priorities and quantitative dosages.

First. The highest priority should now be given to restoring vigorous real growth. Further rises in unemployment should no longer be treated philosophically. Inflation is, to the expert's eye, finally abating a little. It is overly simple to believe that it will flare up dramatically unless we go the whole route of blood, sweat, and tears.

Second. It is false to alibi the rise in long-term unemployment as the inevitable price for winding up the Vietnam war and cutting back on unproductive aerospace programs. Of course, a conversion period has to take place. Of course, people with particular skills and localities specialized to particular activities must inevitably suffer in any wide scale redirection of economic resources.

It is unnecessary and inexcusable to permit the war's windup to induce macro-economic stagnation. A modern mixed economy can afford peace. But if President Nixon reverts to the economic ideology of William Howard Taft, he will strike a blow against the viability of the mixed economy and in favor of the pre-1915 Leninist ideology. The Brazilians, Ghanians, Congolese, Indians—to say nothing of the French, Italians and Princetonians—will take note of the consequences.

And the gallant fight against protectionism, which Richard Nixon and 4,000 economists have been waging, will founder if its major premise is denied—that resources shifted out of inefficient industries will be able to move to more productive work and not onto the roles of the chronically unemployed.

Chapter 2

FISCAL POLICY AND TAXATION

Defined most succinctly, fiscal policy refers to governmental tax and expenditure policies. Management of the public debt is sometimes added as a third function.

To slightly belabor the area of definitions, but not without purpose, it is more meaningful to speak in terms of "discretionary fiscal policy." This suggests a conscious decision-making process for government expenditures, involving both the merits of the spending programs themselves, and the probable effects on the level of economic activity. The same approach would be used in considering tax rates and allocation of tax burdens. A third area of discretionary fiscal policy would be the use of transfer-payment programs, such as social security tax rates and benefit schedules, for economic stabilization purposes.

Within this framework, the title of this chapter suggests that the main thrust of these readings is in the area of tax policy. This is partly true, and is also appropriate for the period of fiscal history with which they are most concerned. But the reader will find that they are by no means devoid of comments and analysis relating to expenditures, both in terms of general level and specific programs. One should see especially the article on "Vital Public Spending."

The entire chapter is a classic lesson in both economics and "political economy." First, the readings show the positive connection between good theory and sound practice, relative to the need for increased taxes, and in terms of both short-run and long-run effects. They also illustrate that good analysis continues to be appropriate to the "facts" as the situation changes. Thus a tax increase can be advocated in early 1966, discouraged at the end of 1966, and again suggested in late 1967 and immediately thereafter.

Second, the selections on "An Open Letter to LBJ," "To Wilbur Mills," and "Upside-Down Economics" reveal the friction and frustration that sometimes result when economic analysis rubs up against the political environment. Good economics need the help of initative from the White House, effective leadership in Congress, and preferably both.

The last reading, dealing with "The Value-Added Tax," stands out somewhat on its own and obviously considers this to be a bad tax. The VAT is seen as a thinly-disguised sales tax.

Many economists feel that the personal income tax, with graduated rates and voluntary compliance, is a great achievement in mankind's efforts at self-government. "Voluntary," in the true sense, of course overstates the situation. But Treasury spokesmen have more than once marvelled at "the miracle of April 15th," as millions of tax returns and tax dollars pour in from a compliant and responsible citizenry. Any kind of sales tax is anathema to this ideal, and the value-added tax falls into this class.

A general retail sales tax is a crude approach to raising revenue, with every cash register a tax collector. Worse yet, it tends to be regressive, taking a greater percentage of total income from those with low incomes than from the more affluent.

The discussion of the VAT provides a simple illustration of how it would work in practice. It is more sophisticated than a retail sales tax, in its mechanics, but its true character is not hard to detect.

As of 1973, the value-added tax has not yet been officially proposed by the Administration, although it has been considered. As suggested in this chapter, it might yet surface in connection with proposed property-tax relief.

With respect to other specific tax policy changes considered in this chapter, the personal income tax surcharge, which was advocated as being needed by the beginning of 1968, was not enacted until mid-1968. It came regrettably late in the battle against inflation, as its greatest impact came in early 1969 when taxpayers filed their yearly tax return. Many families found that an expected tax refund had turned into a net tax liability. Being a surcharge on a taxpayer's normal tax obligation, it increased, by a specified percentage, the amount due. As originally enacted by Congress, then extended and modified, the surcharge was effectively 7.5 per cent in 1968, 10 per cent in 1969, and 2.5 per cent in 1970. Then it disappeared from the scene.

The next to the last reading, "Investment Tax Credit," called for early 1969 suspension of this special tax incentive for business investment in plant and equipment. As noted at the beginning of the article, an anticipated surge in such investment spending threatened to intensify the economy's already inflationary aggregate demand.

Originally proposed in 1961 by President Kennedy to stimulate business investment and the rate of economic growth, the investment tax credit was enacted by Congress in 1962. It has proved successful, both in original intent and as a flexible tool of discretionary fiscal policy.

President Nixon did request its elimination, on April 21, 1969. Repeal of the investment credit was included in the Tax Reform Act of 1969, passed in December, with repeal being retroactively effective as of April 19, 1969.

With the economy needing increased aggregate demand, Congress restored the investment tax credit for an indefinite period, in the Revenue Act of 1971.

RAISING 1967 TAX RATES
December, 1966

There is one major economic question of the day. In the board rooms of Wall Street, the common rooms of Cambridge, and the offices of Washington, we are all asking ourselves: should President Johnson recommend an increase in personal and corporate income-tax rates in January? It is an issue that divides friend and friend, brother and brother. All the industrialists I know are against a tax rise. Most of my banker acquaintances are for it.

Moreover, the battle rages within my own mind. Like Oscar Wilde, who spent the morning putting in a comma and the afternoon taking it out, I find myself oscillating. I oscillate between a concern that we not repeat this year's countenancing of demand-pull inflation, and an apprehension lest 1967 fiscal tightness will come into action just in time to brake an already faltering economic expansion. Let me try to separate the true economic issues from the all-too-powerful political ones.

Last year when the excess of aggregate spending called for a tax increase, the so-called Administrative Budget—an accounting monstrosity—was made to look almost balanced by a mixed bag of meaningless measures. This year the chickens have come home to roost and the Administrative Deficit will appear to be much larger by a misleading amount. None of these silly fiscal gyrations should keep our eyes from the main economic question: taxing to reduce total spending, or not taxing.

THE PESSIMISTS SPEAK

If, as Fortune magazine and 40 per cent of New York business economists believe, 1967 will be a year of economic recession or serious pause, then raising tax rates is economic folly. 1. It is economic folly even if Vietnam spending puts the budget into deficit. 2. It is economic folly even in the face of the argument that, when a nation is at war and its sons are dying on the battlefield, homefront sacrifices are in order. 3. It is economic folly even if 1967 witnesses a good deal of cost-push inflation, inherited from 1966's demand-pull inflation but coexisting with a growth in unemployment and a tapering off of production. 4. It is economic folly even if the Federal Reserve promises to meet any developing recession by some easing of monetary policy.

On the more optimistic side, let's examine the economic outlook as seen by most Washington agencies.

They acknowledge that the "leading indicators" have been generally falling since the spring of the year. Similar declines occurred in 1948, 1953, 1957 and 1960; and in every one of these cases were followed by recessions. But the builders of gross-national-product models also know that declines like the current one occurred in 1951 and 1962, only to be followed by a vigorous resumption of economic expansion. The difference is attributable largely to governmental stimulus offsetting private-economy sluggishness.

THE STANDARD FORECAST

What does the typical GNP forecast say? First, one has to assume something about government expenditure. Neither the North Vietnamese nor the Pentagon Whiz Kids tell the forecasters exactly what future spending will be. So, like the rest of us, they postulate that Federal spending will rise for the next two or three quarters at about its recent rapid rate, to be followed by a halving of the rate of increase in the last part of 1967.

On this basis, the fashionable forecast for 1967 calls for:

- GNP growth of around 7 per cent.
- Three per cent price rises, with real-output growth around 4 per cent.
- Unemployment remaining at about the present 4 per cent level.
- Total profits (before taxes) rising, but at a slower rate.
- Residential construction down again.
- Plant and equipment spending not much higher in 1967 than right now.
- Interest rates still high, credit tight.

Suppose this forecast is about right. Is a tax rise then economically desirable? *My answer is, No.*

The predicted development would be a desirable one even though involving some headaches: continuing balance-of-trade concerns; need for selective credit aids to the building trades, etc. But these are the headaches of vigorous living. In three weeks, I shall weigh the risks involved in the various forecasts and in taking too little or too much fiscal action.

AN OPEN LETTER TO LBJ
January, 1967

Dear Mr. President:

The decision of whether or not to ask for a tax increase in the January budget is the most difficult economic decision you have yet faced. It is also one of the most important.

The risks of doing too much are as real as the risks of doing too little. Let me first list the dire consequences of taxing too much and then of taxing too little.

1. Suppose you recommend an across-the-board increase in tax rates on personal and corporate incomes. And suppose by spring Congress legislates a tax increase of 5 or more billion dollars.

The next taxes might bite in just when our long economic expansion is running out of steam. Either they help to turn a pause into an actual recession, or, what is more likely, the new taxes help to create a period of economic marking time, in which:

- Unemployment rises slowly above the 4 per cent level.
- Profits decline generally.
- That old Eisenhower *gap* between our actual and our potential full-employment production comes back into unwelcome existence.

2. On the other hand, suppose you do not recommend higher tax rates. Then what happened in 1966 could happen again; and, if it does, it will once again be blamed on you.

As a result of mounting Vietnam spending superimposed on excessive home spending for consumer and producer goods, 1967 could—although this now looks doubtful—be a year like 1966 of demand-pull inflation.

This would entail:

- Continued tight money and stagnation in home starts.
- Further deterioration in our current export-import surplus.
- Tight labor markets, with some melting of hard-core unemployment.
- Risks of 1968 cost-push inflation.

How can you guard against either of these grave evils? Certainly not by expecting a consensus from economic experts. On the one hand, such strange bedfellows as Walter Heller, Robert Roosa and Kenneth Galbraith agree that you should raise taxes.

On the other hand, most economists have, like me, veered over to the view that *it has become too late in the expansion to raise taxes.* Most businessmen concur.

How then can you decide between the dangers of doing too much and too little? All economists are agreed that the answer has nothing to do with that accounting monstrosity, the administrative budget. When informed men gather, as the Bible says, "to reason together," their reason tells them that what is important about the Budget is whether it is *inflationary* or *deflationary*, not whether *balanced* or *unbalanced*.

If responsible forecasters expected 1967 to be a year of more than 7½ per cent growth for the U.S. economy your correct decision would be to recommend a tax increase. If, as is now true in both New York and Washington, the prudent expectation is for at best a 6½ per cent raise in money GNP (less than 4 per cent in real GNP) then—politics aside—*economics says you should not raise taxes.* Sound economics says this even though the administrative deficit will look deceptively great for 1966.

You must be warned that there is no real agreement among those who advise a tax increase. Dr. Galbraith thinks it the necessary price for maintenance of expenditure in the public sector and pushing forward with the new programs of the Great Society. Dr. Roosa thinks higher taxes are needed to keep us from going down the road to inflation. Dr. Heller does not think 1967 will be a year of demand-pull inflation: he wants a change in policy mix without contraction —higher taxes only in order to have easier interest rates.

I fear that following the advice of these men will get us none of these good things, but rather loss of momentum in this greatest of all peacetime economic expansions. The stakes are high. Too often in the past, governments have brought prosperity to an end by a misguided concern for budget-balance ideology.

George Santayana said that those who ignore history are condemned to repeat it. With Crane Brinton's help I have improved upon the aphorism. "And those of us who know history are condemned to repeat it with them." By us, I mean all of the American people.

PRUDENT TAX POLICY
March, 1967

When a bunch of experts pick on the Secretary of Treasury for advocating the wrong policy, that is not news. But when the Secretary of Treasury snarls back at his critics, denouncing them in joint economic Congressional hearings as "Monday-morning quarterbacks," that fulfills the man-bites-dog definition of news.

In 31 pages Secretary Henry H. Fowler claims (1) he and LBJ were right in 1966 not to ask for an increase in corporate and personal income-tax rates; (2) they are right to ask for such a tax increase now; (3) they were right to suspend the investment tax credit last September. No doubt if given the chance to bring his last month's credo up to date, Fowler would add (4) and we are *now* right to restore the suspended investment tax credit.

When the intellectual history of our times comes to be written, Abou Ben Fowler will be able to report that not only was he smarter than the experts but that he can modestly take credit for modesty, saying "My claim is much more modest . . . I claim only that . . . we were at all times prudent."

Methinks the lawyer doth protest too much. And with great likelihood before the year is out, the Secretary will be explaining why it will be prudent for Congress to disregard the President's current prudent request for a 6 per cent surcharge.

Don't get me wrong. Some of my best friends are lawyers. But that doesn't mean I'd let them take my appendix out. When President Kennedy was elected in 1960, we had to take the lawyers on his staff back of the barn and explain to them the facts of life. Counselors Sorensen and Feldman blubbered like babies when told that we would have to run a budget d-----t. "The chief's not going to like this," they whimpered.

THE LAW AND THE LIGHT

Until he becomes Pope, a cardinal lacks infallibility. Under Secretary Fowler was often wrong in the years 1961 to 1964. When the Kennedy economists advocated a massive taxcut decision late in 1961, Under Secretary Fowler was opposed. In the subsequent years he was prudently opposed to tax cuts which put the reform of incentives secondary to the promotion of aggregate purchasing power.

Fun is fun, but let us make a deposition that lawyers are no worse than anyone else. Evidence—e.g., George Humphrey and Andrew Mellon—suggests that lawyers make better Secretaries of the Treasury than do businessmen. Faint praise, but praise.

Nor can we put our trust in experts alone. The worst Director of the Budget in recent times was a certified public accountant. Bankers on the Federal Reserve Board have worked out no better than farmers and only a hair better than naval aides.

Economists too make mistakes. How could it be otherwise when one can be found who believes in *any* doctrine you can name? If you don't like the economics you read in Newsweek today, wait a week: something different, maybe better, is sure to turn up.

CASE FOR THE PROSECUTION

Since Secretary Fowler testified last month, each new bit of economic news has confirmed what the experts have been fearing all year.

The economy is so far showing greater weakness than President Johnson predicted for it in 1967.

- The weakness in auto sales has infected retail sales generally. Drs. Ackley, Okun and Duesenberry predicted this would be a low year for consumer saving. So far not so.
- When Pierre Rinfret's private survey suggested a topping out of plant and equipment spending, Washington expressed doubt. Now the SEC-Commerce survey backs Rinfret.
- Inventory piled up in the October-January period at an unhealthy rate. Why should it be expected to have corrected itself by July 1?

Perhaps easier money will bring on a construction boom by the end of the year. But is it wise to base policy upon such a contingent possibility? President Johnson has enough genuine problems in Vietnam. Why take unnecessary risks in the easier area of domestic economic policy?

Secretary Fowler was recently voted "Salesman of the Year." If he can sell Congress higher tax rates in the face of economic weakness, he will deserve the title, "Salesman of the Century." And will risk the contempt of the Monday-morning quarterbacks.

THE NEW TAX SURCHARGE
April, 1967

Finally President Johnson has spoken on taxes.

Now Congress and the American people must make up their minds as to whether additional taxes are needed. Here are my views on the subject.

At the beginning of 1966 I was a hawk on taxes. I expected 1966 to be a year of demand-pull inflation. And so it turned out to be. An across-the-board increase in tax rates is what the modern economic expert recommends when total dollar spending—by government, consumers and business investors—threatens to exceed the value of output that our system can produce at full capacity.

We did not get higher tax rates at the beginning of 1966. Therefore, prices rose excessively. Therefore, the Federal Reserve found it necessary to introduce the tightest money that had prevailed for more than 40 years.

All this culminated in what was called the "money crunch." Few people realize how close the financial markets were a year ago to disorderly crisis.

- Savings and loan associations were threatened with a massive withdrawal of funds. Last summer, official Washington nervously mobilized several billion dollars to meet this bank run should it get out of hand.

- The Mellon bank in Pittsburgh dumped municipal bonds for whatever they would bring, producing paralysis in the bond market.

- Housing construction nose-dived as mortgage funds became unavailable.

- The crucial money supply, which normally grows at an average rate of about 4 or 5 per cent per year, not only slowed down its rate of growth but even turned into a stage of absolute money contraction from April 1966 to November.

In the end, disaster was averted when President Johnson decided to suspend the investment-tax credit and curtail postponable spending programs. No one wants to go through this cycle of inflation and monetary asphyxiation again.

At the beginning of 1967 I was a dove on taxes. Publicly and privately I advised against the 6 per cent surcharge that the government recommended for July 1.

Though not agreeing with those monetary and income-analysis pessimists who predicted an old-fashioned recession for early 1967, I shared the universal concern over the excessive accumulation of inventory at year's end. The ebbing of the boom in plant and equipment was only too apparent in both official and unofficial surveys of 1967 investment intentions.

But, as the Bible says, there is a time and season for everything. Recently, when testifying, I asked the Joint Economic Committee what the name was for a dove who was in the process of turning into a hawk, for I felt myself to be that kind of a bird.

My present position, which I believe is shared by most academic and business economists, is this:

If the economy zooms upward in the months ahead as most experts now think it will—and, of course, this question will answer itself by the time Congress must make up its mind about the Oct. 1 enactment date—then we most certainly should raise taxes to forestall inflation and avoid another "credit crunch."

There are four major reasons why increased tax rates are needed: two involve sound economic analysis; two, which may have merit in terms of psychology and politics, are economically irrelevant. I begin with these last two.

1.   The nation is at war and hence taxes should be raised to show our solidarity with the boys fighting and dying at the front.

2.   Since we shall be running in fiscal 1968 the largest peacetime deficit ever, $20 billion or more, this necessitates an increase in tax rates.

If these are not the valid economic reasons, which are? Already I have stated them.

3.   High tax rates are justified to depress aggregate spending when overfull employment and inflation are threatening.

4.   Fiscal tightness either in the form of higher taxes or cuts in public spending, is desirable if monetary policy is to be employed effectively for easier money and all that this implies for maintenance of housing and other construction.

Since one good reason is enough, why worry about four?

But a hawk can also turn into a dove. No matter what the size of the deficit, if the private economy turns out to be weaker than is required for high employment and normal growth, all bets should be canceled and the surcharge should be dropped.

TO WILBUR MILLS
November, 1967

Dear Congressman Mills:

I am writing to urge you to use all your influence to persuade Congress to pass a tax-increase bill by the beginning of 1968. The economic case for such a measure has never been so strong. If Congress does not act, all the country—including Arkansas—will suffer the harm of unnecessary demand-pull inflation.

In the course of a man's career in Congress, there come perhaps half a dozen crucial occasions when he must make a painful choice between alternatives. The Kennedy proposals to cut taxes massively in the early 1960s provided one such challenge to you personally; and in the end, when the count was taken, you were lined up on the side of the angels. History has pronounced its benediction for this courageous act. And History is again watching you.

Let me review the evidence. You will recall the many seminars we had together when you were on the Joint Economic Committee. The New Economics was then not yet born. But rereading the Congressional Record, I think we can both take satisfaction that we, each in our own way, played an honorable part in developing the modern patterns of American fiscal policy that have worked so well in recent years. Although you were never a zealot for the latest wrinkle of monetary gadgetry, you early saw through the sophistries that passed for financial orthodoxy in the days of Grover Cleveland and Calvin Coolidge.

But I do not have to urge the tax surcharge just because I'm a New Economist. For every Walter Heller who advocates fiscal restraint, there is now also an Arthur Burns. With each week, analysts of all persuasions are increasingly agreed that the period of hesitation which characterized our economy from January to May is definitely a thing of the past. Economists see a clear and present danger of demand-pull inflation for 1968.

To curb excessive aggregate dollar spending, economists recommend:

- An increase in tax rates.
- A cut in government spending.
- Tighter money by the Federal Reserve Board.

And if we do not get prompt action on taxes or expenditure, then the Fed will be forced to be that much tighter in its monetary policies.

The case is a clear one, far clearer than in most years of decision. First, the legitimate fear during the January-to-May inventory pause —that a tax hike might wreck the expansion—is now definitely ruled out. In the face of the Ford strike, gross national product jumped $15 billion in the third quarter—the largest increase since early 1966. A new census survey of consumers' spending intentions suggests an almost frightening exuberance just ahead.

In the first quarters of next year, demand will be swollen because of the make-up effects of the auto strike; and this swell will be aggravated by inventory accumulation in anticipation of a midyear steel strike.

Second, dispute over the long-run problem of the proper level of Federal expenditure can be fatal to the cause of limiting the inflation that threatens in 1968. The 1964 tax cut was held up for two years by a similar dispute concerning "tax reform" (still unresolved!).

Third, if the country cannot make up its mind on cutting expenditures or raising taxes, shouldn't we let it experience inflation?

That is a course of action with dangerous consequences. The inflation we have to avoid in 1968 means an accelerated rise in prices and costs. Aside from the burden placed on fixed-income receivers, such inflation raises the relative prices of our export goods, and reverses the slow progress we had been making since 1959 in improving our international competitiveness and basic balance-of-payments equilibrium. Finally, overheating the economy can jeopardize the longevity of our economic expansion.

If the Fed is left alone to do the job, experience shows that the resulting "money crunch" will place a disproportionate burden on real-estate markets. In 1966 this put the savings and loan associations in real danger of crisis. If this happens again, direct controls may be needed to alleviate such disproportionate effects. And I needn't elaborate on the distrust you feel for those!

Since there is no clear ground swell from the people for higher taxes, what is needed is responsible leadership. *By you.* May I quote Disraeli?

"A leader who never loses a legislative battle is like a miser who never spends his money."

This is a cause worth fighting for.

VITAL PUBLIC SPENDING
November, 1967

The case for a tax increase is based upon the premise that aggregate dollar demand is likely to be so excessive this coming year as to produce undue inflation. Purely as a matter of economic mechanics, inflation can be fought by two kinds of fiscal restraints: higher tax rates, or lower rates of government expenditure—or, of course, a combination. This truth most economists are agreed upon. (Pragmatically, I define a truth to be that which at least two out of three NEWSWEEK experts on economics are agreed upon!)

Now, just which of these two fiscal weapons should be used? Should we rely exclusively on higher tax rates? Exclusively on expenditure cuts? If both weapons are to be used, what should the quantitative mix be?

NEED FOR VALUE JUDGMENTS

Actually, these are not questions that can be given an answer in terms of economic principles alone. Any jury of three economic experts might legitimately come up with three quite different policy recommendations. And such disagreements would be no reflection on the *technical* competence of any of the scholars.

On what then *does* depend the proper policy recommendation? Ultimately, the choice on such matters must depend on the value judgments of the majority of the citizenry.

If the people give high priority to using economic resources to clean up our polluted rivers and atmosphere, the fact that we are waging a war in Vietnam and are facing a problem of inflation should not stand in the way of their getting the program they want. If the people preponderantly desire that minimum standards of welfare be maintained and that the battle against poverty be vigorously pursued, neither war nor inflation provides legitimate economic obstacles to attainment of these goals.

Of course, the fact that more of the nation's resources are being devoted to Vietnam, and the fact that there is such a scramble of spending on goods as to lead to tight labor markets—these are legitimate reasons for taking a fresh, hard look at national priorities. But the following technical fact cannot be overemphasized:

The United States is not today remotely near any limit of tax capacity. If the people desire more of government programs that they deem vital, there is vast scope in the 1968 economy for expansion of *the public sector.*

Note that I have spoken loosely of "the citizenry" and "the people." You can never expect unanimity of the value judgments we are talking about. Some people couldn't care less about the poverty program or redistributive taxation. Others burn for such reforms. And some burn more than others.

So, in a mixed economy like ours, it boils down to the expressed views of the electorate. Majorities come and go. And we have to hope that E. B. White is right in saying:

"Democracy is the recurrent suspicion that more than half of the people are right more than half of the time."

It is necessary to remind ourselves of these abstract philosophical considerations because there seems to be a genuine confusion in much current political discussion. Too often it is taken for granted that cuts in government expenditure must precede or go hand in hand with any rise in taxes. There is no such necessity and it is economic nonsense to postulate that there is. Compared with other Western societies and compared with our affluence and public needs, I find it easier to make the case that America today spends too little rather than too much on government.

THE GOOD SOCIETY

When resources are tight, one might suppose that there is some presumption that all frills be eliminated. Thus, we justify a tax surcharge on the ground that the last dollars taken away from us will cut down on our least important private use of resources. At such times government programs of marginal worth—the supersonic airplane, our confused farm program, and much of our aerospace expenditure would be on my list—are also candidates for the knife.

However, and here I am presenting my credo for the good society, I believe it would be tragic if the new campaigns we have been waging against poverty and inequality—both at home and abroad—were to be abandoned or even curtailed because of the myth of economic necessity.

NEWSWEEK readers know that I favor a tax increase. Let me make clear that I do not favor it at any price. If its costs were a legislative deal to cripple important welfare programs, I would have to point out that a degree of open inflation is not the greatest evil.

UPSIDE-DOWN ECONOMICS
February, 1968

From the standpoint of scientific economics, discussion of the tax rise is at a scandalously primitive level. Red herrings obscure the single analytical issue—will 1968 be a year of excessive demand-pull inflation in the absence of a tax increase? Or will the economy be so weak in late 1968 that a tax hike will add to growing unemployment and excess capacity?

I regard the following arguments as red herrings:

- If you disapprove of the Vietnam war, as do some 350 recently petitioning economists, you may hope to starve out the military by refusing one extra pfennig of taxes. This is, at best, a *symbol* of protest. I cannot recall a single instance in which war has been halted by such a tactic. Inflation easily finances war.

- The proper level of Federal spending hinges on value judgments of voters. Since philosophical views differ, the outcome is always the resultant of compromise. Budget policy for next year has now been formulated. The President has been too austere from the standpoint of those who aspire to the Great Society; for those who think the public sector has long been overblown, the proposed budget is too lax. I do not find it persuasive that changes in the level of future spending are achievable by tightness or looseness of tax policy. How much we tax will determine how big is the eventual deficit, how great the peril of inflation.

SUBSTANCE OF ECONOMICS

Here, then, are genuine issues.

1. *With or without a tax increase, there will be no recession in 1968.* Our record 83-month expansion will be 95 at year's end. Earlier, Senator Proxmire could properly oppose a tax rise on the basis of fear of overkill and recession. That time has gone by; that time has not yet come.

2. *Since fall, the probability of demand-pull inflation has risen.* The first half of this year badly needs the tax surcharge. If toward year's end aggregate demand turns stagnant, that will be a good time to reverse policy and cut 1969 taxes. A change in policy attributable to a change in the developing pattern of the economy is not a sign of vacillation. It is a sign of good sense.

3. *Everyone knows prices will be rising in 1968.* And at more than the 2 per cent rate that our mixed economy has learned to live with.

This quickening of prices is not trouble ahead in the skies. It is already here. One presumes it comes as a surprise to Senator Proxmire. I recall the severe catechism which he submitted me to last summer when I agreed to testify before his Joint Economic Committee. "With excess capacity up, how, Professor Samuelson, can prices rise?" They could. They did. They do. They will.

Some argue that price increases by oligopolistic corporations and unions call for wage-price guideposts, not fiscal and monetary measures. No academic economists agree. The best way to ruin the genuine contribution guideposts can make is to try to use them as a substitute for macroeconomic policies.

SHADOWBOXING OF POLITICS

Some argue prices will rise in the months ahead whether we tax or not. True enough, if you concentrate myopically on the next months. But all experience shows that the rate of inflation *of the next few years* (and it will affect the innocent Wisconsin constituents of Senator Proxmire as much as those of legislators who are hawks on taxes) crucially depends on *the degree of excess in aggregate demand* that is allowed to develop.

We are paying now—in rising prices, wage settlements outstripping productivity, balance-of-payments pressure, soaring interest rates—for failure of Congress to raise taxes two years ago.

In scientific economics, expenditure cuts and tax rises are *substitutes* to fight inflation. Not so in politics. The more the President cuts spending, the more will Wilbur Mills *reward* him with tax increases! This is upside-down economics with a vengeance.

But why am I surprised? When President Kennedy pleaded in 1962 with him for the massive tax that the country desperately needed *for Keynesian reasons,* Mills demurred. After the Dallas assassination, President Johnson, by promising *cuts* (!) in expenditure, made a deal with the late Senator Byrd which finally brought the 1964 tax cut.

It is unrealistic to exaggerate the importance of one legislator, but by my calculation Mr. Mills cost the nation $10 billion in the 1962-63 period. Truly a valuable man.

In 1968, though, he may atone with $10 billion of extra inflation.

INVESTMENT TAX CREDIT
March, 1969

Inflation watchers were rocked last week by news from the SEC and Commerce Department that businessmen intend to increase their plant and equipment investments by almost 14 per cent.

The new outlook for excessive investment spending should, in my opinion, cause President Nixon to suspend the 7 per cent investment credit temporarily. Here's why:

1.   The economy is still on an inflationary binge. To bring the rate of price increase down from 4 per cent toward a more moderate figure of, say, 3 per cent, some actions are

2.   Already the Federal Reserve is being called upon to take Draconian measures to fight inflation. This will mean not only painfully higher interest rates; it will also bring in most of the discomforts associated with the money crunch of 1966—uneven rationing of credit between new and old business, growing and stagnant business, small and large business.

3.   Experience demonstrates that tight money takes for its principal casualty the housing industry. When there is a scramble for more resources than the total resources available, it is right that housing should share in the restraint. But it is not, in my judgment, good national policy to have housing starts cut by 40 to 50 per cent as happened in 1966. In the 1970s, with their bumper crop of young marrieds, we shall pay in higher rents and zooming residential costs for any serious diminution of home construction in the waning

4.   Admittedly, inflation could be fought by adding onto the present surcharge another 5 or 10 per cent tax. But I see no evidence that this would be politically popular or feasible. Nor is it clear that consumer spending is the prime villain in the present inflationary scenario.

5.   Admittedly, inflation could be fought by still further tightening of the Federal Reserve money screw. And the impact of such tightness on the housing industry could be alleviated by special financial subsidies to home construction through the Federal housing agencies, through the U.S. Treasury, or through the Federal Reserve. Since all such measures will add to the nominal public debt, I don't expect that anything but tokenism would, in fact, be politically feasible in this area.

      Even if it were possible to cushion the impact of tight money on residential housing, to get the same restriction of aggregate demand from enforced reductions on plant and equipment spending would, I suspect, require very high interest rates. These will cause difficulties for our partners abroad. And they may hang on to plague us in the years to come when the winds may be blowing up deflation rather than inflation.

6.   In September of 1966, to alleviate the money crunch and moder-

ate what looked like an excessive fixed investment boom, the Johnson Administration did suspend the 7 per cent investment tax credit. Almost at once relief was felt in the money markets of the country. On the whole (despite the protests of the Treasury, which naturally found it a headache), the operation seems to have been a successful one in accomplishing its purpose—namely, ensuring against an overexuberant fixed investment boom.

So historical experience, as well as the common-sense view that firms will invest less when their returns from doing so are reduced, justifies suspending the tax credit.

What are the possible arguments against suspension of the tax credit?

1.   The Nixon Administration might be regarded as a pro-business Administration. Why should it take from business this accustomed source of profit?

2.   Perhaps the inflationary danger is being exaggerated. Perhaps it will involve overkill if suspension of the investment tax credit reduces investment severely.

3.   Vigorous growth requires as much capital formation as we can get. Adjusting to inflation by reducing investment will reduce our future capacity to produce an enlarged total of real national product.

4.   It is a bad thing to use variations in the investment tax credit as a deliberate weapon of stabilization. Why? Because it is plain immoral. Because it involves discretion by government, which is wicked. Because it disturbs business planning.

5.   Suspension creates administrative problems for the Treasury.

In economics, every decision involves pros and cons. Judgment is necessary. My advice to Mr. Nixon: suspend the investment tax credit.

THE VALUE-ADDED TAX
March, 1972

If re-elected, President Nixon will propose a new kind of Federal tax, the value-added tax or VAT. For anyone just poised on the line of indifference between voting for Richard Nixon or for his Democratic opponent, this would be a good reason to decide to vote against him.

Why do I say that? Because I myself am not on the border line and wish to tilt against the Republicans? No: such a reason would be as good or bad without regard to the issue of VAT.

Is it because I think voters should turn against anyone who proposes a new tax or an increase in an old tax? No: I believe that whoever gets elected, George Wallace included, will definitely have to propose increased taxation in the next budget. Even if we return to the goal of full employment, our pressing public needs will require greater resources than our present tax system will release.

People hate taxes the way children hate brushing their teeth—and in the same shortsighted way. In a rational world, the President would have apologized to the American people, instead of claiming credit, for the fact that he and the Congress have lopped off more than $20 billion of Federal revenues. An unholy alliance pushed this through: those who think that the only good tax is a low one combined with those who perceived, correctly, that the economy was stagnating and needed fiscal stimulus in some form or another. History will record that it would have been better if that stimulus had come not from permanent taxrate cuts but from getting on with the spending programs that loom inescapably ahead.

A ROSE BY ANY NAME ...

But let us not stray from VAT to general fiscal issues. A broad sales tax at the Federal level has been recommended repeatedly by Republican Administrations. No bones are made about the reasons: a sales tax is less progressive in its incidence than is a graduated income tax; it is less egalitarian, and hits the affluent classes less hard; and it is argued that the affluent classes are the ones who save and invest and innovate.

Alas, the American people have never bought the argument for a Federal sales tax. It is enough to drive a conservative to despair!

But wait. Maybe one can get by stealth what one can't get outright. How about sugar-coating a sales tax on final consumption by achieving the same thing in the form of a value-added tax? For, make no mistake about it, to the expert in public finance, VAT is a tax on consumption expenditures: a tax not collected at the point of final sales, but rather one collected in less-visible installments.

Here's a finished loaf of bread worth 40 cents. A sales tax of 10 per cent means rich and poor buy it for 44 cents. Nothing hidden. No damned nonsense about equalizing incomes.

Under VAT, the farmer pays a 1 cent tax on his 10 cents' worth of wheat. The miller pays 1 cent on his 10 cents' worth of value-added in milling. (Careful: flour sells for 20 cents, but he is allowed to subtract the 10 cents he paid the farmer before calculating his value-added tax basis.) The baker pays 1 cent tax on his 10 cents of value-added in baking. The grocer pays 1 cent on his 10 cents value-added in retail distribution.

Final score: same 4 cents paid in VAT by rich and poor as in Federal sales tax. Q.E.D.

Final verdict: gutting the graduated income tax smells as bad in one form as another. Maybe fetid smells from hidden places are even worse.

GIMMICKS, GIMMICKS

To get VAT in as an opening wedge, two gimmicks are being tried.

First, the poor are perhaps to be given some rebate on their income tax in the beginning and some necessities may be exempted. Such bait has worked in the past to get state sales taxes in for the first time.

Second, and more dramatic, courts in California and elsewhere have been ruling that poor localities, which are unable to collect as much property tax and revenues to support public education at the levels enjoyed by the affluent suburbs, must receive help from the affluent regions via state or Federal grants. This is overdue: men of goodwill must hope that the Supreme Court will concur.

An attempt will be made to sell VAT as part of a package of property-tax relief, in time of impending court-induced property-tax crisis.

Intelligent liberals will see through the ruse. They will insist that new resources for revenue sharing must come from income taxes based on ability to pay.

Chapter 3

INFLATION, THE EVOLVING SOLUTIONS

The categories of inflation which economists identify and the antidotes they prescribe have evolved with the economic and political experiences of the industrialized nations.

"Tight Money," written in October 1966, outlines the causes of the demand-pull inflation that began in 1965 and fiscal and monetary policy actions for dealing with that inflation. Instead of a careful mix of both kinds of policy, the economy was subjected to a brief jolt of unusually tight money which had little lasting impact on inflation.

Society seeks to avoid inflation on the one hand and unemployment on the other. (Deflation is rather unlikely.) Society does so because both of these conditions impose costs on it. The relative importance of the costs associated with unemployment and inflation depends on the institutional arrangements of the society, its values and, of course, the point of view of the evaluator. By mid-1969, the United States had experienced several years of demand-pull inflation and had elected a new administration partly for that very reason. "Nixon Economics," written at that time, contrasts the views of those who assign greatest weight to the costs of inflation and those who are more concerned with the deleterious effects of unemployment. In addition, the article speculates on the "gradualist" approach, something of a compromise between the other two, of the Nixon Administration.

Within a month (June 1969) the state of the economy could be described as an "Inflationary Slowdown"—prices rising briskly, real growth slowing. The Nixon Administration "game plan" sought, by a gradual slowing of inflation, to create only minimal unemployment. This approach reflected not only a sensitivity to the political and economic costs of inflation and unemployment, but a presumption as to the flexibility of the many markets which comprise the United States economy.

If markets are flexible, they will respond to a reduction in demand in a manner which prevents development of a large amount of unemployment. For the most part this means that the rise in prices (and wages) will slow down or perhaps even stop.

By the end of 1970, the demand-pull inflation had given way to one that could be characterized as cost-push. Markets had proven to be more rigid than expected and the society was discussing "Price Controls."

In an economy based on private decision-making and markets, most economists prefer to attack inflation with monetary and fiscal policies. This is so because these policies impact indirectly on private decisions regarding the allocation of resources. As these instruments have proved unable, within politically acceptable limits, to reduce inflation to levels politically acceptable, more direct policies have come under consideration. Price and wage controls introduce the government directly into private decision-making; and, as the article, "Price Controls," makes clear, they are not without their own costs to society.

The costs of inflation are what society wants to avoid, not inflation *per se.* Price and wage controls have been imposed in this country and have been a mixed success. But if "there seems to be no known cure for creeping inflation that is better than the disease" perhaps we should develop mechanisms which will allow our "Living with Inflation."

TIGHT MONEY
October, 1966

The year 1966 will go down in the history books as a year of mild, creeping inflation. It provides a classic textbook case of the kind of inflation economists call "demand-pull"—in contrast to "cost-push."

Prices have been rising by 3½ per cent per year. The reason is simple. It is not because of union wage increases. Actually, less than half the usual number of wage contracts have come due for collective bargaining in 1966. (Next year will be quite another story.)

Too much aggregate dollar demand—private and governmental, investment and consumption—has been bidding up prices now that labor markets are tight and plant capacity strained.

Economists are generally in agreement on the three main causes:

1. **Escalation of Vietnam spending**
   - —which is superimposed onto
2. **A plant-and-equipment boom**
   - —which in turn was triggered off by
3. **The highly successful Kennedy-Johnson tax cut of 1964-65.**

If only President Johnson had known last January what we know now. The policy prescription for a year that brings an 8½ per cent increase in GNP, plagued by price rises, is easy. It involves

Tighter fiscal policy:

- Across-the-board increases in corporate and personal income-tax rates; suspension of the 7 per cent investment tax credit;
- A squeeze on all expenditure programs deemed marginal (aerospace? supersonic planes? obsolete navy yards? farm subsidies? . . .)

Tighter credit policy:

- Higher interest rates;
- Tighter rationing of bank credit;
- Depressed stock market prices—all this engineered by the Federal Reserve through refusing to let the total money supply grow enough to satisfy the booming demands.

How has it worked out? We got half the prescription, and with a vengeance! Money has been tight. Housing starts are way down. Wall Street is howling. More important, Main Street is hurting.

Half a prescription may be better than none. If penicillin and sulfa are called for, sulfa alone may be better than nothing. But it is possible that twice the dose of what you happen to have in the house can give you a stomach-ache.

When President Truman hurled from Missouri a warning that over-tight money had caused depression in the past and would do it again, President Johnson of Texas listened. And he stopped listening to Secretary Fowler of Washington, D.C.

Micawber-like, Secretary Fowler has been praying all year that with a little bit of luck something would turn down. And he was right. Something did. In the spring auto sales dropped.

Economics, unlike the law, is *quantitative.* One or two industries are not enough. By summer, the second-quarter calm was over. The last half of 1966 is again overstrong.

WHAT ABOUT 1967?

So President Johnson acted in September. To relieve the load on monetary policy, he proposed a temporary suspension of the investment tax credit; of fast depreciation for construction; of back-door borrowing by Federal intermediaries. He also promised expenditure cuts.

The impact of these programs has been about as expected. Money markets have recovered a little.

But suddenly a new wave of pessimism has hit us. Just when business activity is quickening, business confidence is wavering.

"Won't there be a recession in 1967? Even if only a pause, won't this bring falling profits?"

One-third of all business economists voiced such pessimism last month. This month Pierre Rinfret has reported that his private sample of investment intentions shows, in contrast to the 17 per cent growth of 1966, only 3 per cent for 1967.

Meanwhile, back at the ranch, what are the government experts saying? Dr. Ackley, current chairman of the CEA, still warns of overexuberance in 1967. Dr. Heller, his predecessor, still advocates a tax increase.

If the Rinfrets are right, to get the tax cut next January that we should have had last January would be to compound the felony.

But remember this. By New Year the President will know more about 1967 than we can know now. Betting that so shrewd a man will goof is a sucker's game. Fortunately.

NIXON ECONOMICS
May, 1969

When young Dick Nixon was in the Navy, there used to be a saying, "There is the right way, there is the wrong way, and there is the Navy way." In these inflationary times, there are also three ways of economics.

There is the hard-nosed economics which says, "Inflation is an evil. The only way to fight it is to mobilize Federal Reserve monetary policy and government fiscal policy to cut down on aggregate dollar spending. After this cut in dollar demand brakes the real rate of growth of the system, unemployment will grow appreciably. Excess capacity will gradually develop. As men out of jobs undercut the wage scales of those in jobs, and as manufacturers with idle capacity whose costs go on whether or not they produce are motivated to underbid their rivals for scarce orders, money wages will finally stop growing so fast and commodities will come down in price."

Then there is the more humane economics which says, "Yes, inflation is an evil. But curing it by engineering a slowdown in real growth and a contrived increase in unemployment is a still greater evil. In itself this is socially undesirable. In addition, there will result so great an increase in unemployment among ghetto youths as the result of a general slowdown as to cause riots and violence. It would be bad for the nation to let this happen, and it would be bad politics for President Nixon to make this happen."

WHAT MIDDLE WAY?

Obviously, the new Administration is not buying either of these extreme solutions. There is a lot of territory in between them. Just which middle road is Mr. Nixon's road?

From a stain on a man's finger and a list in his left shoulder, Sherlock Holmes could tell what must surely be his social-security number and his favorite Scotch whisky. Would that Holmes were here now to read the inscrutable record of Mr. Nixon's first hundred days of office!

On major questions of fiscal policy, the President seems to have kept an open mind. After originally criticizing the 10 per cent surtax, he reluctantly gave his blessing to its extension. Then as the grim news began to come in on the speeding up of the rate of price inflation, he withdrew his assent, instead recommending that it be cut back in 1970 to 5 per cent.

Was this because of another change of mind, the decision to ask for repeal of the investment tax credit? (I can hardly fault him for this last decision, since in this column I sent him an open letter suggesting its suspension. But where I had, so to speak, suggested only a marital vacation, Mr. Nixon has come out for a permanent divorce.)

Was it thought that a 10 per cent surcharge, plus no investment credit, would create overkill and a recession in 1970? Not if one listens to one of the few Nixon economists who has been heard from in public recently, Dr. Herbert Stein of the Council of Economic Advisers. For we learn from him that the purpose of the repeal is not primarily to cut down on the inflationary pressure resulting from excessive investment spending.

THE OPEN MIND

The new team has great respect for the potency of the Federal Reserve. Do they expect it to have created too great a slowdown by Christmas time? Or, as I would much prefer to learn, do they have confidence that the Vietnam war will be significantly de-escalating by that time?

In the absence of an omniscient Holmes, a Doctor Watson could be forgiven for thinking that scarcely a dent has yet been made in inflation. Can he believe the TV prophecy by White House counselor Arthur Burns that by the end of this year—only seven months away —prices will be growing at less than 3 per cent a year?

The money market is as confused as anybody. Since March, interest rates have been trying to come down from their recent lofty highs. If the war is about to end and if the back of the inflation has been broken, this makes good sense. But are we there yet?

My own guess is that growth will have slowed down by the year's end. But only slight improvement in the rate of inflation will then be realized. As the toll of the slowdown becomes politically uncomfortable, chances are that anti-inflation action will ease and we will be off again to the races.

Mr. Nixon is forsaking fine tuning for gradualism. The opposite of fine tuning is coarse tuning. The opposite of activism is inactivity. Although we give thanks that the President is not closing his mind to the intricacies of the situation, the uneasy thought asserts itself that an open mind is sometimes hard to tell from an empty one.

INFLATIONARY SLOWDOWN
June, 1969

When John Maynard Keynes used to slip off to the Continent for a vacation, the franc was wont to quiver and several Balkan currencies to depreciate. Today, at commencement time, the ordinary risks of Wall Street life are intensified by the prospect that William McChesney Martin and John Kenneth Galbraith may or may not be receiving an honorary degree.

It is not given for all of us to see visibly etched on the face of Clio, the Muse of history, a wrinkle that we have personally put there. But periodically I am called to report to readers of London's Financial Times on the state of the American economy. And since there is alleged to be a small band of Threadneedle Street Irregulars or Samuelson watchers, who take seriously the guesses I put forth, it is a sobering responsibility. For once it is better to be merely right than to be clever.

This midyear what shall I say?

FACT

First, *America is undergoing inflation.* Prices in mid-1969 are soaring at a 6 per cent annual rate. Unless money wage rates rise by 9 per cent, the usual increase in real wages cannot be realized.

Second, *interest rates are, if not sky-high, at least flagpole high.* I know bankers who have been paying more than 10 per cent for short-term funds in the Eurodollar and Federal funds markets. Anyone who knows those bankers cannot be surprised that they have raised the prime lending rate to 8½ per cent per annum.

Although Congressman Wright Patman will not believe it, the high interest rates are more the *result* than the *cause* of the inflation. When you subtract a 6 per cent rate of price increase from a 10 per cent interest rate, you are back to the 4 per cent real rate of interest of more normal times. Not before people return to the expectation of no more than a 2 per cent annual price rise can we expect a return to 6 per cent mortgage and similar charges.

Third, *the real economy is definitely in a slowdown.* In the first half of 1969 real output grew at less than a 3 per cent annual rate, which is in decided contrast to the 6 per cent real rate of growth in early 1968. In my opinion the tax surcharge and the Federal Reserve's tightening of money and credit have contributed to the deceleration in real growth discernible since a year ago.

Most of the usual concomitants of an economic slowdown are beginning to appear. Productivity is deteriorating. Average unemployment is, slowly, rising. As usual, non-white unemployment is rising faster than white unemployment. Profit margins are down and over-all corporate profits are beginning to erode.

The combination of tight money and dwindling profits is taking its toll in Wall Street. Dreams of peace around the corner cannot overpower the fact that it costs you 9 per cent on margin money. At such odds few handicappers can beat the bookie.

What does this all add up to as far as the 1969 figure for gross national product is concerned? The magic number that I cast before the readers of the Financial Times and NEWSWEEK back last December is looking more and more to be a pearl of rare value. All the authorities are beginning to zero in on a GNP estimate for 1969 of $924 billion. If I came within a tenth of a per cent on the basis of incorrect budget and other exogenous data, think how great would have been my accuracy with the correct December figures!

But being pledged to truth not cleverness, I must register some disclaimers. The 7⅓ per cent growth in money GNP will be due a bit more to price increase and less to real growth than I had envisaged. (As they say in forecasting school, what you lose on the turns you gain on the roundabouts.) And I had expected a bit less strength in the first half of the year at the expense of more in the second.

OPINION

How shall we score the Nixon economists? This is an issue on which one can be nonpartisan. The new team can be exonerated completely. For they have in effect done nothing.

It is true that the Fed has caused money to grow at but a 3 per cent annual rate since December, but this "fine-tuning" has been *against* the advice of the Nixon ideologues. Gradualism is their watchword.

On all this I have no complaint. For there is no sight in the world more awful than that of an oldtime economist, foam-flecked at the mouth and hell-bent to cure inflation by monetary discipline. God willing, we shan't soon see his like again.

LIVING WITH INFLATION
February, 1971

Creeping inflation is the malaria of the modern mixed economy. Like malaria, it is uncomfortable to live with, and just will not go away.

But unlike the case of malaria, there seems to be no known cure for creeping inflation that is better than the disease.

If it is going to be around for a long time, what are inflation's known effects? Much of what you read in the papers or hear about inflation at Rotary lunches is scientifically false.

- It is not the case that inflation and deflation are equally bad. Along with falling demand and prices usually comes falling production, or a slowdown in the rate of growth of output. With the total social pie reduced, the trifling gains that creditors get from deflation, when their interest earnings and loan repayments buy more, are more than wiped out by the losses to workers and other capitalists. On the other hand, the inflation that comes from too rapidly rising output does involve a larger total pie to be divided.

- It is definitely not the case that inflation is "primarily a tax upon the poor." A study prepared for the Institute for Research on Poverty at the University of Wisconsin by Doctors R. Hollister and J. Palmer shows that an index number of the necessities that the poor buy does not go up quite as much as do prices generally—particularly those for services. Aside from changes in job opportunity, experience has confirmed the expectation that welfare and other aids to the poor tend to be raised by governments to compensate for declines in purchasing power of the dollar.

THE GORED OX

Who then is hurt by inflation? When the National Bureau of Economic Research assigned Prof. Raymond Goldsmith of Yale the task of working out statistically the net gains and losses that different classes experience as a result of inflation, he came up with a finding that most of us found startling. No single class was hurt *net* by inflation—not farmers, not workers, not profit receivers—save for one class alone. It is the *elderly,* those caught on fixed and inadequate pensions by an unanticipated inflation, who do suffer net from inflation.

Even this finding may be losing its validity with the passing of time. For one thing, social-security benefits are beginning to be escalated in terms of the rising cost of living. One of the beauties of social insurance as against private insurance is the fact that, precisely because it is *actuarially unsound* and is based upon the *real* taxable capacity of productivity of the nation, social security can rise phoenix-like from the ashes of even the most galloping inflation to provide a minimum of assistance for the aged.

There is a further point about protecting the passing investor against forseeable inflation: for many years there has been built into the interest yields earnable on bonds and other fixed-principal investments a definite premium to compensate for inflation. If you cheat me once by springing an inflation on me, shame on you; if you cheat me twice, shame on me.

THE SKEPTICAL JURY

This raises a new and important point. Although creeping inflation is not as bad as it is cracked up to be, it is also not as good as some of the claims that used to be made for inflation. As soon as everyone begins to anticipate creeping inflation correctly, and to make his adjustments to it, along with the disappearance of its evil effects will go the disappearance of its stimulative effects on real growth. Brazil and Chile, with cantering inflations that all have seen through long ago, are not to be envied.

Where then do these scientific findings leave us? They reinforce, in my judgment, the wisdom of moving toward expansionary fiscal and monetary policy designed to keep unemployment from growing any further. Let us make no mistake about it: these policies do involve us in some new risks with respect to reacceleration, or at the least, some risks that improvements in the rate of price increase will not be forthcoming.

No jury of economic experts will concur with the contention of the new Nixon game plan that, by the second quarter of 1972, we are likely to have brought unemployment to 4½ per cent at the same time that inflation has been brought down to a 3 per cent annual rate. Even if this combination were somehow feasible, it could never be reached with Dr. Burns permitting the money supply to grow at only a 5 per cent annual rate and with a fiscal '72 deficit of only $11 billion.

Some lies are mortal sins, some venial sins. At least the recent projections are biased on the side of humanity, and I shall not be the first to throw a stone.

PRICE CONTROLS
December, 1970

The history books will carry 1970 as a year of no economic growth. A year of rising unemployment and falling profits. And despite these travails, nonetheless a year of continuing inflation.

It was not a good year for the forecasters, whether gloomy or not. Not a single member of President Nixon's team of economists added to his professional reputation. The picture outside Washington was not much better—either for the overpessimistic monetarists or the overoptimistic Keynesians. Non-economists did even worse than the economists.

The escalation of the Vietnam war in 1965 produced classical demand-pull inflation—i.e., too much dollar spending chasing a limited supply of goods, with labor markets tight and order backlogs high as even overtime production could not produce as much as was wanted. By 1970, just as the demand-pull inflation was weakening in consequence of tight monetary and fiscal policies, the militant desire of union members to catch up to, and stay ahead of, the inflation led to upward cost-pressure on prices.

No one had a right to be surprised that there was a General Motors strike or that it could be brought to an end only by a whopping wage increase. No more should we be surprised if the steelworkers strive stubbornly next year to win an equally inflationary wage settlement.

NEW DISEASE

If you read the successive editions of my textbook "Economics," starting with the first edition in 1948 and the eighth in 1970, you will see an increasing emphasis on this new disease of "cost-push" or "seller's inflation." Because the world does change, what was good enough economics for your uncle and his uncle isn't good enough today for you. And a 1970 textbook won't be good enough for your nephew in the years that lie ahead.

What can be done about cost-push inflation, this scourge that makes it impossible for us to have both full employment and price stability? What is needed is some kind of a successful "incomes policy" of the sort that will let us pursue fiscal and monetary policies sufficient to produce jobs for all who want to work and yet will prevent those tight labor markets from erupting into never-ending inflation.

In the medical field what we need is a cure for cancer. It is good science to recognize that we don't know such a cure. I think it is good economic science to recognize that our mixed economy does not know how to have a satisfactory incomes policy that will back up monetary and fiscal policy. And neither do any of the mixed economies abroad known how to have a satisfactory incomes policy—not Sweden or Switzerland, not Japan or Germany, not Holland or Britain. Here then lies the unsolved frontier in modern economics.

Introduce permanent government controls on prices and wages? That is the recommendation of J.K. Galbraith. And he is not alone. Any public-opinion poll will show that there is much support for such programs among the electorate.

CLINICAL EXPERIENCE

Prior experience, here and abroad, does not augur well for peacetime price-wage controls. I wish that Dr. Galbraith would analyze that experience—in about a dozen different countries and at various times in the last quarter century. If he can show that the evils involved are less than those involved in alternatives, anyone with an open mind should welcome the demonstration. But one fears he will have his work cut out for him.

Right at the present moment, every country in Scandinavia is experimenting with government controls on prices. The Norwegian experience—introduced, it is interesting to note, by a non-socialist government—is only weeks old. The Swedish experience is only a couple of months old. I wish I knew about bout the Danish experience. The only case where I have heard favorable comments on mandatory price controls is in the case of Finland. In connection with her currency devaluation of recent years, the Finnish Government introduced various measures of price freezing. So far the result has seemed to be not bad. Even the critics of such measures seem primarily to fall back on dire predictions about trouble to come in the future.

Every researcher has seen many false treatments alleged to cure cancer. On the present evidence, I cannot favor price-wage controls. But I must concur with chairman Burns that the President should intensify his leadership in urging limits on wage and price increases.

Chapter 4

INTERNATIONAL TRADE AND FINANCE

International monetary reform is the principal theme of this chapter and, of course, is appropriate for this recent span of years. With more selections than any other chapter of the book, these readings represent fairly complete historical coverage of the period; starting in 1967 with the International Monetary Fund's plan for Special Drawing Rights, as discussed in the first reading on "Monetary Reform," and concluding with an analysis of the situation following the ten per cent devaluation of the dollar in February of 1973, in the selection titled "Dollar Repair." A further "floating" of European currencies, relative to the dollar, followed in March 1973.

In the light of recent developments, Professor Samuelson's earlier analysis of the overvalued dollar and prescriptions for possible reforms, including greater exchange-rate flexibility, speak for themselves. In fact, the very thoroughness and relative length of the chapter suggest brevity in these opening remarks. But as every economics student knows, underlying the international payments mechanism are the real gains of trade itself, to all concerned. This point is repeatedly made by Samuelson, as in the final remarks of "Dollar Repair." In our own self-interest, we should not let these gains fall victim to the difficulties of the payments problem; especially not to the fears and avarice of the "gnomes" of any type.

MONETARY REFORM
September, 1967

The greatest inventions of all are anonymous, as for example, fire, the wheel and cheese. The gold standard itself evolved when the Muse of History's head was turned. Britain used both silver and gold in the eighteenth century. Suddenly, one decade, silver rose in value relative to gold. "Bad money drives out good," says Gresham's Law; and, without the meeting of a committee, silver went out of circulation.

With Victoria on the throne and Britannia ruling the waves, it was natural a century ago for the rising new nations—Germany, Japan and the U.S.—to go on the gold standard too. Actually, it was only for a few decades before World War I that the gold standard prevailed. True, it did not work well, for this was a time of repeated crisis, depression and inflation. But it did work.

The year 1914 ended many things, both good and bad. One of them was the automatic gold standard. Gold payments were suspended during the war itself. Winston Churchill, while Chancellor of the Exchequer in 1925, made the greatest mistake of his career. He tried to put the Humpty Dumpty of gold back on the old prewar parity; but what he accomplished was a decade of English stagnation and, some would say, precipitated the beginning of Britain's economic decline.

BRAVE NEW WORLD

After World War II the world had learned its lessons. The Bretton Woods Conference set up in 1944 the International Monetary Fund and International Bank. Since nations would no longer "play the rules of the game" of the automatic gold standard, new institutions and mechanisms had to be founded. Exchange rates were to be stable, but no longer at the expense of unemployment.

Despite the croakings of Cassandras, world trade has vastly outperformed all expectations since then. There's the rub. The volume of trade has grown much faster than South African or Russian mines can spit out gold. With unanimity, the experts have long been warning that new sources of international reserves are imperative. Call these needed liquid reserves "paper gold" or anything you like. Without them, economic asphyxia is certain in the end.

What to do about this? There has been no shortage of proposals: Triffin plan; Bernstein plan; Roosa plan; several old Keynes plans; or we could raise gold's price (thereby helping the U.S.S.R. and South Africa). Or, following opposite counsel, cut gold's price to teach hoarders that dollars are a girl's best friend. Other experts have schemed up new monetary units and financial institutions to supersede the International Fund and Bank.

FOWLER'S TRIUMPH

Last month the Group of Ten agreed on a plan for a new monetary reserve asset. It operates within the Fund. It supplements rather than supplants gold. It makes sense and will, I believe, be the most important innovation since Bretton Woods. Here is how the plan works:

Special drawing rights (SDR) will come into existence after: (1) the Rio meeting of the Fund and Bank approves the plan later this month; (2) the separate 100-odd nations ratify the agreement in 1968 or 1969; (3) the director general of the Fund declares, in 1969 or 1970, a clear need of additional liquidity; (4) and finally, 85 per cent of the Fund members approve his programs.

The new SDR will be just like legal tender in the hands of member nations. Until they have spent 70 per cent of their allotment, their SDR are as freely disposable as gold itself. Even the final 30 per cent has its controlled uses.

But will nations approve? Shrewd heads say they will. The U.S. has a voting power of 21.9 per cent and we will certainly not veto. France has a 4.3 per cent voting power; all the Common Market, 16.6 per cent. Do not believe that the Common Market votes unanimously with de Gaulle. They haven't in the past and they won't in the future.

The wheel was not invented in a day and the London agreement is no panacea. It's not intended to solve the U.S. balance of payments. Nor can money cure all ills. But money can cure the asphyxia that comes from money shortage.

At a time when so many of President Johnson's programs seem to be going badly, he should be able to take great satisfaction that the initiative for monetary reform that he promoted two years ago should finally have succeeded so well. Our grandchildren will be grateful.

A DEVALUATION PARABLE
December, 1967

After John F. Kennedy's election in 1960, a leading English economist sent him a letter suggesting that his first act in office be a devaluation of the American dollar in joint concert with a devaluation of the pound and the Canadian dollar. (This is fact—the letter was sent to Kennedy via Dr. Heller—but the rest is my academic pipe dream. As will become evident, if I tried to peddle this parable in Washington I would be thrown out on my ear.)

Instead of dismissing the suggestion as impractical, let us suppose that President Kennedy suspended gold payments by Executive order in January 1961. Immediately the price of gold rose in the London market, now that we no longer provided the Bank of England with gold to supply that market. Nervous Frenchmen began to hoard gold—as is *their* legal right. Speculators began to buy gold bars, coins, and South African mine shares.

After hasty meetings in Basel, the Common Market countries also suspended gold payments. Japan soon followed. Wall Street prices fell the first two days following the Inauguration; but as fears of inflation swept the better clubs, stocks soon recovered and headed upward.

INITIAL CHAOS

Meanwhile, what about exchange rates between the dollar, pound, mark, and franc? By bilateral agreement, the pound was permitted to depreciate 7½ per cent relative to the dollar. This was considered wise in view of the fact that English export costs were preventing her from generating the volume of sales abroad needed to pay for her foodstuffs.

Since the mark and the franc were also off gold, there was no fixed parity between them and the dollar. In February 1961, the foreign-exchange rate between the mark and the dollar wobbled from day to day. Because the gnomes of Zurich distrusted "that man Kennedy," Continentals sold the dollar short. Fearing that a too-cheap dollar would enable American exports to inundate Continental markets, many Germans wanted the mark to depreciate as much as the dollar. But Erhard won out in a policy to insulate the Common Market countries from "importing American inflation." This was done by letting the dollar depreciate 12 per cent relative to the mark, the guilder, and the lira.

Only de Gaulle stood aloof, using exchange controls and quotas to keep out our goods, thereby breaking the Common Market treaties.

ULTIMATE EQUILIBRIUM

What ensued from 1961 to 1970?

1.   America's sick balance of payments began to improve. Our exports, which had been growing so costly as to make us lose in share of world markets, now became 10 per cent cheaper. Domestic industries, such as steel, found it easier to compete against Japanese and European imports, now that foreign costs had appreciated in terms of dollars.

2.   With an improvement in our *basic* balance of payments on current account, Kennedy found that he did not have to "tie" our foreign-aid programs. Secretary McNamara no longer had to buy military items in this country even if they were 50 per cent more expensive.

3.   Once the world realized that the dollar was no longer overvalued, New York became the money market of the world. Short- and long-term funds came here in abundance, to be parceled out all over the world wherever true returns were greatest. American companies could, without apology or hindrance, invest in whatever lands they found most profitable. In particular there was no need for an interest-rate-equalization tax to curb loans abroad, or a "voluntary" capital-control program to curb direct corporate investments.

4.   Once chairman Martin saw that the dollar was no longer overvalued, the Fed was emboldened to create the expansionary credit conditions conducive to a great "Kennedy growth sprint."

5.   After America fed out $5 billion of gold from Fort Knox—much of it to France—hoarders had their bellies full. And when de Gaulle's health began to fail in 1969, hoarders became fearful that the other governments wouldn't buy their gold back at any price. So gold fell to $28 an ounce late in 1970.

6.   After de Gaulle's death, the Common Market admitted the U.K. and the EFTA nations. And the world adopted the paper-gold schemes of the IMF.

7.   Best of all, U.S. full employment had been restored by 1963. World output and trade grew throughout the 1960s, breaking all records.

DEFENDING THE DOLLAR
January, 1968

At last it has come—direct controls on international transactions.

The world reacted with some surprise to President Johnson's New Year's announcement that corporate direct investments must now be limited. To the man in the street the gravity of the crisis was underlined by the threat to limit his freedom to be a tourist in Europe.

There need have been no surprise. It was plain that devaluation of the pound had set into motion gold hoarding and distrust of the dollar's present parity. Had the President not done something, it was certain that there would have been a gold drain of several billions in 1968.

Naturally, the President acted. He opted for one more turn of the screw of direct controls. He converted the voluntary program of restricting direct corporate investment abroad into a coercive program, and one with reduced quotas for both banks and corporations. Although this is the most important part of the program, it was eclipsed in the minds of the general public by his vague suggestions that tourism be limited. That part of Mr. Johnson's message dealing with renegotiation with NATO and other partners on sharing the burden of foreign-exchange costs has, quite wrongly, received almost no attention.

INEVITABILITY OF NECESSITY

Critics say: "Instead of offering palliatives, LBJ should strike at fundamentals of the problem." But what do such words mean? America has but three choices:

1. *We could devalue the dollar,* hoping to reduce its value relative to the mark, franc and yen. Speculators wrongly thought this imminent. They believed naïvely that de Gaulle's luck can produce any miracle, even toppling the dollar soon.

2. *We could engineer prolonged stagnation in our domestic economy,* hoping thereby to improve our trade surplus. Though this is the traditional solution preferred by the gnomes of Zurich and Manhattan, no Democratic President could buy it.

3. *Or we could do what President Johnson did, buy more time by introducing more direct controls.*

For years, I have been warning speculators that any failure to restore basic balance in our international payments would result, not in Machiavellian devaluation, but in a jungle of exchange controls. So far we are on the timetable.

The saying "Good Americans go to Paris when they die" illustrates how vital to American life travel abroad has been. Any attempt to prevent Americans from going to Venice and Copenhagen while they are alive is sure to prove politically controversial. Why then did so astute a leader as Mr. Johnson open up this Pandora's box? I can only speculate.

NO MORE GRAND TOUR?

First, there really is big money to be saved if tourism can be reduced. Speaking as an economist, I must point out that the dollar has been devalued *de facto* in many other directions: the military dollar buys up to a third less at home than does its foreign-exchange equivalent; the interest equalization tax is equivalent to a depreciation of the investment dollar. Tourists are getting a subsidized bargain that the nation can no longer afford when they can buy foreign exchange at the $35 parity figure. A tax of $100 on everyone who travels to Europe is completely defensible in terms of practicality—also equity, since it hits those already subsidized.

Second, even if Congress never does finally succumb to its prejudice against the foreign fleshpots and never does legislate curbs on tourism, the President could not have found any other proposal so dramatic as this one. How can inhuman corporations object to capital controls when even the sacred rights of the man in the street are in jeopardy?

Third, our willingness to talk about cutting down on tourism hits the surplus countries of Europe where they live. They love to chide us for our deficits, but they squeal when they lose our profitable business. General de Gaulle may bring glory to France, but if he kills off the flow of summer profits, what price glory? In truth, surplus countries are like the wives of drunkards: they lecture their spouses, but a cure often proves worse for them than the disease.

Finally, will the program work? Experience suggests that direct controls do buy time; but increasingly they spring leaks and create inefficiencies. Economists would prefer the use of taxes on investments to outright fiats. But that would require sensible Congressional action—our biggest deficit today.

STEEL STATISM
February, 1968

The steel industry is mounting a strong campaign for protective quotas against competitive imports from abroad. Last year they were asking Congress for "temporary tariffs." But since they know in their heart of hearts that there is nothing "temporary" about their need for protection from competition, and since once you have asked the state to intervene in your favor you have already given up the principle of believing in free enterprise, the steel industry has now joined textiles, glass and oil in lobbying for quotas to set quantitative curbs on imports.

Let me state the industry's case. Then appraise it.

CLAIM AND COUNTERCLAIM

1.   Steel imports from Europe and Japan have been growing at an accelerated rate. Our exports, which used to be among the highest in the world, are shrinking rapidly.

2.   According to the American Iron and Steel Institute—the spokesman for the industry—these trends will continue into the future. By 1975 imports will take 20 rather than 12 per cent of the total market. These additional imports will displace some 60,000 steel workers.

3.   The basic reason for "invasion" of our markets by imports in this: although America is the world's most efficient producer of steel in terms of total man-hours required—as reckoned in the steel mill and in the factories that make steel-making equipment—our efficiency is still not as much greater than efficiency abroad as are the money wages that American industries have to pay *in comparison with* money wages abroad. U.S. Steel, according to Roger Blough, must pay about $40 a day to attract workers from other American industries; Japanese steel companies need pay only the equivalent of $10 a day to get help. Our mills are more efficient, but not four times as efficient. And they cannot be made so.

4.   For national defense and security, our domestic industry deserves protection. To quote Mr. Blough, "Can we, for example, be assured of the strong industrial base in steel we need for modern defense if one-quarter or more of the steel we require were imported from countries lying uncomfortably close to the Soviet Union or China?"

5.   There is world overcapacity in steel. Steel is dumped here at lower costs than sold at home. No other country lets free trade prevail in steel. Why should we?

6.   A quota, limiting steel imports to the percentage they had in the last three years (about 10 per cent) would improve our future balance of payments, and heaven knows it needs improving.

Here is the economists' reply.

We gain most in international trade when we buy goods made with labor *lower paid* than our own. When an industry does not have an efficiency exceeding foreign efficiency by the average proportion that our money wages exceed foreign wages, we lack "comparative advantage" in that industry. And we gain in American living standards by letting that industry shrink.

By its own admission, steel lacks comparative advantage. Just as U.S. Steel buys power whenever it cannot produce it as cheaply, the U.S. should buy its steel in least-cost markets. This way our products made of steel can be most numerous and our real standard of living be highest.

If the steel lobby said "Give us quotas and they will cut into profitable American exports *elsewhere* by an equivalent number of billions of dollars," no literate congressman would listen to their pleas for protection. (Naturally I exclude congressmen from Gary and Pittsburgh.)

VERDICT FOR DISMISSAL

America still has a surplus of exports over imports amounting to billions of dollars per year. This demonstrates that other industries do have the comparative advantage steel lacks. True, our cold-war offshore needs and our foreign-aid desires are so large—particularly when coupled with the wish of our corporations to make direct investment abroad—that our private export surplus is too small for our needs. Tariffs, quotas and direct controls can temporarily bridge the gap. But neither in the short nor long run does steel have a special case for protection. And let us remember that a quota is the most malignant form of protection, much worse than a tariff.

When the time comes that steel must stand in line with the merchant marine for subsidy in terms of national defense, it will be hard to distinguish it from a nationalized industry. That time is not remotely near.

GOLD DETHRONED
April, 1968

Early in March chaos prevailed in the London, Paris and Zurich markets for gold. Speculators and hoarders bought gold frantically at a pace that could not be permitted to continue. Something had to give. The London gold market was shut down. The gold pool, which France had earlier abandoned, was discontinued.

In mid-March the Six, comprising the leading nations that had formed the gold pool, met in Washington and, as was inevitable, agreed upon a two-price system for gold. I.e., they agreed to stop selling gold to private markets while continuing to buy and sell at $35 an ounce on all transactions among their own official central banks and among other nations who agree not to deal with the private markets. (Even France is welcome to rejoin the club!)

Once we stopped feeding the private markets at $35 an ounce, the price of gold in Paris and Zurich leaped upward, reaching $44 prior to the post-weekend announcement by the Six. Since that time, the price weakened to the high thirties, as speculators took a quick profit and as the hope faded for de Gaulle's doubling the price of gold.

LONG-RUN GOLD PROBLEM

The mid-March agreement put off the gold crisis. As everyone says, it buys us more time. I think something enormously more important was accomplished, something which actually exceeded my expectations:

- *The Six have taken the first step toward demonetizing gold.* The leading nations have served notice that they will not in the future necessarily buy gold back from the hoarders and speculators. *Caveat emptor.* Foreigners who hoard or speculate on gold at prices above $35 an ounce must now be on guard lest they lose their shirts.

If gold is to be phased out as kingpin of the world's monetary system, the achievement of last week's Stockholm meetings—which carried forward negotiations for creating "paper gold" (i.e., Special Drawing Rights under the International Monetary Fund)—becomes fraught with significance. And no one knows this better than de Gaulle, who tried, but failed, to sabotage the Stockholm agreement and who still sulks in the background.

What is the future of international finance? To judge the outlook, I think we must distinguish two problems: (1) gold and total international liquidity reform; (2) chronic U.S. balance-of-payments deficits and overvaluation of the dollar at its present parity.

The long-run gold and liquidity problem stems from the simple fact that, while international trade grows more than 6 per cent per year, goldmine production grows barely 2 per cent. The rational solution to this discrepancy is to develop "paper gold" that will substitute for and serve as a supplement to gold, in its function as an international reserve.

Supplementing gold has taken place domestically in all the leading nations, and the proposal to create SDR's is promising and deserves universal support. Now is no time to antagonize de Gaulle by know-nothing Senatorial action denying gold sales to those in arrears on World War I debts.

LONG-RUN DOLLAR PROBLEM

Even if gold and liquidity were no problem, we would be faced with the fact that the United States has run chronic balance-of-payments deficits for more than a decade. The causes run deep and are quite incurable at the existing foreign-exchange rates. They are:

1.   The productivity miracles in Europe and Japan, which have been narrowing for a decade the technological gap between American and foreign productivity and lowering our export competitiveness.

2.   The great flow of direct investment in other countries by American corporations hoping to profit by combining their know-how and capital with foreign labor.

3.   U.S. Government military expenditure—most particularly on Vietnam!—and expenditure on foreign aid.

Except to abandon Vietnam and get rid of the dollar's overvaluation by a 10 to 15 per cent depreciation relative to the mark and other
surplus currencies, there is nothing we can do to end our chronic
deficit. I fear time buys us nothing but time. The good work of
mid-March may well be frittered away as our cooperative allies find
unwanted dollars thrust on them.

Conclusion: end the Vietnam war and begin negotiations aimed
at depreciation sufficient to overcome overvaluation of the dollar.

THE FRENCH GALBRAITH
July, 1968

"Fifteen years from now it is quite possible that the world's third
greatest industrial power, just after the United States and Russia, will
not be Europe, but *American industry in Europe.*"

With this blast of trumpets, J.-J. Servan-Schreiber begins his
book, "The American Challenge," recently the best seller in France
of any book, fiction or nonfiction. (Indeed, as will presently become
clear, I am not sure in which category it belongs.) Its thesis is simple.

Military warfare has been succeeded by economic warfare, and
the Americans are occupying Europe. Wellington's belief that Water-
loo was won on the playing fields of Eton gives way to the new view
that victory emerges from the seminars in management at the Harvard Business School. Were Stalin appraising the power of the Pope
today, he would ask: "How many computers does he have?"

Europe is not given much more time. For "by extrapolating
present trends, it seems clear we Europeans . . . [though] we will grow
even richer . . . will be overtaken and dominated, for the first time in
our history, by a more advanced civilization."

THE TECHNOLOGICAL GAP

Who is Servan-Schreiber? Only 44, he served with the Free French
Air Force; wrote an exposé of French atrocities in Algeria based on
personal experience; and is editor of L'Express, the popular French
newsweekly. He is one of Europe's "new men." According to Arthur
Schlesinger Jr.'s foreword, " 'The American Challenge' may do for
European unity very much what Thomas Paine's 'Common Sense'

did for American independence." (Fortunately, as Samuel Johnson observed, in writing introductions one is "not under oath.")

The student riots and general strikes that have recently hit France postdate the writing of the book, posing new problems undreamed of in the author's philosophy. The American corporation invader may wish to bypass French soil as high-cost scorched earth, unreceptive to his industrial seed. Hence, it is well that the author has addressed himself to all of Europe—Germany and the Common Market countries generally—and not just to France.

All of Europe has become obsessed in recent years with the concept of "the technological gap." Nobel prizes go these days to Berkeley and not Berlin. The supersonic planes that only a fool would think to build are built here better. Industrious Americans edit the letters of Horace Walpole more elegantly than proper Englishmen can afford to do.

Worst of all is the "brain drain." Hitler's push of intellectuals to our shore has been succeeded by the pull of American paychecks. Now a Fermi or a Segrè can hope to coax Nobel prizes out of Berkeley equipment. The roads that lead to Rome also lead away from it.

THE BIG BONER

One hates to spoil a pretty story, but talk of the ruin of Europe is tommyrot. The amateur who shuns the conventional wisdom must take care lest he swallow the novel nonsense.

Assertion: "From the end of the cold war and the launching of the first sputnik, American power has made an unprecedented leap forward. It has undergone a violent and productive internal revolution."

Fact: From 1950 to 1968, Europe and Japan have *narrowed* the productivity gap between America and themselves at a rate unprecedented in all history. Theirs has truly been a "miracle sprint." Since sputnik, America's balance of international payments has chronically weakened. Effete Europe has run chronic surpluses, outselling us at home and abroad.

The miraculous progress of the less-than-most-affluent nations has been the big story of our times. No one predicted it. Not Marx. Not Spengler. Not Toynbee. Not even my old teacher Joseph Schumpeter.

That Japan outgrows Russia is perhaps not surprising. But who could have expected this of Austria and Italy? Even Britain, whom we all pity, has averaged faster growth in the postwar era than ever she did in Victoria's glorious days of free enterprise.

Servan-Schreiber correctly perceives that American workers have ceased to possess monopoly access to modern managerial methods and equipment. That Europe's living standards can grow faster than ours merely by imitating our technology is the corollary he misses. It is Europe's vanity, not her pocketbook, that is hurt by America's new supremacy in pure science.

Can 500,000 French book buyers be wrong? *Mais, oui.*

GOLD
October, 1968

The annual meetings of the International Monetary Fund and International Bank have ended in Washington. It was all relatively peaceful.

As Sherlock Holmes explained to the police, the remarkable thing was that the *dog* did not bark. The remarkable thing last week was how *little* gold was discussed.

This is in sharp contrast with the period following last November's devaluation of sterling and with the gold run of just last March, when speculative hoarding in Zurich and Paris caused us to hemorrhage gold at the rate of a billion dollars a week.

The setting up of the two-tier system of gold pricing terminated the immediate crisis. Once the IMF and the leading nine nations of the world sealed themselves off from the free markets and agreed to deal only with each other, and at the official $35-an-ounce price, speculators no longer faced a one-way, sure-thing gamble.

If they pay $45 an ounce for gold today, they might just find that tomorrow they can only sell it at $38. That may seem a small loss, but when you remember that these deals are done on margin with highly leveraged borrowings, the loss is seen to be a possible 50 per cent or more.

SMOOTH SKIES

So far, the two-tier system has worked. The original fear that some small central bank might bring down the two-tier system by buying at the official price and making sneak sales to the free market in order to capture the differential never made much sense. And subsequent experience has shown that the two-tier system will be vulnerable only to a falling out among the principal nations within the club itself.

Here is where France and de Gaulle become important. I have spoken of the Nine rather than the Ten because France tried to sabotage last March's Washington and Stockholm agreements. That was when France, in the general's words, was an island of serenity in a chaotic world.

The student revolts and general strike of last spring revealed how thin was the veneer of French serenity. Far from being in a position to intervene offensively to topple the status quo of gold parities, France has had to come cap in hand to beg for stabilization loans. This, too, has contributed to recent international stability.

But, of course, the most important factor producing the present lull has been America's dramatically improved balance of payments. Why this improvement? And can it last?

Certainly the improvement has not been in our trade balance and private balance on *current* account. Because of recent overheating in the economy, imports have soared beyond our exports and we remain far from the comfortable trade surplus we enjoyed prior to the Vietnam escalation.

The improvement has been exclusively on *capital* account. Continental investors have been gobbling up Wall Street "bargains." There has also been good reception by Europeans of convertible bond financing by U.S. corporations trying to comply with our mandatory foreign investment controls.

SOME DOUBTS

Since the barometer is steady, can we not look forward to a speedy implementation of "paper gold" in the form of new Special Drawing Rights (SDR's) in the IMF and permanent equilibrium? I must voice some doubts. What comes in on capital account can also go out. The continued attractiveness of American stock prices is not a condition one can rely on!

The next President, whether Nixon or Humphrey, has no hidden weapon to improve our trade balance. If the Vietnam war and its drain of offshore dollars does not come to an end, our international partners will become restive over having to take on unwanted dollars.

Here is where comes the genuine threat to the two-tier system and the promise of international liquidity reform via SDR's. What then?

A question I am increasingly asked is: Will President Nixon devalue, and throw the blame on his predecessors? Here is my answer:

One can bet that only a leader supremely self-confident and willing to take calculated risks would make such a move—as was proven in the case of Harold Wilson when first in office and when for eight hours our government was not in communication with the British while they threshed out the wisdom of an immediate devaluation.

Whether or not a dollar devaluation would be desirable in the long run from an economic and political point of view, nothing in Nixon's Congressional or Vice Presidential career indicates that he is such a man.

GOLD BLUES
September, 1969

On Cape Cod I recently ran into a New York banking friend. Although the sun was shining and the wind brisk from the southwest, his face was gloomy.

"A fool and his money are soon parted,"he informed me sadly. "Yes, and there's no fool like an old fool," I replied unkindly. For, as I suspected, he had a sorry tale to tell of his new losses in betting on an upward valuation of gold.

Here are the sordid details:

1. In October 1960, when it was still legal for Americans to hold gold abroad, Morgan (as I shall call him) put up $20,000 in margin money to buy $120,000 worth of gold at $40 an ounce. By February 1961, a month after the Eisenhower executive order required Americans to get out of their foreign positions, he sold out his position at $35 an ounce, losing $15,000 of his $20,000.

2. In the summer of 1961, at the time of the Berlin Wall crisis, Morgan put a few thousand dollars into marginal Canadian and South African gold-mining stocks. He quickly doubled his money in these. (That is his only transaction without loss.)

3.   Precluded from engaging directly in gold operations, Morgan decided that silver was the next best hedge against currency depreciation and arbitrary government. With that extraordinary sagacity that only a pre-1929 economic training can give, he managed to catch silver at the high. The result, several painful margin calls of the pre-1929 variety and loss of five times his initial investment.

COSTLY IDEOLOGY

You would think that to be enough. For Morgan did not work his way up from the Yale Daily News to the vice presidency of one of our biggest banks without developing a certain respect for money and some instinct for knowing when to cut his losses. And if it was money alone that was involved, I daresay the whole matter would have ended there.

Scratch a banker and you draw the blood of an idealist. Morgan thoroughly disapproves of the New Economics. Within his arteries there is a constant battle going on: sometimes reserpine wins; more often the contemplation of deficit financing sends his systolic pressure up to unsafe limits.

Each month Morgan reads the confidential newsletter of Harry Schultz from London. He marks its predictions of an imminent rise in gold price, and circulates Xerox copies among his younger colleagues. And poor Morgan cannot help putting his money where his heart is.

So naturally, when there was a gold run last year, egged on by General de Gaulle and his septuagenarian expert Jacques Rueff, Morgan gave it one more good college try. He bought American-South African Investment, listed on the New York Stock Exchange, in March 1968. He could hardly have picked a more unfortunate moment. Apparently a number of his contemporaries from Yale and Princeton were then having the same golden thoughts, for Morgan had to pay a premium over net asset value for his stock exceeding 50 per cent.

When Morgan and I met on the Cape, he had thrown in the towel.

THE NEW ORDER

Who can blame him? De Gaulle is gone. The South Africans are sweating out their ability to get rid of the gold they have been holding off the market. Rumors of gold filtering into Zurich from the Soviets will not die. Even the franc devaluation could not cause a ripple in the London and Zurich gold marts. The two-tier gold system has been flourishing.

Later this month the International Monetary Fund and World Bank meetings will implement the agreements to issue "paper gold" in the form of SDR's (i.e., special drawing rights in the IMF that nations can use within that club in place of gold for settling international balances).

This does not mean that our international problems are at an end. After the German elections, the mark ought definitely to be appreciated. I still think the dollar is somewhat overvalued at the existing parity, and that it would be in the interests of all to have a multilateral realignment of key rates.

And I am hopeful that we can someday move toward some kind of "crawling peg" mechanism that will permit limited exchange-rate flexibility and adjustment in any annual period. For without these changes, the system of "paper gold" starts out under a grave handicap.

But these are all sensitive subjects with Morgan, and we confine our discussions to spinnakers and that southwest wind.

INTERNATIONAL FINANCE
October, 1970

The international year in finance has its own calendar, ending and beginning in September with the annual meetings of the International Monetary fund and the World Bank. Copenhagen was the 1970 meeting place for civil servants, central bankers, private financiers, and run-of-the-mill economic experts.

This year's report is not bad—no dramatic news is good news here.

1. *The two-tier gold system is working well.* Gold hoarders lost 8 to 12 per cent on their holding this last year. South Africa has had to seek refuge for her mines' outputs in distress sales to the IMF lest the free-market price quoted to jewelers, dentists, and the Mafia sink below $35 per ounce.

2.   *The Special Drawing Rights, consisting of new liquid reserves (so-called "paper gold") created in limited amounts by the IMF, got off to an excellent start.*

3.   *The U.S. balance of payments continues to be in over-all deficit*—in the sense that our *private surplus* of exports over imports on *current* account is still far less positive than it was in 1964 before the Vietnam escalation. The current surplus of only a couple of billion dollars falls far short of what would be needed to finance (1) our governmental military and foreign-aid offshore purchases and (2) the huge new investments abroad that our corporations would like to make each year.

THE SICK DOLLAR

Fortunately, the dollar itself and short-term dollar securities are assets that foreign agencies, private and public, would be very happy to accumulate each year in the billions. And they would desire even more billions if they could believe that the future parity of the dollar were likely to be maintained or improved—not relative to gold, because gold no longer counts now that it has essentially been demonetized, but relative to the main other currencies such as the mark, yen, franc and guilder.

Therefore, it is genuinely normal for a key currency like the dollar to run a substantial and chronic so-called basic deficit.

But enough is enough. Foreign investors and central banks, given their *free* choice, would presumably not wish to take in the many billion dollars of deficit that would result if we got rid of our piecemeal government controls introduced to alleviate our balance-of-payments shortage. Indeed, these many interferences, which are both inefficient and inequitable, still do not suffice to keep us from forcing on foreigners more dollar obligations than they wish—particularly since those foreigners rightly fear that the next changes in currency parities are more likely to be more favorable to the yen and mark than to the dollar.

Thus, the *dollar is an overvalued currency.* How much it is overvalued would be revealed if we (1) stopped tying foreign aid and let those funds be spent anywhere, (2) eliminated mandatory capital controls on corporations and the banks, (3) let the interest-equalization tax lapse, (4) revalidated the military dollar by discontinuing the practice of buying goods at home even when they cost 50 per cent more than abroad.

Here is a test. If, like the Canadians in recent months, we were to let supply and demand determine the parity of the dollar relative to the other currencies, who can doubt that the result would be an appreciation of the mark and yen, and a relative depreciation of the American dollar?

HEALING FLEXIBILITY

The best news from Copenhagen is the growth in interest in some kind of exchange-parity flexibility. At last, all realize that the Bretton Woods system of inflexible parities is fatally flawed and leads inevitably to overvalued or undervalued currencies and to financial breakdown.

The 78-page fund document on exchange adjustments represents a move toward flexibility in its suggested further study of (1) more frequent, small adjustments in exchange parities to correct fundamental disequilibrium more promptly, (2) some widening of the bands around parity in which exchange rates can flexibly adjust and (3) temporary floating of a currency as a transition to a new parity in the 1969 German manner.

This is progress, and the path of policy for America is now clear. Once and for all we should stop following uneconomic policies—import quotas, idiotic SST's, you name them—whose only rationalization is to defend a parity of the dollar that is indefensible, and which is in any case not worth defending.

Has Vietnam taught us nothing about cutting our losses?

THE SHAKY DOLLAR
April, 1971

To put it frankly, the dollar is what economists call an "overvalued currency." This is in contrast to, say, the German mark, which economists call an "undervalued currency."

A currency is neither undervalued nor overvalued when it is selling at a parity such that its balance of current exports of goods and services in comparison with imports is large enough to finance the net short- and long-term capital investments that people and governments (including our own people and government) *voluntarily* want to make on balance.

The word "voluntarily" is emphasized because, in a healthy state of equilibrium, no German exporter is supposed to have to ask himself: "Is this export in the interests of the German nation? Of mankind?" And no American, tempted by a trip to Rome, or for that matter to Monte Carlo, is supposed to have to ask himself: "Is this trip what Treasury Secretary Connally would recommend? Am I letting President Nixon down? And am I depriving some New York hotel workers or Las Vegas card dealers of job opportunities when I take this trip?"

MAKESHIFT MEASURES

If the dollar were not overvalued, there would be no need for an interest-rate equalization tax, which penalizes an American who wants to buy a security abroad. And no need for mandatory quotas on investing abroad by corporations and banks.

There would be no need for the rule that our quartermasters must buy supplies in America even though they cost 50 per cent more than similar quality items from foreign sources. Tying of foreign aid, which compels those we help to buy higher-price, lower-quality American goods, is a practice we used to lecture the world against back when the dollar was undervalued. But that was almost fifteen years ago and now the shoe is on the other foot.

By every rational test, the dollar has been an overvalued currency for almost fifteen years now. Is the situation improving? No, it is not. I thought there was perceptible, slow improvement going on in the years 1959-1964; but the escalation of the Indochina war, and its aftermath, blew that progress. Since 1965 the situation has, if anything, been deteriorating.

Expert opinion expects 1971's basic-payments deficit to be even worse than 1970's. Previously, in the tight-money days of 1969-70, the situation could be papered over by the fact that our banks were willing to borrow in the Eurodollar markets at rates of 10 per cent and higher: foreigners are delighted to hold dollar obligations if they are perfectly safe and pay such astronomical interest rates.

Now that America's recession requires the Federal Reserve to ease interest rates at home to bring down the rate of unemployment our banks are flush and don't wish to borrow Eurodollars at any rate. Since private individuals abroad won't hold the dollars we keep spitting out each year, they pass the hot bricks on to their government's central bank.

BETTER THAN GOLD?

Do the central banks of Germany, Japan, France, Italy, Belgium and Holland really want all those dollars? Up to a couple of years ago, many economists kept insisting that the world was on a dollar standard—that the dollar was better than gold, than marks, or anything else. According to this comfortable doctrine, this gave us the license to create money for all the world to finance our wars and living standards.

Most experts now take an alternative line, leading to the same comfortable conclusion: "OK, so the central bankers, given their free choice, would prefer gold (official-tier, not free-market-tier, gold) and paper gold (SDR's) to some of their dollars. But they know well they can't have free choice. So they have no alternative to piling up dollar holdings in future years—until they finally wise up to overvaluation of the dollar via-à-vis their own currencies and unilaterally or in concert appreciate their currencies back to an equilibrium parity."

Since the opposite to "benign neglect" of the international deficit could be "malignant preoccupation," I do not dissent. Still, justice long delayed is not justice. International equilibrium long delayed builds vested interests that could make the final solution harder to achieve.

In Germany vested interests are becoming entrenched in the export industries. In the United States more and more industries clamor for quotas. Long before spontaneous currency appreciation abroad occurs, the protectionist poison may have entered deep in our system.

DOLLAR CRISES
May, 1971

The first part of the monetary crisis is over. The mark and guilder are floating; their exchange rates against the dollar vary from moment to moment depending on supply and demand. The Austrian schilling has been appreciated relative to the dollar (and other currencies) by 5 per cent, the Swiss franc by 7 per cent.

Here, the man in the street learned there was a monetary crisis from the headlines telling him that the Germans had stopped buying dollars at the old parity. Titillated a little by the crisis, he wondered whether this was a disaster which would affect his livelihood or nest egg.

Abroad, the crisis was regarded as a blow to the prestige and economic strength of the United States. Even our friends felt it couldn't have happened to a nicer guy than the richest and most arrogant nation in the world. What robbed a little from their *Schadenfreude* was the calmness with which our government, citizenry and stock market took the news.

How do these events appear to the economist? What does he expect will happen in the future?

THREE CAUSES

The basic long-run cause of the crisis had nothing to do with the speculators. It lay in the basic fact that the dollar has long been an overvalued currency, running chronic balance-of-payments deficits that involve piling up of unwanted dollars abroad.

The intermediate-term cause of the crisis was the fact that America, to fight its recession and reduce unemployment, has had to have interest rates lower than those needed abroad. If our banks will no longer pay 9, 11 and even 13 per cent for Eurodollars, foreign corporations and individuals are no longer willing to hold as many dollar obligations as last year; they pass on the hot bricks to their central banks, which must buy them if the Bretton Woods rules of the game are adhered to.

Consequently, the official settlements deficit has swelled at the expense of the private liquidity deficit. Cool money observed our debonair policies of benign neglect of the international balances, and the mounting restlessness of foreign governments over holding ever-increasing dollar reserves. The tinder was set.

The match that set off the speculative explosion was the rumor that several economic institutes in Germany were about to issue a report favoring appreciation of the mark. Germany has its Hellers and Friedmans: when they speak with one voice, the world listens. So too does Karl Schiller.

Who were the speculators? They were American corporations and banks, and, in lesser degree, American individuals. They were Frenchmen, Germans, Scots, Tunisians—anyone who wished to take a flyer which promised little downside risk if no parity changed, but which promised a quick gain (of many times 10 per cent if borrowed money was used on short margins) in case the Deutsche mark were revalued.

Isn't there a law against this sort of thing? No: when the Bretton Woods scheme is working according to its normal manner, all this is quite according to Hoyle. Moreover, some of the corporations kidded themselves that they were not looking for speculative profits but were only undertaking protective hedges against higher German prices for the things they will have to buy later.

The IMF rules have not been working well as far as the dollar is concerned for a long time. The U.S. does have mandatory capital controls on its international corporations. But, so long as a company can keep within its foreign-investment quota on Dec. 31 and other window-dressing dates, it is free to take a flyer in any currency speculation.

THE FUTURE

To economists, change in dollar parity is a good thing, not a bad thing. It helps to reduce our payments deficit and raise the competitiveness of our domestic industries. A move from disequilibrium to equilibrium is good also for the surplus countries. Germany stops giving away goods for bits of green paper it doesn't want; it also insulates its price level from imported inflation.

However, the outcome of the crisis has not solved all the monetary problems of the world or of the dollar.

1. I hope the German Government will not set an official parity for a long time. Let the gamblers sweat.

2. The outcome could well have been exchange controls, not a floating currency. That danger remains.

3. There remains the matter of the undervalued yen.

DEVALUATION ECONOMICS
August, 1971

Another dollar crisis has been brewing. Its immediate spark was the Reuss report of the Joint Economic Committee, pointing out that the dollar is seriously "overvalued" and that something ought to be done about its parity relative to other currencies.

So what else is new? That the dollar is overvalued enough to keep our goods from being internationally competitive in the needed degree has been known for years by the readers of these pages.

What is new is that a Congressional committee has dared to utter the forbidden words "devaluation of the dollar." What does this mean?

First, we must distinguish between "dollar depreciation" and "dollar devaluation." Dollar depreciation involves merely a change in the foreign-exchange rate between our currency and that of another —say, the mark or the pound. Thus, even though the official price of gold remains at $35 an ounce, if the exchange rate rose to $2.80 per pound instead of the present $2.40, we would say that the dollar had depreciated relative to the pound; or, what is the same thing, that the pound had appreciated relative to the dollar.

Those who have been preaching the comfortable doctrine of "benign neglect" of America's balance-of-payments problem have obviously been expecting that other countries would eventually appreciate their currency relative to the dollar when finally they tired of accepting our dollar deficits.

WE OR THEY?

Thus, most economists have been expecting a future depreciation of the dollar relative to the currencies of the surplus countries—Japan, Germany, Switzerland, Austria, and probably France and Italy. This involves no revaluation of official gold. And economists couldn't care less about the free gold price in Zurich or the alleys of Tangier.

Suppose we agree that the dollar's parity should change vis-à-vis the other principal nations. How can this be brought about?

No one of them is eager to appreciate its currency unilaterally. It is practically impossible for them to meet in secret and announce this as a *fait accompli.* Speculators would pounce upon any rumor of such a collective meeting. Besides, unilateral currency appreciation is politically unpopular with the export industries in the surplus countries.

So usually it is *after* a speculators' crisis that the mark or the Swiss franc gets appreciated.

How much simpler it would be if the dollar *itself* could by a stroke of the pen get adjusted. But that is just what the Bretton

Woods and IMF setup cannot allow: the dollar is the archstone of the present financial system.

What irony that the king of the jungle should be cut off from the remedial options that every low creature can enjoy.

This raises the question:

Why not raise the dollar price of official gold and of paper gold (special drawing rights), say, from $35 an ounce to $40 an ounce? At the same time, the price of official gold in terms of the yen, mark, guilder and franc is not to be raised by this 15 per cent amount.

Now we are talking about a devaluation of the dollar (i.e., a drop in its value relative to official gold). But note: we are talking also about a depreciation of the dollar relative to those currencies that have not revalued gold as much as we have.

THE IMPOSSIBLE DREAM

I am not saying I favor this solution as against other solutions. What I have long been saying is that this is not the unthinkable program that statesmen and experts claim it is.

First, it could not automatically help the South African or Russian miners of gold. The official gold tier can be sealed off forever from their profiting from devaluation.

Second, it would not undermine paper gold or SDR's. They are always to be revalued *pari passu* with official gold.

Third, this kind of revaluation need not favor those countries that have been hoarding official gold. Those nations that have played ball with us in past crises could, by agreement with our authorities, be permitted to share in the "revaluation profits" implied by writing up the official price of gold.

Fourth, it is silly to say that every other country will insist on raising its gold price as much as we do. For, just as we, the deficit country, benefit from dollar depreciation, they, the surplus country, will benefit from appreciation of their currencies.

QUESTIONS AND ANSWERS
October, 1971

In lecturing, I meet certain key questions that perplex the public. Here are my answers.

Q. Was the NEP necessary?

A. Yes. The old game plan was performing disappointingly.

Q. How's the new program doing?

A. Let's begin with the wage-price freeze, which understandably most concerns the common man. At the halfway point, the 90-day freeze appears to be working a bit better than might have been expected.

- The index numbers of wages and prices will register less inflation in this period than earlier. And, I suspect, than later.

- A confrontation with organized labor has been averted.

- The program is popular and compliance is good.

Q. Do you agree with the first computer models that expect 1972 to be a great year? Dr. Otto Eckstein, a Democrat, has a computer estimate that NEP will raise real GNP growth to 7 per cent, up from a pre-NEP 5 per cent for 1972.

A. A lion tamer must not let the beasts frighten him. All a computer does is tell a *consistent* story: a consistent truth or, if the programmer's guesses are unlucky, a consistent fiction. Computers as a group speak with forked tongue—each one tells a different consistent story.

Most first-pass models merely assumed that President Canute has spoken: ergo, inflation will be curbed. Thus, if you put in half the inflation rate and the computer works with pretty much the same dollar relations, then all the gains come down below the line in the form of improved real-growth rates.

I don't think the post-freeze controls, strong as they will be, can work such miracles. The back of my envelope shows less inflation progress and less induced growth.

- Anyone who was betting on 5½ per cent unemployment by the 1972 election must still fear 5+ per cent by then.

- I expect prices to be 4 per cent higher a year from now, not 2 ½ per cent higher. Without NEP 5 per cent could have occurred.

Q. How's the floating dollar?

A. Ideally, the dollar should float downward—or, what is the same thing, surplus currencies such as the yen, franc and mark, should float upward—by 10 to 15 per cent. Ideally, there should be no 10 per cent import surcharge. Ideally, the new parity structure should be built-in flexibility to correct new disequilibriums in a gradual way.

Q. Ideally, ideally. Actually . . .?

A. Actually, the yen is up only 7½ per cent. Other currencies scarcely half that much since August.

To freeze parities here would be tragic. However, there is plenty of time to move toward viable parities if we avoid premature stabilization.

Q. Do you favor the import surcharge?

A. Like all free traders, I opposed it as a barrier that adds nothing useful to dollar depreciation. But the stubbornness of the Japanese and French makes me admit that this is the only bargaining ploy that has given them pause.

Still, I fear the import surcharge. I fear that protectionist sentiment will saddle us with it long after parity bargaining is over. I fear a new round of retaliatory trade restrictions abroad.

Q. Should we revalue gold?

A. Here the President goofed. The IMF, the French, the Japanese, the whole of the Big Ten, want the drop in dollar parity to come in part through writing up the dollar price of paper gold (i.e., Special Drawing Rights) and official gold (i.e., gold in the governmental tier and not in the world of Swiss numbered bank accounts and hot money). Why fight the whole world dogmatically? I have always been in favor of milk of magnesia on the proper occasions.

Q. You've sold out to South Africa?

A. No. Never again can they get more than $35 an ounce for new-mined gold sold to the official tier. Gold from Russia can't get in this tier at any price.

Q. Why not abandon gold?

A. I hope we will eventually. But Mr. Nixon can't advance that day by insisting on the old $35 gold parity. He should be proud to be the second President (FDR was the first) who devalued gold from a disequilibrium parity—just as he should be proud to be the second President (Ike was the first) to cut our losses in a senseless war.

DOLLAR WOES
March, 1972

Last December in Washington the principal nations arrived at a monetary agreement that brought to an end the crisis and chaos that followed upon President Nixon's Aug. 15 suspension of gold convertibility. The world heaved a sigh of relief.

- Now an international depression could be averted.
- With the dollar substantially depreciated fruitful and mutually profitable trade could continue among nations.
- Equilibrium in America's balance of payments could be restored in a couple of years as the medicine of exchange depreciation gradually cured the illness of America's chronically overvalued dollar.
- Removal of the Nixon 10 per cent import surcharge was to be the first step in a general attack on quotas, tariffs and capital restrictions everywhere.
- Some much-needed flexibility in exchange rates was provided by the new IMF rule permitting currency rates to move in a widened range of 2¼ per cent around the new parities.

Most informed people, experts or not, thought this to be a pretty good agreement: not perfect, but definitely several steps in the right direction. Still left on the agenda for later negotiation were the important issues of further reform of the IMF rules to institute *gradual flexibility* in exchange parities and the whole band around parities—so-called gliding bands or crawling pegs.

For later agreement, also, was left the issue of resuming some kind of future convertibility of dollars held abroad.

DOUBTS

Who opposed the December agreements? The Administration team, understandably, considered it a triumph. The opposition Democrats largely had to concur.

The French would have preferred more than the token raising of the official price of gold, from $35 an ounce merely to $38. But de Gaulle was dead and Pompidou was willing to compromise.

The gold bugs, whether in South Africa or in Arizona Rotary Clubs, thirsted for a doubling of the price of gold at least. And for resumption of gold coinage and gold holding. But what else is new?

Finally, libertarians, who think the only good currency is one that is freely floating, were as disappointed that the crisis ended in halfway reforms as Trotsky was when the moderate Kerensky regime succeeded the Czar.

Three months have passed since the agreement. International finance has been far from peaceful. Instead we are in a continuing crisis.

"Isn't the December agreement coming unraveled?" "Won't the price of gold be doubled soon?" "Won't the dollar be depreciated again soon?" These are questions constantly in the news. Nor are they on the tongues of Continental gnomes only.

Why this flare-up of monetary uncertainty? Why is the price of free-tier gold near its peak, at $50 an ounce some 30 per cent above the official IMF tier price? Why is the dollar near its floor in the admissible band around the new parities? Most important, why did the cool dollars that had gone abroad in 1971 not return in the expected multibillion-dollar reflux early this year?

Let me answer as best I can these important questions. And let me give my best estimate of the odds that we shall soon see a further depreciation of the dollar, in terms of other currencies or in terms of gold.

SELF-FULFILLING PROPHECIES

First, the odds are 99 to 1 there will be no doubling of the price of official gold. Just because a rumor is denied in Washington doesn't mean it's true. (The free-market gold price could go anywhere—to $80 or down to $34 depending on what some gnomes, peasants and gangsters are thinking about the crisis.)

Second, three months is too short a time to throw any light whatever on the question of whether the dollar was depreciated too little or too much relative to the mark, yen, franc and pound. No jury of experts could have insisted on greater depreciation than December's average 12 per cent. But all the expert jurors know this exchange depreciation is a medicine that takes two or three years even to indicate whether it is going to be able to cure the disease of international deficits.

Third, American and non-American corporations fear that new exchange controls on the dollar loom ahead. Such a run on the dollar could, with odds 40 to 60, become a self-fulfilling prophecy.

SAD FACTS, HIGH HOPES
October, 1972

Autumn brings colored leaves and annual meetings of the International Monetary Fund and International Bank. When officials and bankers assemble in Washington, they will look back on more than a year since President Nixon suspended gold payments in August 1971. The ensuing crisis received a respite last December at the Smithsonian Institution in Washington. The dollar was then officially depreciated relative to the yen by 17 per cent, relative to the mark by 14 per cent, relative to the principal currencies of the world by an average of 12 per cent.

Disaster was avoided in 1971. But 1972 has not yet brought any return to international equilibrium. The American deficit of exports over imports has, up to now, shown no improvement. The economists' prescription of dollar depreciation has not yet shown visible signs of improving the patient's condition.

Both last spring and this summer, there were moments when it looked as though the Smithsonian interim agreement would break down. Britain had to give up defending pegged parity of the pound. As the pound floated, doubts grew about the viability of the dollar's parity. Speculators (i.e., frightened treasurers of multinational corporations) dumped dollars.

Foreign governments and central banks grudgingly swallowed billions of those unwanted dollars. "It's our paper I.O.U.'s for theirs," one German banker proclaimed in the hope of debunking talk of more dollar depreciation to come.

CONFLICTING GOALS

An uneasy calm between storms now prevails. Final decisions on monetary reform are still to be arrived at. This next year of negotiations will be a hard one.

France and the U.S. are still at loggerheads on ultimate goals. France wants gold set back on the throne, with its official price doubled. (Who said General de Gaulle is dead?)

What do we want? First, we want time for the Smithsonian medicine of exchange depreciation to work. And second, if over the next two years it turns out not to work, we want a larger dose of its same prescription—further downward flexibility of the dollar's exchange rate.

What don't we want? We don't want to depress our economy in order to wipe out our balance-of-payments deficit.

We don't want to convert the $70 billion that have fled abroad into gold. Or into paper gold (Special Drawing Rights) that is supposed to be just as good as official gold for every purpose.

We don't even want to convert these dollars—which sit so heavily in the stomachs of foreign central banks—into U.S. Government bonds that carry a guarantee against loss on future devaluations and depreciations of the dollar parity.

ULTIMATE TARGET

What we seem to be praying for is a miracle—the following kind:

1.   U.S. productivity improvement plus control of inflation at home superior to that in Japan and Western Europe is to reinforce last December's dollar depreciation to give us a whopping surplus in the balance of merchandise exports over imports. Invisible earnings from abroad by our giant corporations are to soar, so that our current balance of payments turns positive for several years to the tune of $10 billion per year.

2.   Yet all this is to take place so smoothly as not to cause Germany, Japan or other surplus nations undue distress in their export industries and domestic economies.

3.   As our surpluses bring dollars back to America and conviction that the dollar is more likely to appreciate than depreciate, capital movements will reinforce rather than thwart the strength of the dollar.

4.   Once the American balance of payments has been put in order, we can with renewed prestige use our influence to expedite needed long-run reforms: flexible exchange rates via crawling pegs or other devices; gradual phasing out of gold in the international monetary mechanism; orderly evolution of the system of paper gold, along with some "link" that funnels to underdeveloped countries more of the new liquidity than they deserve in terms of their present economic performance.

5.   Finally, in strength and not weakness, we can relinquish the special role of the dollar as the key international reserve currency.

Miracles are not sure things—or even likely outcomes. But dreams do point up the ends that means should strive for.

THE RIGHT TO HOARD GOLD
December, 1972

There was a little-noticed plank in the Republican platform that the Nixon Administration didn't much like. The right of American citizens to hold gold was to be reinstated as soon as it became feasible.

Nothing is surprising in this. Just as little boys dream vaingloriously of being able to be invisible and exercise all sorts of magical powers, elderly people of means have always dreamed of being able to have an asset that would insulate them from government controls. What can be better for this purpose than a gold hoard?—particularly if you are not squeamish in a pinch about engaging in a little perjury concerning the magnitude of your holdings.

What I find more surprising is the unanimity of a subcommittee of the Joint Economic Committee recommending that the right of private persons to hold gold be reinstated when feasible.

Congressman Henry Reuss of Wisconsin, who chaired that subcommittee, is a liberal who has been on the side of the angels in connection with international monetary reform. He is not one of those enamored of corporate democracy, in which a man with a million shares has a million times the voting power of a man with one share. Nor would he wish to restore that earlier state of affairs in which wealthy people, when they became critical of domestic management by government, would remove their funds from the country —thereby bringing on a financial crisis that would return the authorities to their orthodox senses. (Do I exaggerate? Ask any student of French history.)

DEMONETIZING GOLD

Indeed, Congressman Reuss is in favor of ultimately phasing out gold as a substantial element in our monetary system. And so am I.

But I think that a premature restoration of the right to hoard gold will most likely *set back* the cause of demonetizing gold. Here's why.

We must remember that several countries still hanker for a return to the gold standard. France, for one.

Even those nations who would not mind phasing out gold are apprehensive over whether it can be successfully done. (And make no mistake about it: going back to a gold standard would be better than some alternatives that might ensue if the present attempts to reform the Bretton Woods system of international finance should fail —for example, the alternative ot a regime of exchange control and fettered world trade.)

Every prudent man must therefore realize this: there is a *not negligible probability* that, at some future date, the members of the International Monetary Fund will be going back to a modified metallic gold standard.

I do not point out the above fact because I like it.

THE UNPALATABLE PROSPECT

Suppose, therefore, the U.S. sells much of its Fort Knox gold on the open market at prices above the official $38 an ounce. And suppose other countries do likewise. Will the end of the story be (a) demonetization of gold and (b) transfer of real purchasing power from would-be gold hoarders to deserving official treasuries? I much doubt it.

More likely is the following realistic possibility.

1. If gold becomes legal to hoard, there will be a tremendous increase in the demand for it. And why not? Only a few sheiks, French bourgeoisie, gangsters and speculators now own any appreciable amount of gold. Under a regime of freedom, you and I will want to hold a little—just for prudence's sake. And the car dealer down the street may want to hoard a lot!

2. In consequence, the price of free gold *may well rise rather than fall.* Canny governments will then be slow to sell off their gold at giveaway prices. And recrimination will fall on the heads of those officials who gave to the hoarders a great bargain.

3. At the meetings of the IMF, those nations now on the fence with respect to gold will find their respect for it rising as its free price rises. Making the post-Smithsonian mechanism of cards work will be more, and not less, difficult.

Thus, Italy was reluctant last summer to settle its debts with its Common Market partners in metallic gold rather than "paper gold" (Special Drawing Rights in the IMF). Think of the new scope for Gresham's Law to operate, once official gold becomes as valuable to a nation as the free Zurich price!

In short, all that glitters is not a good idea. Here is a change that we should go slow in making.

DOLLAR REPAIR
February, 1973

The 10 per cent devaluation of the dollar is, I think, a good thing. The dollar was overvalued for a dozen years prior to 1971. American goods and services were increasingly noncompetitive with Japanese, German, and foreign goods generally. The result was a chronic deficit in our international balance of payments. And also an extra temptation for American capital to want to go abroad in the pursuit of better yields.

However controversial this diagnosis may have been prior to the 1965 escalation of the Vietnam war, by the end of the 1960s anyone could see it. You didn't have to be a canny speculator or the treasurer of a multinational corporation with a M.B.A. from the Wharton School of Finance.

Yet we couldn't do much about it under the setup of the Bretton Woods system. All we could do was point out to the Japanese and the Germans that is would be in their interest as well as our to appreciate the yen and the mark relative to the dollar.

The Germans, despite some obvious political difficulties in a country traumatically frightened of any "tinkering with the currency" by memories of past inflation, did undergo mark appreciation several times after 1961. The Japanese are another story. Theirs is a system that can act only after full agreement has been reached among the interlocking establishments. When you are growing at 10 per cent a year, why agree to any change in the status quo?

TIME RUNNING OUT

Disequilibrium, like a corpse in the closet, can't be wished away. That final run on the dollar in August 1971 forced President Nixon to suspend de jure convertibility of the dollar. At the Smithsonian in December 1971, the dollar was depreciated relative to most currencies by about 8 per cent; and relative to the yen and mark by around twice as much.

Such dollar depreciation was a good thing, not a defeat for the dollar. It simply put a more realistic price on the goods that America has to sell—a changed price made necessary by the miracles of productivity growth in the Common Market and Japan.

Why didn't the Smithsonian medicine work? First, economists know that depreciation is slow medicine. It is medicine that actually may make the patient seem more sick rather than less in the first year. So the jury expected to have to wait two or three years to learn how well the prescribed dosage would work out to restore balance-of-payments equilibrium.

Fourteen months is enough time to show that depreciation is no quick-acting miracle drug. The run of nervous money away from the dollar meant the world was not to be given the two or three years needed to complete the Smithsonian experiment.

This time the United States acted unilaterally. If the yen and mark won't rise, the President can lower the dollar relative to the paper and official gold of the International Monetary Fund. Instead of $38, it now takes $42.22 to equal an ounce of official or paper gold. But of course, de facto, the dollar is not convertible even into official gold.

What is more important: the Japanese yen is now allowed to float upward—to be appreciated by market supply and demand. Your Sony TV and Toyota will cost more; maybe you'll buy a Detroit Pinto, and spend your money on a trip to Cape Cod.

NO MIRACLES

Will the new extra dose of medicine work? We know better than to expect instant results. Time will tell. Yale Provost Richard Cooper might turn out to be right in his belief that this is an overdose of depreciation—one that will move the dollar in a couple of years from being overvalued to being undervalued.

I hope we are now nearer to long-run reform of the IMF system. What is needed most is earlier flexibility of exchange rates to correct over- and undervaluations before they become chronic and malignant. The fact that Canada, England, Italy and Japan now have floating exchange rates is a definite approach toward flexibility (repeat, flexibility, not chaos).

I think the whole world is better off now than it was last month. That includes Japan, which should begin to make long-overdue adjustments toward becoming less of an export-oriented economy.

Let's hope that we don't spoil it all by letting our new campaign to bargain down foreign tariffs and quotas result in all nations winding up saddled with trade-killing barriers. There is an underswell of protectionism pervading the land, which it would be dangerous to cater to.

Chapter 5

GROWTH—POPULATION
AND THE LABOR FORCE

The first two articles of this relatively brief chapter, on "Population," and "Falling Birth Rates," deal with a subject which American economists as a group have tended to neglect. Typically, if an economics major wanted seriously to study the statistical magnitudes and relationships of population theory, it was first necessary to find out the location of the Sociology Department.

This neglect was a matter of choice, even though T. R. Malthus, one of the "classical" economists following Adam Smith, was the author of the gloomy thesis that unchecked population growth will outstrip mankind's means of subsistence. Looking back from the bicentennial of the independent United States, we see not overpopulation but relative labor shortage, and much ingenious economizing of labor through new technology.

But as the first reading points out, the reality of the Malthusian threat has been a matter of time and place. Considering less fortunate parts of the world, it has been a case of "for them alas yes, for us happily no." Even in the prosperous United States, the post-World War II baby boom brought to life the ominous geometric progressions of neo-Malthusians. These first two articles point out that we have now been riding a downward trend in the birthrate for some time, and evaluate the economic significance of this.

It is not meant here to ignore or be indifferent to the rate of population growth in global terms. Economics has indeed been concerned, in consideration of world economic development. But the discussion of this chapter is couched in terms of the domestic economy.

The last two articles deal with "The Brain Drain" and "The Four-Day Week." These are economic considerations in a most basic form; the allocation and utilization of a scarce resource, in this case labor. It is observed that labor, if free to do so, and whether super-brainy or not, will move to where it can maximize its own welfare. If this involves particularly talented and productive people, and threatens to become a misallocation in terms of world efficiency, it also becomes a problem.

"The Four-Day Week" comments on this interesting movement in business, toward scheduling a work week consisting of four ten-hour days. It is looked on with favor in the reading, particularly for the increased variety it adds to working arrangements, and for possible gains in the small joys of life itself.

It is also noted that the four-day week need have no adverse effect on the performance of the economy. If it is possible that the extended leisure of a three-day weekend could somehow lower Gross National Product, it is also true that a gain in leisure might be equal in utility to something presently counted in GNP. And for those driven by a terminal work-ethic to somehow combine two four-day jobs into a virtual eight-day week, modern economics can assure plenty of moonlighting opportunities for as long as a person can stand the pace.

POPULATION
June, 1967

As psychologists estimate intelligence, John Stuart Mill probably had the highest I.Q. of all time. At 3 he could read Greek; by 6 he had written a short history of Rome; at 8 he studied the differential calculus; and it was not until 13 that he mastered political economy.

But Mill omits to mention in his modest autobiography that he was arrested as a boy for distributing birth-control pamphlets. The evils of overpopulation he perhaps detected in his parents' large family. And like all the classical economists, he was obsessed by the fear that the labor supply would outstrip natural resources and lead, by the law of diminishing returns, to a bare subsistence wage.

To Mill, overpopulation was not a future evil but one already present in his own time. At what we now recognize to be the period of greatest Victorian progress, when life expectancy was rising as a result of scientific advance, not all of Mill's I.Q. could prevent him from uttering the quite erroneous opinion that it was doubtful if all of scientific progress had up to his time lightened the load of a single worker.

STOMACHS AND ELBOWS

Well, we all know that braininess is no protection against misinformation. But Malthus and Mill did have a valid point, as experience in India, Japan, Haiti and China shows.

Unless offset by technological progress, population at compound interest rates of growth can lead to poverty and pestilence—to life that is nasty, brutish and short. And even if the law of diminishing returns is thwarted enough to permit living standards to rise, still in many cases they would have improved still faster had soaring numbers not absorbed much of the potential for progress.

With respect to advanced nations, like those of America and Western Europe, the Malthusian bogey is not so acute. Look around you in the subway or at the club and you will see that we generally eat too much. Some lima beans substituted in our diets for creamy milk and filet mignon would lower our cholesterol levels and add to life expectancy.

True, our pistons are exploding petroleum products at a rate that cannot be maintained indefinitely; but doubtless physicists will learn how to use nuclear fission and fusion in the future to stay ahead of our energy needs; and before cheap oil shales are exhausted, our schoolchildren will be synthesizing hydrocarbons from the atmosphere and the oceans.

What exploding population means for modern society is lack of privacy. The problem is no longer that with every pair of hands that comes into the world there comes a hungry stomach. Rather it is that, attached to those hands are sharp elbows.

When you crush more molecules into a balloon, the temperature rises. When you pack more people onto the same beaches, prairies and hills, the social temperature rises.

PILLS AND PROSPERITY

Fortunately, our birth rate has begun to fall in this decade. But it is still at levels other nations would call high.

Some trace this return to sanity to the pill. Since the drop antedates the pill, others simply write it down as a return toward sanity. I suspect that there is a genuine change in fashion. Fewer couples want fourth or fifth children, and most are better able to achieve their desired targets. (After the war, polls of my MIT students showed they wanted an average of five children; paradoxically, many of them were only children! The new generation is coming from the large families of the war eras, and without the incomes of Nelson Rockefeller they don't want his size family.)

What will the economic effects of slower U.S. population growth be? Surprisingly minor, I would guess.

1.   Pollution of air and water will get worse however maternity oscillates. As noted, privacy remains a problem.

2.   But it is not true, as market analysts insist, that population growth is needed to keep our capital investments high and our incomes growing at a full-employment level. True, Gerber's baby foods have already felt the pinch. But Congress can always contrive the budget deficits needed to provide high demand. That is its job, not the obstetricians'.

Who'd want to bring innocent babies into a society so stupid it must use the boudoir as a boondoggling device for perpetuating prosperity?

FALLING BIRTH RATES
June, 1972

At last America is nearing the critical point at which the birth rate has fallen so low as to be below the magic replacement rate of 2.11 children on the average per completed family. (Why 2.11 and not the two needed to replace the two parents? Because some children die before reaching the age of marriage, and because some people never marry at any age.)

There has been nothing sudden about this decline in the birth rate. Ever since the peak of births in 1957, the statistics have been showing a declining trend in the birth rate. We don't have to look in the almanac or census to realize this.

We have only to look around us and note how many fewer pregnant women there are around these days. We have only to talk to young people to realize that the fashion has changed: the target number of children, which had been dropping for the middle classes from 1900 to 1939, without prior warning soared in the World War II and postwar years. Large families were in—way in; and not merely for hillbillies or slum dwellers, but for Princeton and State U graduates as well.

Today, the pendulum of aspiration has clearly swung back toward fewer or no children. The average age of marriage is again rising. Being single is again respectable. The traditional role of women is changing.

It would be nice to know the reasons for this sociological change. But even though we cannot be sure of the reasons, we may be able to project with some confidence that the drop in the birth rate will be a long-lasting trend, not just a transient wobble.

CHANGING PRACTICES

Certainly improvements in techniques of birth control play a role. The Pill, loop, sterilization, legal abortions, all contribute to the decline in births. A presumed increase in frequency of sexual intercourse is more than offset by effective use of birth control.

The loosening up of the Catholic Church since Pope John has meant both a sharp drop in aspiration goals of Catholic couples and a sharp rise in their ability to achieve their projected goals for family size. Another generation of convergence between Catholics and the rest of the population in these matters would result in practically no remaining differentials.

Birth rates of blacks, although still higher than those for whites, are also converging down toward those of whites. The differentials that existed in the 1920s between the rural masses and the educated middle classes are narrowing significantly.

Does economics provide any rationale for the drop in birth rates? Not particularly, I have to guess. We have experienced only mild recessions since 1957, no real depressions. Economic insecurity, if it could be objectively measured, has probably never been less. (Possibly though, the large pool of liquid savings, which people came into the postwar period with, has been gradually depleted relative to living-standard needs. This might help explain the drop. Even more important is the dawning realization of how much it costs a family to educate its children these days.)

Still, it is the general malaise in society, the feeling that things are getting worse rather than better, and the future more bleak, that constitutes the most significant force working against the high birth rate. In short, it is to sociology rather than economics that we must look for an understanding of the changing demographic trends.

ECONOMIC EFFECTS

Would a stabilizing of the birth rate at, or even a bit below, the replacement level be a good or bad thing, economically speaking?

To a first approximation, I think we can regard this new trend as a neutral factor. Economics is the handmaiden of the people, not their master. In this age after Keynes, if people want to have the population grow slowly for half a century and then gradually decline—and this is what is implied by births falling below the replacement rate, rather than near-term zero population growth—then modern mixed economies do have the knowledge and skill to formulate fiscal and monetary policies to ensure against grass growing in Main Street and mass unemployment resulting from slower demographic growth.

For the rest of this century, the old and young will be blessed with a relatively large number of people of working ages to help support them. In the next century, as past age bulges wear off and the average person grows older, the crunch on social security and old-age pensions will occur.

In brief. The people can have what they want in population trends.

THE BRAIN DRAIN
December, 1968

Adam Smith said, "Of all baggage man is the most difficult to transport." Today his dictum is anything but true.

If you're looking for partners in a string quartet, the best choice in the world is through the Los Angeles phone book. But don't ask your respondents to produce a birth certificate from Boston or Williamsburg. Most likely they were trained in the conservatories of Vienna, Paris and Prague.

Today American physics and chemistry are pre-eminent. It was not always so. Thanks to Hitler who, like George Wallace, had no use for intellectuals, many of the world's brainiest scientists migrated to our shores in the 1930s. Most remained. And it is the students they trained—whether from Paducah or Poona—who are doing the experiments and inventing the equations that will earn the Nobel Prizes of the future.

Fortunately, the Hitlerian influence is gone and Europe has settled down. Except for Czechoslovakia, from which we can soon expect a new stream of talent, few need come to our shores to avoid discrimination and to attain freedom of belief.

THE MIGHTIER DOLLAR

Yet the brain drain continues. Outstanding scholars, managers, engineers and artists continue to our shores because they can earn a higher standard of living here. And there is nothing new in this. For every Pilgrim who boarded the Mayflower to achieve freedom of religion, there have been hundreds of peasants and artisans who booked steerage because they knew a cousin with a better job and standard of living in Detroit or Fresno.

Throughout our history, alongside the brain drain, there has gone on the brawn drain. The dirty work of building our transcontinental railroads was done by imported Chinese and Irishmen. Sicilians weeded our truck farms; Mexicans still give us cheap tomatoes. If your mother and grandmother were spared dishpan hands, it was probably because of someone named Bridget or Jemimah. And let us not forget that those who hoed our cotton and made aristocratic living possible down on the old plantation did not come to our shores seeking freedom of worship and Tom Paine's "The Rights of Man."

Where is the balance to be drawn between immigrants as supermen and misfit ne'er-do-wells? Australia's first families were dumped from England's prisons. The Georgia colony had similar origin. Some of Quebec's most illustrious forebears came from Devil's Island. Often, in talking to Swedes or Italians in the old country, one senses an air of patronage toward their fellow countrymen in America, a belief that those who couldn't make good at home were those most likely to go abroad.

TO HIM WHO HATH

But it is the drain to America of the best-trained and most gifted people that most concerns other countries. When County Cork or Mississippi loses a potential Nobel laureate, complaints mount. Few tears are shed for immigrants who enter our cities, who go upon the relief rolls here.

We can expect more complaints. 1.   Our recent revision of immigration laws will accentuate the brain drain. The old rationing quotas were designed in 1924 to keep out people different from the original Western European settlers of this country. The new laws discriminate in favor of ability regardless of geographical origin. 2.

Our society has generally become more of a meritocracy. Antecedents count for less today. If a Japanese can split the atom better than a Virginian, today he'll get the physics chair at MIT—and even at Charlottesville. (By contrast, John Maynard Keynes could never have become a professor at the University of Paris since he had not been trained in the Faculty of Law there. After France had lost the flower of her manhood in World War I, she paid for this parochialism.) 3.

America has become the training ground for advanced students from all over the world. If Americans get Cambridge fever and resist going back to Urbana, why shouldn't students from Bombay do likewise—particularly when salaries and working conditions are infinitely better here. We suck out the best talent from the developing nations, enhance it by training, and then—too often—alienate it permanently.

What to do about the brain drain? Chaining men to their homelands is indeed to treat them as mere baggage. And yet can we give no weight to the pride and interests of the have-not nations? The best compromise will be hard to find.

THE FOUR-DAY WEEK
November, 1970

Kenneth Galbraith once told my wife that he does nothing he doesn't want to do. Somebody makes out his income tax and takes care of his investments. He serves on no committees that are boring. Each morning, as religiously as Pablo Casals plays Bach fugues, he writes at his home in Cambridge or at his Vermont or Swiss retreats. Then he walks to his deskless office, or spends the afternoon on the Gstaad ski slope.

Blessed is the man who never fights a traffic jam. Despite Samuel Butler's observation that the clergyman's home is often an unhappy one because the clergyman is there seven days a week, I deem more days off a boon. Although it is not given to all of us to enjoy the affluence of Galbraith, thanks to a new social invention some of us can cut down on our commuting time by 20 per cent.

I am referring to the burgeoning movement called the four-day, 40-hour week. Until I was asked to write a foreword for a book of that name, I had not realized how many businesses all over the country have been pioneering in this direction.

VARIETIES OF EXPERIENCE

Here are only a few examples.

- The Kyanize Paint Co. finds that its workers much prefer a three-day weekend though they work longer on the other days. The company benefits because 4 times 4 batches works out more smoothly than 5 times 3.

- At the Roger Williams General Hospital in Providence, a better supply of nurses is possible because the opportunity to work fewer days is available. Fewer shift changes aid patient care by minimizing the information loss between different nurses on the floor.

- At Lawrence Manufacturing, in the town where Lowell girls used to work but where recruitment of textile workers has become almost a losing proposition, the cry is now heard, "Thank God it's Thursday!"

- The 4-Day Tire Chain of Newport Beach, Calif., finding that tires get sold mostly on Thursday through Sunday, has made a virtue of necessity and now works the foor-day week.

I could go on with other examples of manufacturing, retailing, and banking establishments, but I must not kill off the sales of Bursk & Poor of Cambridge, Mass., the fledgling publisher of the book. In that work various experts describe the movement. And, judging from the advance sale of tens of thousands of books, the subject is one of widespread interest.

What interests me is the economics of the problem. How will it affect national output? Wage standards? The quality of life?

As people get more prosperous, they naturally tend to take some of their extra real income in the form of more leisure. The long-term trend of total working hours, per week and in terms of years of a lifetime, has been downward. The four-day week is in line with this trend just as the five-day-week movement was years ago in this country and recently in Russia.

To the trade-union movement, which has been generally sympathetic to the four-day week, the shortening of hours is all-important. The ten-hour day, or even the nine-hour day, is to them a less favorable aspect.

A general economist has no need to deplore nor to encourage the trend toward shorter hours. If we use the knowledge of the newer economics, we can insure that there will be enough jobs to go around even if people should take it in their heads to work a 50- or 60-hour week. If, instead, people decide they want more leisure, the fact that this will slow down the rate of growth of the GNP is only a reflection of the inadequacy of the way we measure that magnitude. If leisure were somehow reckoned in the GNP, much in the way that we reckon in the other good things of life—apples, oranges, back rubs, ballet, and football games—there would be seen to be no true reduction in real GNP from shorter hours.

VIVE LA DIFFERENCE

What interests me about the four-day week is its advantages to those who take it up first. Often in economic life it pays to be different.

How much better to work a couple of hours longer and beat that 5 o'clock traffic jam. Better still, if one doesn't have to go into New York every day, one can better stand the prospect of riding on the Penn Central. And if one has weathered that ordeal, why not amortize the investment over more hours of effective work? Particularly when that gives you the chance to see the winter sun, and get on a first-name basis with your children?

So cheers for any new development that widens choice in this too-confining world.

HUMAN RANSOM
September, 1972

A highly educated person who wishes to leave the Soviet Union has just had sprung on him a new exit fee: the payment of $25,000 to reimburse the state for his education. This new proposal of human ransom has met with international outrage and done much to harm the slowly improving public image of the U.S.S.R.

Of course, such extortions are not without precedent. Hitler's Nazi Germany often exacted its pound of flesh, nicely gauged to what the market would bear, before it would grant exit visas to refugees.

The ante-bellum American slave down South, like the Russian serf, was the chattel of his owner. He could not leave the plantation or estate: more than that, he could, so to speak, be extradited back to it; and any bounty hunter could pick up some pieces of silver as a reward for helping in his repatriation. Karl Marx had some choice words to say about this barbaric practice.

But surely I exaggerate? Suppose one says arbitrary edicts against migration are evil things, but free, voluntary money bargains are part of man's heritage of liberty and freedom.

To argue in this way is to misunderstand the profound sense in which money is coercive and an instrument of force. It's a topic worth developing.

WHAT SIMPLE SIMON LEARNED

Let the reader complete the adjective missing in the following sentence. "I could not go to college because my parents were -----."

One answer important in history would be, "black." Other admissible answers would be, "Jewish," "Catholic," "untouchable," and so forth. But quantitatively, without question the single answer that, since Adam and Eve, would cover most cases would have to be "poor."

Economists use the expression "rationing by the purse." What a welter of human misery those innocent words can cover. Marie Antoinette could as deservedly have gone down in the annals of infamy if she had only said, "Let them *buy* cake."

Suppose Abraham Lincoln, or for that matter Jefferson Davis, had said to the slaves, "You can buy yourself out of bondage." The hollowness and callousness of the offer would have been self-apparent, particularly if the putative purchasers had been living in a socialist society in which accumulation of personal wealth had been made the exception rather than the rule.

All this hawking of human flesh is absurd. Were it otherwise, Governor Rockefeller could make a gold mine out of Sing Sing prison, and Governor Reagan balance his budget by going public with a hot secondary issue of stock in San Quentin.

This does not seem to be a decision that the Russians have thought out carefully at the highest level. Obviously, there is no reasoned possibility that those in Russia who wish to emigrate can, in any significant number, by themselves, pony up the fees asked. So as far as applicants are concerned, it is simply a transparent device to refuse the more educated exit visas. In terms of the reaction of domestic or foreign public opinion, there can be no advantage in declaring a prohibitive price over simply refusing exit permits by decree.

OUTSIDERS TO THE RESCUE

What other possibilities then are there? The Soviet authorities cannot think that an appreciable amount of money can be forced out of Israel itself. In view of the stringency of internal funds there, to say nothing of scarcity of foreign exchange (since payment in Jaffa oranges is but a fanciful possibility), no well-informed Soviet authorities can really expect anything much from this direction.

We are left then with the final possibility that the Soviet Union seriously hopes to force more affluent Jews outside of Israel, or other well-off believers in freedom, into raising a kitty to buy exit permits for the would-be migrants.

Ethics and public opinion aside, is this a perspicacious gambit? In terms of Soviet cost-benefit analysis, is the feasible yield to be reckoned in millions of dollars, tens of millions, or hundreds? One suspects that, after the authorities do their homework, they will choose to revoke this decision. Only the Chinese hope not.

Nothing said here is to deny that educating people is indeed a way of creating human capital. But still it is one thing to have a Yale Plan in which students agree *in advance* to be taxed on future incomes to repay tuition loans. But that would never justify Kingman Brewster's incarcerating the members of the 25th Reunion Class in the Yale Bowl until their relatives provided the wherewithal to spring them.

Chapter 6

WALL STREET
AND THE ECONOMY

Both this chapter and the next deal with "the stock market." This is partly in the narrow sense of the organized stock exchanges, especially the New York Stock Exchange, but also in the broader sense in which the expression "stock market" refers to all securities markets and the securities industry in general.

The emphasis in this chapter is upon the relationships between events in the stock market and events in the economy; and between the total performance of the stock market and that of the economy. Alternative cause-and-effect hypotheses are considered, as to whether the behavior of the stock market determines what happens to the economy, or *vice versa.* The reader can await the view of the chapter on this, although some might be quite sure in advance that the answer is overly obvious. *Post hoc, ergo propter hoc?*

Backing off from the extreme argument that the stock market dominates the entire economy, it is true that the movement of security prices might have positive or negative implications for economic policy objectives. This is illustrated by the selection on "Stock Prices."

Can the price movements of specific stocks be predicted by charting their past performance? Or can it somehow be determined clearly that particular stocks or stocks in general are underpriced, overpriced, or "just right"? This is considered some in the first reading, "Science and Stocks," and again in "Thinking About Stocks."

The articles on "Reforming Wall Street" and "Martin's Monopoly" indicate some accomplishments, but also continued need, in reforming both specific rules of the stock market and the structure of the securities industry. Reforms and rule changes are supported which will increase competitive efficiency, so that extra services of brokers will be priced in accordance with their extra costs. Some progress has been made toward increasing competition in commissions charged by brokers, in place of a fixed-rate schedule, at least on moderately large transactions. With respect to mutual funds, it is also noted in the chapter that "give-ups" are now prohibited by the Securities and Exchange Commission. Give-ups were the practice in which a broker, executing a large order for a mutual fund, would give up part of a commission to another brokerage firm which helped to sell the fund's shares.

The Martin Report was submitted to the New York Stock Exchange in August 1971. Although it did call for stock market reorganization involving greater public control, the report as a whole is assailed here for continuing the essentially monopolistic, non-competitive internal structure of the NYSE.

These two chapters have the flavor of a conversation with a sophisticated investor/economist, with little forced attempt at being elementary, or as sequential as a textbook. To a student reader who happens also to be a raw recruit to stock market literature, the readings might seem at times to be rather lofty stuff. Hopefully, in this case, concurrent class discussions and reading will fill in the base.

SCIENCE AND STOCKS
September, 1966

Stock prices on Wall Street are down 22 per cent from their all-time peak early in the year. If you look only at this indicator of business conditions, you would think the country is in a recession.

But if you look at real output growth you would conclude we are now enjoying great economic prosperity. And if you examine the 3 to 4 per cent upward creep of average prices, you would suspect that our economy is overheating.

Can economic science explain the paradox of rising commodity and hesitant stock prices? Indeed can economic science throw any light on gyrations of Wall Street prices?

Since the SEC requires full disclosure in these matters, let me at once enter a disclaimer. The way to fortune as a speculative plunger is not via the Ph.D. degree in economics. That is a fact of experience. Prices on the bourse, unlike the planets or the tides, are not subject to exact explanation, much less prediction.

Having made this confession of modesty, I must assert arrogantly that there simply does not exist—outside of economic analysis of business and industrial conditions—any better way to understand the general behavior of share prices.

SENSE AND NONSENSE

I know that technicians claim to make money by searching for esoteric patterns in market charts. But I also know that honest men think they can cure cancer with snake oil. Every objective study has failed to validate prediction devices that rely on anything different from *informed common sense.*

Let me merely relay the view of Holbrook Working, who spent a lifetime studying prices. Dr. Working reported most technicians and chartists will be found, on close examination, to have holes in their shoes.

What are the few common-sense regularities about stock prices that have stood the test of historical experience? Here are three with current relevance.

Stock prices and money national income do, over long periods of time, show roughly corresponding movements. In great depressions, equity prices collapse. In great inflations, equity prices do—eventually!—rise.

But stock prices do show more ups and downs than gross national product or business indicators generally. To prove that Wall Street is an early omen of movements still to come in GNP, commentators quote economic studies alleging that market downturns predicted four out of the last five recessions. That is an understatement. Wall Street indexes predicted nine out of the last five recessions! And its mistakes were beauties.

Item: Just before the great postwar inflation, common stocks tumbled in 1946, perpetrating what denizens of the Street call the "biggest mistake the market ever made." Others nominate 1939-42, 1962 or 1965 for this dubious honor.

PRICE-EARNINGS PUZZLE

"Don't argue with the tape," you say? Nonsense, the tape is arguing with itself every moment. For every seller there is a buyer. When statisticians feed equity price changes into an electronic computer, it literally cannot distinguish them from coin tossings. Try it on your IBM 7090.

Although present and probable future corporate profits are admittedly the most important determinant of intermediate market movements, no way exists to determine what is the proper price-earnings ratio.

President Hadley of Yale used to say: "God Almighty does not know the cost of moving a ton of freight from New York to Chicago." I doubt that the devil himself knows what is the equilibrium price-earnings ratio on stocks. Eighteen to 1, as so long held? Fifteen to 1, as Secretary Douglas Dillon once rashly averred? Twenty-five to 1? Or 14 to 1, as the tape enunciates now that high interest rates imply high P/E ratios on bond investments. No one knows.

Years ago when a friend asked J.P. Morgan, "What should I do about my stocks? I can't sleep nights." Morgan replied, "I'd sell down to the sleeping point."

In these days of Vietnam uncertainties, that talked-about 1967 recession cannot be counted upon to materialize. Those out of the market seem more jittery than those still in. Perhaps Morgan would advise them to buy up to the sleeping point.

TAIL OF THE DOG
March, 1968

Thus far this year the stock market has been falling. The Dow Jones industrials have declined more than 10 per cent from their high of last September, which itself compares with the all-time peak of 1,000 touched as far back as early 1966.

There has been an element of paradox in this Wall Street drop. Certainly the last six months have not been a period of sluggish business. The year from mid-1967 to mid-1968 looks to be one of the most buoyant in our history, buoyant enough to involve price inflation at an uncomfortable 4 per cent annual rate.

Nor has this been one of those periods of so-called "profitless prosperity." Profits actually turned up at about the time that stocks began to falter, and receded in 1967 by only about 4 to 5 per cent instead of by the 10 to 15 per cent so widely feared on the Street.

Recent experience then provides one more example that, whatever is the causal relationship between aggregate business activity and the course of stock prices, it is not an exact one-to-one identity.

CAUSE OR EFFECT?

Despite the failure of perfect concordance, the vast bulk of experience throughout history and in many different countries shows that there is a strong and positive intercorrelation between share prices and general business activity. Let me review some of that evidence.

Stocks are not a perfect inflation hedge. But in extreme inflations abroad, stocks have performed better than money or bonds.

During the prosperous 1920s, stocks were booming. At the Depression bottom, you could buy the blue chips for a dime on the dollar. After World War II had doubled the wage and price level and had shifted the American economy into the growth patterns typical of post-Roosevelt mixed economies rather than of McKinley-Coolidge systems of laissez-faire, stock prices finally surged in what has perhaps been the greatest Wall Street boom of all times. If you have not done well as an investor this last quarter of a century, you are not cut out for this kind of work. But only the very young or the hopelessly romantic can expect it always to be so easy.

But have I perhaps confused cause and effect? Is it the GNP rises that push up the Dow Jones index? Or rather the rises in stocks that pull up—by its mustache, so to speak—the economic stystem?

In my view the stock market constitutes the tail of the dog while real output constitutes the body. Although most economists today agree with me, there was a time when many experts attributed primal causal importance to the stock market itself.

Ernest Henderson, the remarkable founder of the Sheraton Hotel empire and just recently deceased, long held ingenious theories to explain the business cycle. In 1962 he warned President Kennedy that the severe drop in equities then taking place would entail a serious recession.

He had a point. Just as Newton's apple has an upward pull on the earth, stocks must be admitted to have a feedback influence on the economy. Events from 1929 to 1932 were particularly much affected by the simultaneous collapse of real estate and equity markets. President Kennedy advisedly weighed the possible dangers to his recovery stemming from a drop of total market values then exceeding $100 billion (and which MIT's expert, Franco Modigliani, estimated might cut down consumption spending by some $5 billion *if long persisting*). This Wall Street stock collapse was one straw that helped break the back of President Kennedy's resistance to a massive tax cut.

MESSENGER, NOT MISSILE

Still, economics is a quantitative science and we must weigh causes carefully. The ups and downs of stock prices do affect the optimism of the 23 million people who own some stocks. But the possible quantitative effects upon consumption and investment spending are minor in comparison with the other key variables. Errors in estimating the changes in housing starts, Federal Reserve policy, military and civilian expenditures, inventory fluctuations—all these are individually and collectively much greater than the most extreme effects that can be plausibly attributed to stock values.

To deny to stock prices causal primacy is not to deny that they often serve as leading indicators. And this raises the question: does the January-March market drop mean that Wall Street sees something we don't see? More on this another time.

ANTENNA OF A MOUSE
May, 1968

Recently I compared the stock market to the tail rather than the body of the dog. Intervening events have confirmed the view that Wall Street oscillations are more the effect than the cause of business activity.

While both staid and glamour stocks were plunging downward this winter, the American economy was booming as never before. In reflection of the displacement of New York by Washington, consumer income soared during the first quarter, as higher social-security benefits and minimum-wage rates came into effect. The propensity of the consumer to spend his income also rose just when stocks were falling.

Meanwhile, what was happening down at the office? We know now that expenditure plans on plant and equipment were undergoing a sizable upward revision in consequence of the general economic overexuberance.

All this growth had to be good for profits. And it was. Despite mounting unit labor costs, 1968 profits are rising to record heights.

RUSH FOR THE ENTRANCE

Wall Street found it hard to remain bearish under these ebullient conditions. It welcomed every excuse to climb back off the limb on which it found itself. Even before the two-tier system for gold was introduced in mid-March, the most nervous money was sneaking guiltily back into equities. When an unpopular President announced his retirement and wish to negotiate an end to an unpopular war, the Whiz Kids of Wall Street fought for the entrances and the short sellers covered in panic.

Volume of turnover has skyrocketed, exceeding even the records set in 1929. Who is getting rich these days in Wall Street? Not the bulls. Not the bears. Not the crabs.

It is the bartender who is enjoying the cocktail party most. Bonuses were terrific last Christmas. Next Christmas they will be colossal. The gravy is even filtering down to the interior decorators and architects who are designing those new branch offices and boardrooms.

No wonder the anti-trust division is vying with the SEC to topple the oligopolistic system of commissions that the New York Stock Exchange has been able to impose for lo these many years. If I buy 100 shares of General Motors and you buy 50 times that amount, we both have to pay exactly the same commission *on each 100 shares* even though the total costs of both transactions are hardly different! No wonder the insidious system of broker "give-ups" flourishes. The laws of economics and corruption cannot be repealed by the executive committee of the exchange.

Whom the gods would destroy they first make mad. The exchange will rue the day it rebuffed the SEC proposals for reforms on commissions and give-ups, reforms which most academic observers regard as mere love taps.

One cult of technical chartists believes that high volume presages rising stock prices. This is less idiotic than much of the technical witchcraft encountered on the Street. But even here I suspect there is a major confusion between cause and effect. Most people, I have observed, have a rendezvous to tithe their winnings with their friendly broker. When they are making money, they itch for even more and he is glad to accommodate them with helpful hints. Thus it is primarily rising prices that generates turnover, not vice versa.

With GNP growing in an inflationary way, we have no need to look for esoteric explanations for the Dow-Jones revival. Still, the move toward retrenchment in Vietnam must certainly be taken into account.

SEE HOW THEY RUN

Today Wall Street is a dove and not a hawk. This the news flashes tell us. I believe this to be good for the reputation of capitalism. But I must warn against reading too much into the fact that the ticker rises on each dovish headline and falls on each hawkish development.

There is no integrated mind in the marketplace. The proper image is that of a colony of related cells, or of a centipede whose various legs know only dimly what the others are doing. Whether or not peace will be truly beneficial to the GNP, profits, and the Dow-Jones index, once the denizens in the marketplace have become conditioned to expect that peace news is bullish, they will grab for their phones on the whistle for peace in the same way that Pavlov's dogs salivated when they heard the dinner bell.

Although earnings may dip temporarily when peace comes, I expect that higher price-earnings multiples can be applied to those earnings.

REFORMING WALL STREET
September, 1968

Last year I pointed out in this column that something was rotten in Wall Street. This public service brought down on my professorial head considerable vituperation.

But time is vindicating my concern. Under fire, the New York Stock Exchange has now agreed to lower commissions on transactions in excess of 1,000 shares and has outlawed the nefarious practice of "give-ups."

And the Securities and Exchange Commission has agreed, on an interim trial basis, to accept the new commission schedule of the exchange.

Hence, in this new day there is no longer anything rotten in Wall Street? A muckraking columnist can now turn his attention elsewhere?

BAROMETER FALLING

With all respect, this is nonsense. The housecleaning in Wall Street is just beginning. I know it. Manuel Cohen, chairman of the SEC, knows it. The attorneys of the brokerage community know it. And, most important of all, the Antitrust Division of the Department of Justice knows it.

For make no mistake about it. It was not the fulminations of columnists that brought about a single cent's reduction in commissions. And, despite the propensity of the industry to complain about the SEC, it has, if anything, been soft in exercising its undoubted administrative powers. What has blown the whistle on the monopoly has been the new interventions by the Antitrust Division.

Since capitalism is too important to be left to the tender mercies of the capitalists, all who really cherish the efficient working and survival of an enterprise system must once again be indebted to the Antitrust Division. Space does not leave room for a full listing of all of the evils and defects of the present financial scene. So let me sample the more important structural weaknesses.

- *Competition doesn't work to bring costs down to the efficient minimum.*

The New York Stock Exchange is an island of privileged monopoly. *It* limits its members and access to its floor. *It* sets minimum fees. If U.S. and Bethlehem Steel tried to act the way the New York and American exchanges act, Roger Blough would be in jail before you could say Merrill Lynch, Pierce, Fenner and Smith.

When the SEC asked Congress to put limits on the *maximum* loading fees that the mutual-fund industry could charge, the industry hired experts to testify that the present up-to-9 per cent loadings were the product of free competition. Senators were assured that competition could be relied on to ensure the public interest.

Now the industry is hiring experts—some of them the very same experts—to testify that taking away the stock exchange's monopoly powers to set *minimum* fees will result in "ruinous competition" and chaos. Balderdash!

- *"Give-ups" and "churnings" of portfolios are direct consequences of the uncompetitive fee schedule.*

When a brokerage firm is sued and fined for decimating a widow's net worth through excessive buying and selling—that makes the headlines. But what about the non-criminal propensity to overtrade that goes on all the time and on a vast scale?

An acquaintance who runs a go-go fund explains that he could not motivate salesmen to push his fund if he did not generate more commissions from turning over the fund's portfolio than his trading judgment told him was profitable in its own right. For a long time no one complained, as the go-go boys seemed to coin instant wealth for their clients. This year the gravy ended. This year most of the large go-go funds have been falling behind the exchange index of all stocks. But even if they had not, that would be no excuse for rigged commission schedules and give-ups.

AGENDA FOR CHANGE

> • *Mutual-fund loadings and particularly front-end loadings on periodic investment plans are so high as to create powerful vested interests.*

These loadings are not the product of free competition. The law keeps you or me or Merrill Lynch from bringing the loading on 100 shares of, say, the Dreyfus or MIT fund down to the 1 or 2 per cent rate that would result under competition. Such price-maintenance regulations should go.

Next moves are up to the Justice Department, the SEC and Congress. Except as a first step, the new commission schedule is a token reform. Give-ups were only the visible part of the rigged schedule. Abolishing them only drives the evil underground and may even lessen the loopholes through which competition operated.

Can we hope to hear from the Presidential candidates—both of them?

STOCK PRICES
March, 1969

Last week I had a phone call from a reporter on The Wall Street Journal. "Doctor, what is going to happen to the stock market?"

Having worked hard for that Ph.D., I can never resist flattery. So instead of giving him a quick answer, I settled for a profound one, replying, "It will fluctuate."

"Yes," said he impatiently, "but are you and your sons buying or selling?"

"Both," I answered, "we are buying cheap and selling dear. We are culling out poor quality from our portfolios, exercising at this time of all times selectivity."

One should not be facetious about serious matters. And I would not have engaged in this double talk, even in jest, if the recent decline in Wall Street were a matter of serious economic concern.

WHO'S LAUGHING?

Actually, now is the time when more is not better. We are in a period of overmuch inflation. Private capital formation is, if anything, still too strong. The Federal Reserve is trying to tighten up on money spending. The new Nixon Administration is trying to reduce the rise in prices from a more than 4 per cent annual rate to a more moderate number.

Why then should I, as an economist, shed tears when the Dow Jones average drops from 950 to 900? This is not like the spring of 1962 when a decline in stock prices might have put the early Kennedy recovery in jeopardy. Even a further sizable drop, say to a Dow Jones index of 800, could not, in my view, be deemed a bad thing for the American economy.

I realize that a stock decline would seem like a bad thing to speculators who are borrowing money in order to increase their leverage. And when some 26 million people, who are the group who own some common stocks, read their newspapers, they will feel a bit poorer when stocks are at a lower rather than a higher level. Hence I will be accused of wanting to shoot Santa Claus when I look with cheerful acceptance on a drop in equity prices.

Does nothing worry me? Yes, if I thought that stock prices were going to halve in value, that would give me pause. (From 1929 to 1933 stocks dropped 80 per cent on the average. Many used to attribute the Great Depression of the 1930s to the great crash of October 1929; but expert opinion today reverses causation, tracing the deep drop in equities in 1933 to the drop in GNP that Herbert Hoover and the Federal Reserve Board permitted to take place in 1930 to 1932.)

However, in the cold of winter I refuse to worry about the heat of summer. There is no reason to expect that Wall Street prices will collapse to anything like only half their present value. And in this troubled age I must ration my worrying time.

In one respect only should economists in Washington be worrying about a 10 or 20 per cent drop in share prices. A falling off in volume of trading, so that the record keepers can catch up, should be a welcome thing. And so should pricking of the bubble of speculation on the American Exchange and over-the-counter, in which fried-chicken and nursing-home franchisers coin instant wealth. I salute an end to frenzied finance, in which conglomerates take over companies several times their size by issuing their own overrated stock jn a self-fulfilling Ponzi game.

Only in connection with our balance of international payments, in which the deterioration of our surplus of exports over imports on current account has been papered over by the inflow of foreign capital into the American stock market, should chairman McCracken, Secretary Kennedy, or counsellor Burns keep a watchful eye on the broad tape.

WHAT TO DO

Suppose capital does leave. Should that persuade chairman Martin and the Fed to ease up on credit?

Far from it. Trying to patch up our balance of payments by monetary policy would require even higher domestic interest rates, tighter rather than looser credit.

Moreover, we have too long been hamstringing desirable programs at home out of consideration for our chronic international deficits. It is time to stop playing that game.

Let us do the right thing for vigorous and sustainable growth at home. And if that reveals the present parity of the dollar is not tenable, let us get on with the task of removing the fundamental flaw in the Bretton Woods currency arrangements by introducing flexibility in the mechanism of foreign exchange rate determination.

THINKING ABOUT STOCKS

August, 1970

Nine years ago my employer, MIT, gave professors the option of putting half of its contribution toward our pensions into a sliding-scale, commonstock fund, rather than in the usual "safe" collection of bonds and mortgages. What was I to decide?

Though I thought the market a bit "high" in mid-1961, I also knew that I was a busy man who would not soon think about the matter again. So reasoning that a good habit is better than perfectionism in timing, I chose the equity option. How has it turned out?

At intervals I receive a chit from the pension fund showing how the two parts of my nest egg are doing. By 1969, the stock portion was ahead by a little. In view of subsequent Wall Street weakness, I suppose the fixed-principal bonds are now ahead.

In appraising this experience, please take note of the following:

1.   The 1961-70 decade, more than most, was free of ups and downs of the business cycle. Real GNP grew steadily.

2.   This was also a decade of inflation—creeping in the first half, trotting in the last.

3.   A pension fund is free of all taxes—income or capital gains.

4.   From the nature of accumulating pension moneys, here was almost a pure case of "dollar averaging." Regardless of anyone's opinion about the Dow Jones index, roughly the same number of dollars went to buy common stocks each month. Yet there was no magic in such arithmetic, despite the truism that more shares were bought at low than at high prices.

ANY MORAL HERE?

Now the last thing I want is to get a barrage of letters from brokers and counselors, flexing their muscles and demonstrating that I'd have been better off to have put my money with them. No doubt true; but then there are a legion of portfolio managers who have done worse, and I am satisfied that our committee followed the standard rules of prudence.

Nor do I wish for anyone to draw the inference that (a) I am complaining and regret the 1961 decision, or (b) that "variable-annuity" pensions have been proved by experience to be undesirable. For actually, this may well be the only decade in this century in which an equity fund would not be clearly ahead.

The hypothesis I wish to put forward is this:

After a long period in which common stocks are at a discount—because people remember the Great Crash and Great Depression and have not fully realized the extent of the postwar inflation—*there may finally come an era in which stocks are pretty much fully priced and in which interest rates have risen to take proper account of the inflation to be expected.*

When that day finally comes, the New York stock market will cease to be a one-way street. Long sideburns on a money manager will then no longer be enough.

BUT WHEN?

The important question is how to recognize when the hypothesis of fully discounted stock prices applies. On the ancient principle that, to learn what your wife will become, look at your mother-in-law, I have examined the experience of stock markets in France, West Germany, Italy and the U.K.—all of which have been characterized by inflation and growth.

How would you have done (a) buying their stock indexes across the board, as against (b) putting your money all through the 1960s in the Eurodollar market at rates of interest varying from 5 to 12 per cent per annum? I have not made the calculation accurately, but back-of-the-envelope computations suggest that it would be a close-run race.

What are dangerous clinical symptoms to watch for? When dividend yields fell below bond yields, that was not yet a signal of equity overvaluation—for the reason that part of earnings are not distributed as dividends but are plowed back into corporations to produce systematic capital gains.

It is a more dangerous signal when the ratio of earning-to-stock-price (the reciprocal of the price-earnings ratio) falls persistently below the interest rates on bonds. However, in an age of *inflationary bidding up of the real assets of corporations,* a stock fund might still outperform a bond fund even though both have equal earning yields. But the danger point is then being approached—especially when Wall Street expects certain kinds of inflation to put pressure on costs and profits.

What all this suggests for personal investment I hope to return to in a future column.

MARTIN'S MONOPOLY

January, 1972

Something is rotten in Wall Street. By this I do not mean that the Dow Jones index is likely to collapse in a crash. For half a dozen years now, everyone in the securities industry has realized that the existing system is not viable and that reforms are long overdue.

Sometimes a single individual can, by his penetrating diagnosis and synthesis, provide the strategic insight that galvanizes a nation into action. The case of Dr. Abraham Flexner's famous 1910 report on the state of American medical schools is a notable example. No Congressional commission authorized his effort; but so compelling were his facts and his analysis that he had no need for backup by government.

When William McChesney Martin Jr. agreed to do an unpaid report on the reconstitution of the New York Stock Exchange and the financial industry generally, some may have hoped for another Flexner report. After all, Martin was for nearly two decades the respected chairman of the Federal Reserve Board. Before that he had been, at an age when he was still subject to the draft, the first paid president of the New York Stock Exchange, having been picked for that job at a time when the Great Depression and the peccadilloes of the Richard Whitneys of high finance had put the exchange in the doghouse of public opinion and suspicion. If Wall Street did not clean its own stable, or at least cosmetically pretty it up, the handwriting was on the wall for the government to step in with regulation more severe than Roosevelt's SEC has ever yet seen fit to apply.

A SECOND DANIEL?

Mr. Martin has made his report. It is a grievous disappointment. Far better than the absurdities of the present situation should prevail until the end of time than that the explicit recommendations of Martin, and, what is more insidious, the logical implications of his philosophy, should be frozen into law.

The harm that a private monopoly of the financial establishment can do, even when policed by the Securities and Exchange Commission, is great. And the nation has indeed suffered under such a regime. But competition from third markets, from regional exchanges, from violations of the spirit of the cartel if not of its letter, have intervened to limit the power of the monopoly. So things have not been as bad as one might have feared.

What the Martin report does is to propose, quite baldly, *that the full power of the government be invoked to perpetuate and police monopoly pricing of the services of the securities industry.* And all this has been proposed, I am sure, in naïve good faith, under the guise of unifying the competitive market.

GOVERNMENT CARTELIZATION

Naturally, the Martin report has begun to come under widespread attack. Let us analyze the issues.

The crucial issue is this: how do we get brokerage-services charges at their *true competitive costs,* in particular recognizing the basic fact that a transaction that is five and ten times as large as the usual 100-share round lot involves nothing like five and ten times the telephoning, bookkeeping and other true costs?

The solution is for Congress and the SEC to permit, nay to *require* through the full force of antitrust and public regulation law, a competitive commission structure that reflects the true costs involved.

This means striking down as illegal the exchange's old-boy club rule against competitive commission setting for transactions less than $500,000.

It means encouraging regional exchanges, over-the-counter and third markets, to cut down on the excess rates quoted by exchange members, if they can do so *while maintaining full disclosure of all transactions* on a unified, SEC-regulated tape.

It means forcing the exchange to admit institutional members if, thereby, they can bring down the costs to the widows, orphans and broad public *they* serve. (If the competitive rates are achieved, presumably there will be no need for institutions to become members. But that is for them to decide.)

Mr. Martin, not understanding competition, comes out 180 degrees wrong on each one of these issues. What a tragedy for the nation!

Aside from the social evil of the Martin proposals, they will represent a Pyrrhic triumph for the financial establishment if adopted. Economists of all persuasions will join with Naderian critics to pursue the vulnerable industry relentlessly. Until, finally, a future government is sure to lower the boom. finally, a future government is sure to lower the boom. . . . ?

TODAY 1,000, TOMORROW ...?

December, 1972

The old, tired Dow Jones average of 30 industrial stocks finally made it over the hurdle of 1,000. Wall Street tried to get excited over the event; but to tell the truth, one juicy rumor from Henry Kissinger would do more for the bulls than would piercing any historic ceiling.

In terms of basic economics, just where does the stock market seem now to stand? This is a convenient time to review some of the salient relationships.

What is surprising is not that the Dow Jones index broke 1,000, but that it has taken so long to do so. As long ago as 1966, the Dow marched up to the 1,000 level. And again it did so in 1968.

Even if you think stocks were on the high side in 1966 and 1968, remember that a lot of irreversible inflation has taken place in the last six years. Real growth may have been on the disappointing side in the first Nixon term; but still it has been positive in recent years.

To reproduce the machinery and plant of American enterprise would cost you much more today than in 1968. Yet the price tag of such assets in the capital markets has not advanced much.

AS THE COUNTRY GROWS

And what's so remarkable about the Dow? True, its 30 firms are sizable. But a better sample of what has truly been happening to stocks is provided by the Standard & Poor's 500-share index or the New York Stock Exchange's comprehensive index of all its listed stocks. Both of these indexes long since surpassed their 1966 and 1968 peaks, without anybody's noticing it.

The public was badly burned by the 1968 drop in stock prices. And so were the performance-minded *Wunderkinder* who were running mutual funds and pension accounts. Brokerage houses have been folding up as share volume failed to measure up to bloated expectations. Nor is the end in sight.

But all this commotion conceals the fact that the *average* dollar committed to common stocks has continued to appreciate over the years—and by more than the Dow Jones index. This is true, even though it is also true that most stocks are below their own earlier peaks.

If investment analysts knew more probability theory, they would realize that each stock can at most drop by 100 per cent. But each may increase by 200, 500 or any positive per cent. Therefore, a portfolio of many stocks rises even when most of its holdings drop. The way fortunes grow is by losing a little on several items while making a lot on a few!

THE ROAD AHEAD

Is the moral of all this that one should simply sit and hold a diversified group of common stocks and forget about their day-to-day quotations? Actually, one could do worse.

But more important for those who are out of the market is the ever-recurring question: "Has the market already had its rise? Will it fall on its face just as I jump into it?"

I cannot tell whether the rise since just a year ago of the Dow index from 800 to 1,000 signifies that equity prices have already allowed for the undoubted economic expansion that still lies ahead of us. It would be rash to expect a 25 per cent gain in every year.

What I can do is enumerate the important variables one should watch in forming an opinion on whether Wall Street is too high or too low.

- Forget technical charts of historic ceilings or resistance levels. No scientific proof of their worth has ever been forthcoming.

- Try to form a reasoned view on the future of real gross national product and the price level.

- Calculate the probable range of corporate profits corresponding to your GNP estimates for 1973 and 1974.

- Estimate how high interest yields on bond alternatives to common stocks will be in the future, so that you can guess how high price-earnings multiples may average out.

- Remember that the marketplace is future-oriented. So, in judging how share prices will move between now and the end of 1973, realize that the answer must be sensitive to your GNP guesses for 1974. (For 1974, that far ahead? Yes, alas.)

After you have done your homework on these matters, you will not be able to predict the stock market with accuracy. But you will be able to look yourself in the mirror and say, "Come what may, I've acted with prudence—utilizing the only evidence that can ever be available to risk-taking investors."

Chapter 7

WALL STREET
AND THE INVESTOR

This chapter has already been linked to the preceding one, by introductory comments made there. Little need be said about its general nature, other than the obvious reminder that the emphaisis shifts to the individual investor and away from general economic considerations.

The first reading, on "Reforming The Funds," might at first glance look like a carryover from the previous chapter. But the reforms are beneficial to the investor, and the comments on front-end loads found in mutual fund periodic-investment plans are quite personal and informative. This is picked up again later, in "Prudent Investing."

The chapter is indeed of a direct and personal "what to do and how to do it" character, and these introductory remarks should stand in its way as little as possible. But it should be observed that there also is something of interest on institutional investing, especially in the selection on "Bold Investing." In addition, while the readings make the direct and practical suggestion to purchase shares in no-load mutual funds, rather than those that have a sales-charge, the extra time spent discussing mutual funds' performance is worth the effort. It provides perspective on the relative effectiveness of "professional management," and alerts the investor to the "cult of performance" phenomenon of the second half of the 1960s.

It might seem surprising to some, and overly conservative, to have the readings express such a strong preference for putting the equity portion of one's investment funds into no-load mutual funds, as against a moderately diversified group of directly owned stocks. In response, it can first be said that this approach is not absolutely ruled out. See the conclusion of "Prudent Investment, I." Also, the advisory type commentaries clearly are aimed at those with investment funds of only moderate size. Brokers' commissions must be paid on the direct purchase or sale of stocks, and these have been increased for smaller investors. In that connection, if the goal is ever realized of having competitively determined commission rates reflect the marginal costs of services provided, investors as a group might have to take the bitter with the sweet. It might be a case of smaller transaction rates up, larger transaction rates down, and a further economic incentive for small investors to go the mutual fund route. Finally, the selection on "Mutual Funds" does observe that the diversification possible in a small investment portfolio might be inadequate in reducing risk, compared to that offered by a mutual fund.

The last reading, "Personal Finance," concludes with some suggested new vehicles which are needed by the small investor. One of these would be an extremely diversified stock fund, with no sales charge or management fees, to be operated by a public agency or nonprofit foundation. Another suggestion is that the federal government finally come through with a bond of guaranteed purchasing power, geared to the situation of those with modest annual savings.

REFORMING THE FUNDS
March, 1967

A sword of Damocles hangs over the investment-company industry. The SEC is now asking Congress to curb its lucrative practices.

It all began with a few irrelevant scandals. Some rascals in St. Louis cut a few corners: having sold shares in their mutual funds to the public, they proceeded to overtrade with the proceeds—to buy and sell, sell and buy, thereby generating huge commission charges.

If the public was to be bilked, to whom should the spoils go? To the brokerage firms that charge as high a rate of commission on thousands of shares as on a transaction of a hundred shares? Obviously one does not risk jail to benefit a stranger. Instead friends were given phantom jobs by complaisant brokerage houses, so that the kickback of commissions could appear in the legal form of salesman's commission. No salesman goes to penitentiary just because he received a high fee for little work done; otherwise our jails would have no room for arsonists and murderers.

Crooks only provide the *reductio ad absurdum* to inherent weaknesses. When the New York Stock Exchange enforces monopolistic rules that keep commissions on large blocks of stocks higher than the competitive costs of providing such services, someone has to reap the discrepancy. What is more natural than for the mutual funds to bribe the brokerage firms into promoting their shares harder in return for lucrative brokerage business bestowed on them? Reciprocity, it's called.

BILL OF INDICTMENT

The SEC hired a disinterested group of experts from the Wharton School at the University of Pennsylvania to examine mutual-fund practices, and to make recommendations for reform if any seem indicated.

It is a law of life well known since this century began: the way of the muckraker is dirty; you cannot point out the dubious practices of a lucrative industry without calling down upon yourself a torrent of filthy abuse. But Prof. Irwin Friend, Penn's respected expert in finance, has been able to weather with philosophical amiability the criticisms leveled at his report by the mutual-fund industry. Sitting pretty with four aces in your hand does wonders for a philosopher under attack.

The SEC investigations have merely documented what every experienced person has always known about mutual funds.

1. Like life insurance, shares in mutual funds are *sold,* not bought. The commission, or "load," runs to about 8 per cent, which the buyer pays. On periodic investment plans, the first-year load runs to 50 per cent! If you change your mind and withdraw from the scheme you lose half your money. A fantastic revelation? Perhaps. But how many realize that the same first-year load has always been charged by your trusty life-insurance agent? Salesmen must eat, and it's a long time between sign-ups.

2. Management fees for mutual funds are sufficiently high so that those lucky enough to have a contract with a large fund own a prize that can be sold off for tens of millions of dollars. (Gerald Tsai, the wonder boy of Wall Street, stands to make more than a million per year if the public deems his Manhattan Fund a winner and chooses to invest hundreds of millions in it.)

TURNING OVER A NEW LEAF

Well, what's so scandalous about all this? Many lucky people make fortunes by selling an expensive product door-to-door, e.g., encyclopedias, vacuum cleaners, pasteurized milk and cosmetics. And often owners of life insurance companies or savings and loan associations prosper, even though they show no particular excellence in calculating life expectancies or mortgage safety, provided only that they can attract paying customers.

The difference is this. Since 1933, we have come to regard the investment business as a public utility. *Laissez faire* does not apply to it, because it involves irreducible uncertainty. Neither industry self-regulation nor the forces of inter-firm competition are deemed suitable to its regulation. Special tax privileges have been accorded mutual funds by Congress, and Congress has the right to make sure the industry is properly run.

Ceilings on load charges and management fees are overdue. The citizenry will benefit, and only the special interests will be hurt.

PRUDENT INVESTMENT, I
July, 1967

William McChesney Martin Jr., the chairman of the Federal Reserve Board, has a sensitive nose for something rotten in Denmark and Wall Street. Recently he warned against speculation and a reoccurrence of the 1929 pattern of stock manipulation to gyp credulous investors.

As a result of SEC and other investigations, in the fullness of time Congress will no doubt legislate out of existence some of the more flagrant practices of the mutual-fund industry. But all that must await upon another time. What I am concerned with here is this question:

"What can a prudent man—the sort of person who studies consumer reports before he buys a high-fidelity set—do to protect himself in handling his affairs? What pitfalls should he avoid in investing?"

Being a college professor does not qualify one to engage in the-practice of financial counseling. So, be warned not to take on faith all you are told—including the following pontifications and case studies.

ONE BORN EVERY MINUTE

Beulah Shoesmith was a great teacher of high-school algebra—as is testified by the many distinguished mathematicians and scientists who occupy professorial chairs at our leading universities.

This constitutes a bountiful inheritance that she left behind her. But it was not her only inheritance. Miss Shoesmith also amassed a tidy fortune. Since she always wore the same dress when I knew her, this may have been the result of thrift. But I am inclined to doubt it. When I asked my brother to find out more about how this underpaid teacher acquired a fortune, he was able to come up only with the rumor: "She had a good broker."

Well, we have all been looking for that good broker. And take it from me, he does not exist. Any broker calling the tune for his customer's investments has a fool for a client.

Do I exaggerate? Of course I do. But in a good cause. Needles exist in haystacks, but the prudent man should act as if they did not.

Mark Twain was a great writer and a funny man. Well named, he was also a funny investor. As he himself put it, Mark was a sucker for every inventor who ever came through Hartford, Conn.—literally ruining himself by investments in publishing ventures and typesetting machines that never worked. But when a neighbor named Alexander Graham Bell came for help he was too smart to put his money into such an impractical and newfangled gadget.

Doctors are the worst. A New York friend confided to me that his psychoanalysis is anything but an unqualified success: "Whereas I want to talk about my mother, *he* wants to talk about Texas Instruments."

Anecdotes do not constitute social science. They must be documented by some notion of the frequency of their occurrence. A chap who spends all his working day with doctors—the poor fellow is a "detail man" for, you should excuse the expression, an ethical drug house—assures me that if you scratch an M.D. you find a sucker. Apparently, you can hardly keep their minds on antibiotics and cholesterol reducers, so eager are they to find out whether your firm is about to bring out a winner.

The point of all this is that the heaven of speculative success is an exclusive club, to which many feel called but for whom few are chosen.

It is not that you will ruin yourself seeking capital gains, for it takes gross ineptitude to lose much in stocks these days. (Commodity speculation is another matter. There is a case of dog eat dog: what you win comes out of the hide of him who loses, in contrast to the stock market where everyone can be a genius in a growing country; in corn and soybeans, as in Reno, most dogs lose.)

THE MORAL IS ...

But recall, we are addressing the prudent investor: the man or woman who chooses not to overpay, who puts value on his time, who invests not to prove he is smarter than the crowd but for a future purpose.

Unless you enjoy digging out information about different companies, reading Moody's brokerage letters and government documents, you probably are better off letting others make decisions for you. Either buy a few blue chips or diversified giants—General Motors, IBM, Textron, Standard Oil, Sears—or let a mutual fund or bank take over.

How does the prudent man get others to manage his money most efficiently? That's another story for three or twice-three weeks hence.

PRUDENT INVESTMENT, II
September, 1967

Q. *I am that intelligent but inactive investor who is too busy and inexperienced to invest wisely. How much of my savings should be in common stock?*

A. That has to be answered by you, depending on temperament and circumstances. If you are timid and wishy-washy, the sort who looks back with regret every time a stock drops in price, equities are not for you.

Q. *Is 100 per cent in stocks wise?*

A. Surprisingly, perhaps yes. The Wisconsin University Alumni Foundation has done well being completely in equities, indeed much better since 1925 than the usual college fund. And McGeorge Bundy, president of the Ford Foundation, recently scolded nonprofit groups for timidity in holding low proportions in equities.

But few are as audacious as Bundy, and you will probably sleep better if you aim to put 60 to 80 per cent of your surplus savings—after life insurance is taken care of—into common stocks. I know older trust officers will raise an eyebrow at this departure from 50-50. But remember we live in an age of growth and inflation.

Q. *I've picked my equity fraction. Next?*

A. First we can settle what to do with your fixed-principal assets. Put them into an insured-savings bank or savings and loan association.

Q. *No bonds? Is that patriotic?*

A. It has been unpatriotic of the government to offer such niggardly interest in recent years. The SEC should get after them!

Q. *What about corporate bonds?*

A. Leave them to speculators and sophisticates. Settle for 5 per cent. Over the long haul, borrowers have not done better than depositors.

Q. *Now we have only the problem of common stocks left. How shall I pick them? With a Ouija board? I saw you quoted in the newspapers as telling congressmen that one might as well throw darts at the financial page as pay an expert. Were you serious?*

A. Separate fact from opinion. The papers never give you the fine print of what the experts say. I did report that studies by computers at Chicago and Yale have found that in the last 40 years the best brains in Wall Street ended up with performance results averaging no better than you get from picking stocks by writing down the name of every share on a ticket, putting these in a hat, and then drawing from the hat blindfolded.

Q. *So you recommended that to me?*

A. Of course not. For two reasons. If you and twenty other people did that, you might average out *among all of you* as well as Wall Street advisers would do. But you are you, not 21 people. You don't want to run the risk of being one of those who, by chance alone, does most poorly. Besides, brains might beat chance in the future.

Q. *Sounds as if we should all form a pool and mutually get the safety that comes from diversification.*

A. The fellow who invented the wheel had nothing on you. If mutual funds hadn't already been invented, you could get a patent.

Q. *Seriously, are mutual funds the answer to my problem?*

A. Seriously, yes.

Q. *Then why is the SEC picking on them?*

A. We're trying to bring down their costs to you prudent investors.

But this brings me to your problem. Most mutual funds are sold at a commission of 6 to 8½ per cent. Shun these so-called "load" funds.

Q. *Can I really get as good buys with zero load? What's the catch?*

A. No catch, any more than in buying for less at the supermarket by avoiding stamps and selling inefficiency. No-load funds have proved to do just as well on the average as load funds. So why pay more? Throw your dart at any or all of the following funds: Scudder, Stevens & Clark (Common), de Vegh Mutual, Loomis-Sayles Capital Development, Rowe Price New Horizons, American Investors. I've put the "go-go performance swingers" toward the end. Any library has a Wiesenberger book that gives their addresses. Just send them your check for any amount. Withdraw when you please at no penalty!

There are even "negative-load" funds that sell at a discount from asset value: e.g., Tri-Continental (20 per cent), United Corp. (11.8 per cent, dividend tax-free).

Q. *Let me review. I put part of my money in the savings bank. The rest I put in one or more no-load or discount funds. Then what?*

A. Sleep.

ALIBIS, ALIBIS
April, 1969

Gloom and disillusionment prevail in the corridors of high finance. Performance, the bitch goddess of the institutional investor, has turned her sluttish back on the *Wunderkinder* of Wall Street. At the headquarters of one of Boston's most swinging funds, the ominous sign is up: TO BE UNDER TWENTY-NINE IS NO LONGER ENOUGH.

Whom the gods would deflate, they first make proud.

When savants from the University of Chicago testified before Congress and the SEC that the best portfolio managers that money can buy have done no better since 1925 than the stock-market averages—and that is the same thing as saying that they have performed no better as a result of their research efforts and company interviews than they could have done by staying at home and throwing darts at random at the financial pages—the young pilots of our go-go funds laughed all the way to the bank.

BUILDUP

"Yes," they admitted, "From the birth of Christ up to 1958, professional money managers were not able to out-perform the Dow Jones index. But now we are in a new era. Anyone can be a good *buyer* of stocks; we have mastered the art of being good *sellers* as well. And that means we may turn our portfolios over several times a year, instead of sitting there with old, tired-out du Pont."

Joking aside, what are the objective facts about performance?

1. I do believe that in this decade, more or less for the first time, a young and intelligent group were able to invest somewhat more successfully than the general average.

That may sound like a trivial statement, but it is not. It was not true twenty years ago, and it is still not true today, that the amateurs in the market are always wrong—that all you must do to beat the averages is learn from odd-lot data what the ribbon clerks are doing, and by doing the opposite you can beat the comprehensive stock-exchange index.

2. Having, so to speak, devised a better mousetrap, the innovators found that the world did beat a track to their door. The people with money said, "If we can't beat the people with brains, let's join them." So the new crew got backing, as the following items illustrate:

- After establishing a track record with the Fidelity Fund, Gerald Tsai went public with his Manhattan Fund, becoming a millionaire overnight.

- Some bright young fellows fresh out of the Harvard Business School did well with their Ivest Fund. The Wellington Fund, a slumbering Philadelphia giant, which recognized how all the new money was flowing toward Dreyfus and other hot performers, let the young Bostonians write their own ticket. And though the Philadelphians paid through the nose, the salability of the new product justified the exorbitant price.

- McGeorge Bundy of the Ford Foundation, no financial genius but a swinger who knows a swinger when he meets one, scolded our universities for their mediocre and listless portfolio performance. And since charity begins at home, his alma mater, Yale University, responded to the call. (And high time, I say, since Yale, with Vassar, had decades ago embraced the stupidest of all investment strategies—the so-called "formula plan"—which resulted in selling equities early in history's biggest boom, in order to keep an old *balance* between stocks and bonds!) Yale put another graduate from the Fidelity stable in charge of its portfolio; and through the issuance of the Omega Fund, anyone who wishes to can climb onto the Bundy bandwagon.

More examples could be supplied.

LETDOWN

The denouement of all this has been that the performers have recently been doing worse than anybody in Wall Street. Newton's law of action and reaction states with precision: "The better a fund did in 1965–66, the worse it has been doing in 1968 and 1969." The few exceptions are what every statistician expects in "noisy" data.

Indeed, the mutual funds *in general* have, from New Year's to April Fools', performed worse than dart throwers or the New York Stock Exchange index. Fidelity, Tsai, Yale's Omega, Ivest, Enterprise —yesterday's darlings all—were at last count down with the losers.

And it couldn't have happened to a nicer bunch of guys.

(In a forthcoming column, I hope to state the moral of it all— which is not merely that luck favors the lucky, or that dart throwing is the better way of life.)

BOLD INVESTING

May, 1970

In the course of his difficulty with an ungrateful sovereign, Cardinal Wolsey is supposed to have warned: "Be careful what words you put into the ears of the King, for you will never get them out again."

McGeorge Bundy, who is both adviser to princes and prince in his own right, might reflect on these melancholy words. Using his leverage as president of the Ford Foundation, Bundy has been an effective force in getting colleges and nonprofit organizations to reform their stodgy investment practices.

Aside from the influence of his own personality, which combines excellence of intellect with decisiveness of character, Bundy commissioned the 1969 Barker report "Managing Educational Endowments,"

which has had in the field of college-portfolio management something of the impact that the famous Flexner report had 60 years ago
in the field of medical-school reform.

And, gad, such a message was long overdue. In fact, about fifteen
years overdue. Throughout the longest stock-market boom in history
—pretty much from 1942 until recent times—college treasurers often
lacked the wit or will to protect their sustenance from the ravages of
inflation. They sat in the railroad station reading The Wall Street
Journal, so to speak, while the train of irreversible market advance
disappeared around the bend.

FEEL FREE

The report begins: "The record of most American colleges in investment management has not been good . . . We believe the fundamental reason [for college endowments doing strikingly worse than large,
general growth funds, i.e., 8.7 per cent per year versus 14.6 per cent,
1959–1968] is that trustees . . . have applied a special standard of
prudence . . . which places primary emphasis on avoiding losses and
maximizing present income . . . [rather than on] the clear-cut objective of maximum long-term total return, which we believe should be
the primary endowment objective of every board of trustees."

No one can quarrel with the advice that colleges should not have
to avoid low-dividend stocks like IBM, just because they think they
are in need of greater current "income." In an age of inflation, recurring capital gains can be prudently tapped, in disregard of ancient
taboos against trenching on capital.

Also one can agree that decisions should be made by profession-
als, who must be freed from the need to maintain short-term liquidity and from prescribed ratios of bond and once-safe types of assets.
And it is certainly folly to expect *each* security in an optimal portfolio
to be itself nonvolatile.

In a genuine sense it is these sage, noncontroversial precepts that
constitute the report's primary message.

BE BOLD

But the report has also, understandably, had another kind of impact.
It stresses long-run *performance,* and we all know what the connota-
tions of that word had become by 1969.

The record of ten swinging funds is set against that of the typical university. Well, he who takes credit for the sun must be prepared to be blamed for the rain. How have those great mutual funds, with their eye on the ball of long-term growth, done since 1968? Using a slide rule, one can bet the picture is a dismal one.

But don't make the mistake of judging by *short-term* results, we will be told. Like the astronomer who uses peripheral vision to best see a distant star, one should not concentrate directly on safety, lest one lose it. And the report reminds us that, blindly sticking with the Dow Jones averages from 1928 to 1968, one would have "realized an annual return from dividends and appreciation of 8 per cent." And that, "there are many substantial public investment funds that have been managed without regard to ordinary income over the years and have produced a compound annual rate of return of 12 per cent or more for at least ten years."

It is not my purpose here to use the hindsight of the last year to berate anyone for causing other people to lose their money. (I was, myself, disconcerted to learn from a NEWSWEEK reader that one of *my* columns had persuaded him to put retirement money into no-load funds that have declined with the general market.)

I do fault the report for its cavalier treatment of *long-run* riskiness. My dissent would have been stronger on this score than that of the two committee academics.

And I remind Mac Bundy that the bad advice people get they remember longer than the good.

PRUDENT INVESTING
August, 1970

In my last column, I promised to discuss the problem of rationally investing in an era when the merits of stocks have finally become widely appreciated.

It is well to distinguish between the sophisticated, aggressive investor and most of the human race. Let me first dispose of the sophisticate.

If you have at least half a million to invest and have the time and inclination for the game, you may beat the crowd by (1) putting most of your funds in half a dozen to a dozen stocks at a time; (2) ruthlessly moving from any and all of them into a new set as you discern better investment opportunities; (3) on occasion going completely into cash or, at other times, borrowing to go more than 100 per cent into equities, depending upon your reasoned guess as to the general market's future trend. The performance of even the sophisticates will be only as good as the quality of the information they dig out and their ability to analyze the future impact of such information.

If you belong to that small elite, you have no need to read further. But most people kid themselves if they think that they can successfully emulate such investors. What about the ordinary person with anywhere from $5,000 to $100,000 to invest and whose business or family has first claim upon his time and energies?

HOW MANY STOCKS?

First, you must work out a general philosophy between stocks and fixed-principal securities. Unexciting as it may sound, deciding on some general ratio—such as 60-40 between new money going into stocks and interest-yielding investments—may be the path of prudence. Next decade you can shade this ratio up or down, depending on how men of prudence then feel about inflation and interest rates.

Second, on the stock side of your portfolio, you probably are better off letting someone else make your security selections. For most people this means buying mutual funds(or their equivalent in the trust department of banks). Why delegate? Because commissions to the small men are going up; and buying a few shares of this and that on the basis of friends' or brokers' tips may well result in doing worse than throwing the proverbial dart at the randomly moving array of stock prices.

Which mutual fund? A good rule is, "Never buy from any salesman"—unless you know yourself to be feckless and unable to save money except when coerced by fast talk and heavy penalties. This means no periodic-payment contracts, with or without life-insurance deals—for the reason that the "loading" on such schemes is very heavy indeed, as much as 50 per cent of first-year payments in some cases. Remember, salesmen have to live . . . on you if you need their services.

If you do buy a "load fund," paying 6, 7 or 8 per cent initial commissions to either a salesman or a broker, you might as well stick to it. It is criminal to go from one load fund to another, losing 8 per cent at each turn in the delusive attempt to catch a winner.

"No load" funds do neither significantly better nor worse *as a group* than do load funds. A no-load fund involves no commissions when you buy or sell. You can find a list of no-load funds in any library or in any good newspaper: merely look in the daily listing of all funds for those with identical bid and asked prices. Pick four or five such funds; sign up for their bank-custodian plans, to hold your certificates and (if you wish) automatically reinvest dividends.

Many no-load funds exist which are "balanced" and maintain about a 60-40 equity-bond ratio. But do you want to pay management fees, which both load and no-load funds involve, for someone who merely invests in government and other bonds? (Speaking of savings bonds, buy them only out of patriotism. Financially, their yields have tended to lag.)

MAXIMIZING INTEREST

It is a scandal that so few mutual funds have arisen to enable the middle classes to earn high yields on short-term commercial paper, bank certificates of deposit, Treasury bills and Eurodollar loans.

So most of your non-equity money will probably have to go into an insured savings-and-loan or bank account. Shop around for high rates. It's surprising how many let banks pay them below-market rates.

Finally, a judicious flyer in a diversified list of high-yielding bonds might be worth the risk.

Do these rules seem rather simple? Yes. But like most rules, easy to state and hard to follow.

MUTUAL FUNDS
August, 1971

Redemptions of mutual funds exceeded purchases in May, something that has not been recorded in the last 30 years. Doubt has entered into the house of golden dreams.

Let's take a fresh look at the investment industry, now that the euphoria of "performance" has abated.

First, Congress and the SEC have failed to limit front-end load charges on ordinary sales. These commissions are skimmed off the top of *your principal.* You can still pay 9 per cent commissions on ordinary purchases.

Second, management fees—the substractions from the dividends *your* money earns—are higher than they need be. Competition will never bring these fees down. If it is to be done, it will have to be by regulation.

Third, portfolio turnover and brokerage commissions have been higher than can be scientifically defended. These deadweight burdens come right off the top, where it hurts most, namely, from your potential (lightly taxed!) capital gains. Often excessive turnover comes from excessive ignorance and misplaced self-confidence. Not rarely it comes from pecuniary conflicts of interest: brokerage firms that sponsor mutual funds are prime candidates for suspicion; give-ups, and their equivalents via the regional exchanges, result in sales activities that benefit the management companies but not the fund's shareowners.

Fourth, thanks to "enemies" of the industry but friends of the public, some of the worst abuses in the financial industry have been partially corrected. Kicking and screaming, the stock exchange has been dragged into "self-regulation." Give-ups and kickbacks have been curbed. Under antitrust threatenings, commission rates on large transactions have been lowered a little of the way toward their actual costs.

REQUIEM

This is only the beginning; 1,066 members of the private club called the New York Stock Exchange are coming to realize that access to the market is not like the question of whether loudmouths, hippies, Catholics, Jews, blacks, or Yale cads shall be admitted to the local squash club. In the future, large institutional investors—insurance companies, banks, pension and mutual funds—will either be allowed to be exchange members with immediate access to the floor, or will be given some equivalent status.

Legalities aside, the academic statisticians have been vindicated in their claims that even the largest money managers show no ability to select stocks that will beat the general market—once you correct, as you should, for the greater riskiness and volatility in the stocks that the performance-minded portfolio managers tend to buy. Gerald Tsai, the onetime miracle investor shown to have feet of clay, was no exception: the whole club of performance gunslingers have been proved by the post-1968 market to have looked good only because they were bidding up each other's stocks in a rising market.

WHAT TO DO?

I am not registered as an investment adviser with the SEC. I am not omniscient. But here, I believe, are some lessons justified by the experience of the last few years.

1.   Stocks are not a one-way street any more. Bonds or savings-and-loan shares may do as well in the next five years as common stocks. Maybe not. To the man of caution, this suggests putting a fraction of your permanent savings in common stocks but not all.

2.   A small man—anyone with a portfolio of, say, under $100,000 —is unlikely to do as well investing his own money as he can do in a no-load mutual fund. Commissions are getting to be higher on his own small transactions. His means guesses may be as good as the feet-of-clay mutual managers, but as a small man he cannot get that diversification which reduces risk. (Diversification does not reduce the risk of a falling general market: nothing can, except to have some of your principal in savings accounts or bonds.)

3.   There is no evidence that buying a *load* fund—i.e., one sold to you by a broker, insurance agent, or fund salesman—brings you anything for your 5 to 9 per cent commission charge in the way of superior performance or safety. A few years ago several irate salesmen, who no doubt felt I was taking the bread out of their mouths, wrote purporting to show that I was wrong in saying this. But the jury of science does not bear them out.

A no-load fund that owns most shares on the market, minimizing turnover, commissions, and management fee, is a needed public utility.

PERSONAL FINANCE
April, 1972

Most people save in good times in order to be able to spend in bad times. When you begin work at a low-paid job, you can't save much. When you are old and retired, you still have to eat; and so you use up that which you were lucky enough to accumulate—along, of course, with your social-security benefits.

Really few people, these days, are in a position to leave anything appreciable to their heirs. If you took care of your kids when they were young and helped them to get an education—and haven't had to depend on them in your old age—then you're ahead of the game.

All that sounds like common sense, even though it doesn't cover the J. Paul Gettys of the world or the local miser down the block. But it does agree with the findings of economic science, as for example MIT's Franco Modigliani in his econometric studies of life-cycle saving.

This means that how you handle your little nest egg is a pretty serious matter. I once said sagely to a colleague: "The only money you should speculate with is the money you can afford to lose." He reproved me with the words: "There isn't any such money." I had a point: a 30-year-old doctor coining it can afford to take risks a widow must avoid. But he also had a valid point: most people who read this column will suffer in their old age if they risk and lose their one and only lifetime savings.

Perhaps that's why I get so many letters whenever I venture to discuss optimal investment decisions.

PATHS OF PRUDENCE

What valid advice can I give? Not very much, and only then with genuine humility. It appalls me when I get a letter in the mail saying "After you spoke well of no-load mutual funds, I lost my shirt in one." Or, "How come the past president of the Econometric Society didn't warn in his NEWSWEEK column against the 1970 Wall Street collapse?"

But with plenty of disclaimers and warnings, let me try to be responsive to the questions asked most often.

1. It is even more true today than it was yesterday that most people should *not* quarterback their own investments. Now that stock-exchange commissions are being rationalized in terms of true costs, the little man pays more when he buys and sells a few thousand dollars worth of stocks than when this is done on his behalf by a mutual fund, insurance company, trust department at the local bank, or his employer's pension fund. If you have a flair for speculating and can afford to get your kicks in doing so, you don't need my advice.

2.   If you do decide to own a diversified portfolio of stocks, it remains true that no-load mutual funds and discount closed-end funds have done as well or better than the typical fund sold by your local mutual-fund or insurance salesman. (Some people need him desperately; but if you don't, why give away two years' income in commissions?)

3.   Insurance programs, including policies that involve saving, are a better buy than they used to be now that their interest earnings are having built into them an allowance for inflation.

NEEDED REFORMS

We still need a no-load, zero-management-fee mutual fund that gives the investor convenient ownership in the hundreds of stocks that make up the bulk of listed and over-the-counter issues. There is no evidence that professional money managers can beat the overall market averages without embracing leverage and risky volatility. Will the stock exchange, the SEC, the Post Office, or some philanthropic foundation pioneer this vital social service?

It is hard to beat the interest your local bank or saving and loan pays on fixed-principal savings. But as long as we are dreaming, let's ask the SEC to provide a broad-based bond fund to step up interest returns to small savers.

The time is overdue for the government to issue stable-purchasing-power bonds. Thus, each of us might be allowed to put up to $5,000 a year into bonds that guarantee us as much in goods when we cash them in as their principal will buy now.

Example: put $100 into such a bond now. If the price index goes up by 40 per cent in the next ten years, cash it in for $140 in 1982. In exchange for this hedge against inflation, agree to less interest.

Once the mechanics of saving are improved, we can concentrate on the really tough question: how much to put into common stocks, land and housing—to say nothing of stamps, paintings, diamonds or antiques?

Chapter 8

SOME REFLECTIONS ON EQUITY

Our is a mixed economy in which both markets and governmental policies determine the products that will be produced, how they will be produced, and to whom they will be distributed. It might be said that society, having applied the standard of equity and found the functioning of markets to be unsatisfactory, has sought to change that by introducing policies which alter the outcomes appropriately.

One of the most successful equity policies has been "Social Security." Beneficiaries contribute (i.e., are taxed) but receive benefits in excess of what they pay in. It is a centralized system of social insurance, with an element of inter-generational transfer of income, that has been a success—perhaps a counterexample to the anticipated benefits of revenue sharing.

During the Great Depression, in which the social security program was born, a myriad of social welfare programs were established to assist those with low incomes. These policies sought to amend the outcome of the economic system by transferring income not to persons who, generally speaking, fulfilled an age requirement but rather to those who were in need. With the end of the Depression the welfare system lived on. This system consists of transfers in kind (the goods and services themselves), restricted income transfers (income which must be spent for specific purposes), and some of what might be thought of as unrestricted income transfers. No one seems satisfied. Many are urging, for different reasons, that we move toward a system of largely unrestricted income transfers with none of the anomalies which plague the existing welfare programs. The "Negative Income Tax" is such a proposal.

Governments tax in order to be able to alter the distribution of income (i.e., to transfer as discussed above), to get command of the real resources it needs, and to carry out the policies necessary for avoiding unemployment and inflation. Regardless of the reason, generally it is agreed that taxation should be equitable. Equity is a difficult quality to nail down; but, lack of a consensus on all its implications for the tax laws notwithstanding, there is a growing feeling that this nation needs real "Tax Reform."

There are those who argue that the inequities we see around us, and particularly the poverty, are not just an unpleasant contrast to the affluent majority but are the *source* of that affluence.

Many speak of racism in this country toward nonwhites, and most recognize that poverty is disproportionately a nonwhite phenomenon. Can we best understand this by relying on an analogy which interprets "Racism as Colonialism"? Does the affluence of the majority rest on the exploitation of the minority? The analogy has a surface appeal but the facts suggest otherwise.

One interpretation of the economic discrimination that some critics see visited on all but white males is that it represents a form of market imperfection. Women, for example, have been systematically excluded from many jobs; and in the article, "Prejudice," we hear some first-hand evidence of the economic implications of this.

SOCIAL SECURITY
February, 1967

Which program of the modern welfare state has been, by all odds, most successful? Undoubtedly, the social-security program. And it is a remarkable fact that both expert and layman will agree on this judgment.

It was not always thus. Just 31 years ago the social-security system came into operation. This New Deal measure was hotly contested. The insurance industry fought the program tooth and nail. Suicidally, the Republican Party denounced the concepts of old-age insurance and unemployment compensation as acts of the devil—the opening wedge to socialism. Even many of the pioneering exponents of social insurance came to blows over details of the program and bitterly resisted entry by the Federal government into this area of activity.

History has by now rendered its verdict. Those who said that a centralized system would break down from the sheer weight of the bookkeeping were proved wrong in the first year of the program. The punchcard machine in Baltimore did the job at costs far below those of the original estimates, and even farther below the costs involved in the largest of our private insurance companies.

THE MYTH OF STATES' RIGHTS

Our experience with social security is instructive for other progressive programs, past and yet to come. Consider, for example, the role played by "states' rights." This is a large and diversified country; and what could be more natural than to think that, just as each province is entitled to its own folk dances and customs, so the different states ought to be encouraged to experiment with their own varieties of social legislation.

A pretty theory. But what is the pragmatic truth? Every informed person knows that the Federal part of social security—the old-age insurance system—has worked out efficiently and equitably, free of graft and arbitrary bureaucratic intrigue. But, when it comes to the state-run unemployment-compensation program, we find 50 different systems that differ primarily in trifling details. Instead of creative, regional differences, the only significant disparities involve the attempt of the least humane regions to steal industry away from the rest, penalizing those areas most concerned to maintain decent standards.

An acute moralist said, "Patriotism is the last refuge of a scoundrel." If Dr. Johnson were alive today, he would add, "And states' rights is the first refuge of a reactionary."

The notion that grass-roots government is good government is a myth. The courthouse gangs of the country and the political machines of our cities, at the two-thirds mark in the twentieth century, are both irresponsible and unresponsive. Experts in the discipline of public administration have learned that the hand from Washington, far from being the hand that deadens, is the hand that purifies—that introduces civil service and minimal auditing of the petty cash.

SOMETHING FOR NOTHING?

Social insurance makes sense because we are all in the same boat. All of us are going to die; most of us face a period of retirement before death. It is a good way to run a railroad to take account of this basic symmetry.

The beauty about social insurance is that it is *actuarially* unsound. Everyone who reaches retirement age is given benefit privileges that far exceed anything he has paid in. And exceed his payments by more than ten times as much (or five times, counting in employer payments)!

How is this possible? It stems from the fact that the national product is growing at compound interest and can be expected to do so for as far ahead as the eye cannot see. Always there are more youths than old folks in a growing population. More important, with real incomes growing at some 3 per cent per year, the taxable base upon which benefits rest in any period are much greater than the taxes paid historically by the generation now retired. And social security, unlike actuarially funded insurance, is untouched by inflation: after Germany's terrible 1923 inflation , private insurance was wiped out but social insurance started all over as if nothing had happened.

Social security is squarely based on what has been called the eighth wonder of the world—compound interest. A growing nation is the greatest Ponzi game ever contrived. And that is a fact , not a paradox.

NEGATIVE INCOME TAX
June, 1968

It is not really true that economists can never agree. Last week more than 1,200 economists, from 150 different colleges and universities, signed what may be a historically significant petition.

The time has come, these economists stated, to take the next logical step in the fight against poverty—to introduce in the American system "a negative income tax."

Among the Presidential candidates—Nixon, Rockefeller, McCarthy, Kennedy and Humphrey—there is considerable support for the plan, but not under this unappetizing name.

So call it by the sweeter-sounding, and more informative, name of an "incentive income supplement."

HUMANITY WITH INCENTIVE

Here, in brief, is the meaning of the program:

1. Just as a family today, with income far above the poverty line, fills out a tax report to the authorities, and family below the poverty

line will be required to prepare a report stating (a) its private income and (b) its family size (number of children and other dependents).

2.   If this total income is below the poverty line—say $3,300 in 1968 for a family of four—instead of collecting a tax, the government will provide a dollar supplement.

3.   It is important to emphasize that the final formula adopted is arranged so that even the poorest person has a definite incentive to add to his earnings. For example, in one popular form of the plan, 50 per cent of each extra dollar that a family gets by making the effort to work stays with it. This is in important contrast to much of the present-day welfare systems and to many alternative proposals of a Guaranteed Minimum Income.

Does this negative income-tax proposal sound radical? Impractical? Extravagantly costly to the nation?

Actually, it is none of those things. This is a coolly thought-out program that is becoming increasingly popular both with Democrats and Republicans. Arjay Miller of Ford Motors, Joseph Wilson of Xerox and other leading businessmen recently endorsed it at Arden House. Any plan that simultaneously commands the allegiance of professors Milton Friedman and John Kenneth Galbraith must have a lot going for it.

First, how much would it cost? An appreciable beginning could be made by the new Congress in the year just ahead for $5 billion net—i.e., $7.5 billion gross minus $2.5 billion saved on present welfare. Specifically, for this price tag we could wipe out half the disparity for a family of four between what it is able to earn for itself and a $3,000-a-year income level. (For extra children, the stipend is naturally larger. For individuals or small families, where the need is less, the income supplement would, of course, be smaller.)

Such a program would represent a good start. It would be far superior, in efficiency, generosity and humanity, to the children's allowance scheme recommended by Daniel P. Moynihan. It would cost less than a fifth as much as a program that simply handed out to every family a guaranteed income sufficient to keep them exactly at the poverty line. And finally, the negative income tax, far from being competitive with the efforts to increase the employability of those now out of work, could in fact be a powerful complement to such important manpower programs.

PROSPECT FOR ACCEPTANCE

Is Congress likely to act in this matter? The chances look good.

The time has come to act. In the words of Prof. James Tobin of Yale, the present welfare system is "a disaster." It tackles the poverty problem unevenly. A Mississippi welfare recipient receives barely a fifth of that going to a New York resident. There is not remotely as large a difference in the cost of living to explain this. And the present system is a costly one: although it covers but 30 per cent of those in poverty, it perpetuates that poverty by killing off all incentives to work. The man on relief who takes a part-time job may find it the most expensive error he has ever made if its extra income throws him off the rolls. Indeed, in 28 states of the Union, the kindest thing some husbands can do for their families is to go AWOL to allow them to qualify under present perverted standards.

Economists are virtually unanimous on this matter because they have reckoned the price tag against the urgency of the need and the fiscal capability of our GNP and tax system. As Victor Hugo said, "Stronger than all the armies in the world . . . is an idea whose time is come."

RACISM AS COLONIALISM
July, 1968

In one of his speeches Senator McCarthy compared our domestic Negro problem to that of colonialism abroad. Just as the English exploited the Indians in the nineteenth-century days of Empire, so the white middle classes in America are supposed to be now exploiting the black population.

Perhaps no one should be expected to take campaign oratory seriously. Still, this notion of domestic imperialism is an arresting one, and I should like to play with it to see what insights it may give into our most important social problem.

For make no mistake about it. No. 1 on our agenda for action today is the problem of the poor, whether we be bleeding hearts anxious to do good or be nervous Nellies anxious to protect our affluence.

THE EXPLOITER EXPLOITED?

In considering the problem of British imperialism, the testimony of Rudyard Kipling may be of interest. Kipling is not much in fashion today; but in his heyday—1890 until, say, 1930—he was one of the best sellers of all time. Pick up any book of quotations, or consult your memory, and you will be surprised at how great has been Kipling's influence on our language.

"Oh, East is East and West is West, and never the twain shall meet." "The female of the species is more deadly than the male." "He travels the fastest who travels alone." "And what should they know of England who only England know?" "A woman is only a woman but a good cigar is a Smoke." "Of lesser breeds without the Law." All these catch phrases of everyday speech are due not to Shakespeare or Ben Franklin but to Rudyard Kipling. The critics may despise an author but, if the masses read him, his is the last word. For what do they know of literature who only literature know?

Moreover, in the case of Kipling, his is also the first word. Above everything, Kipling is an author for children; and it is in the impressionable years of infancy that our basic attitudes get set. "Kim," "The Jungle Book," "Gunga Din"—these have had more influence on foreign officers dealing with India than the syllabuses they studied at Oxford, in the same way that Uncle Remus and Huck Finn had more influence on the last generation of Supreme Court Justices than Gunnar Myrdal did.

Although Marx and Lenin may have regarded imperialism as exploitation of the natives by the empire builders, this was not at all Kipling's view of the matter. Born himself in India, the son of a civil servant-teacher, Kipling's view is best summarized by:

> *Take up the White Man's burden—*
> *Send forth the best ye breed—*
> *Go bind your sons to exile*
> *To serve your captives' need;*
> *To wait in heavy harness*
> *On fluttered folk and wild—*
> *Your new-caught, sullen peoples,*
> *Half-devil and half-child.*

It is significant that these words were addressed to us Americans at the time of our Philippine imperialism.

Today, of course, none of this will wash. Kipling cannot be

resurrected into the forum but is condemned forever to lurk in the nursery. Yet before we laugh him out of court, let us admit the testimony of George Orwell, himself no Colonel Blimp, but like Kipling, India-born and Burma-tested.

"[British civil servants in India] were at any rate people who did things . . . they could have achieved nothing, could not have maintained themselves in power for a week if . . . [their] outlook had been that of say E. M. Forster [author of the prophetic "A Passage to India"]."

PLUSES AND MINUSES

I do not know whether on balance Britain benefited from owning India. The computation is a difficult one. Certainly the Dutch were not crippled by losing Indonesia, or the Belgians by losing the Congo. France is better off without empire in North Africa and Indochina, just as America would be after leaving Vietnam. Just as there are few indispensable men, there are few indispensable nations. Were the world to lack the resources of the Indian peninsula and also its hundreds of millions of people, would Western living standards be the lower? White South Africans probably enjoy a higher standard of comfort because each lives on the toil of seven black men. But is it likely that the top two-thirds of our people would be impoverished if the poorer third—black or white—did not exist?

What remains then of the concept exploitation? Having quoted McCarthy, Kipling and Orwell, let me finally quote Paul A. Machiavelli: "The poor have property rights in the rich." This is a fact, not a target.

TAX REFORM
August, 1969

It began most recently with some casual remarks by the outgoing Secretary of the Treasury, Joseph W. Barr. People were fed up with inequities in the tax laws, he said, and the mail signaled a "taxpayer's revolt" ahead.

Earlier in 1968, Robert Kennedy had begun to campaign on the issue that rich men, with hundreds of thousands of dollars of income, were able to escape *all* taxes because of loopholes in our tax laws. On the eve of his assassination, Robert Kennedy was deliberating the wisdom of some kind of a minimum tax rate that even millionaires would have to pay.

But such a program involved political risks at that time and required a considerable amount of courage. For the early attempts by John F. Kennedy's New Frontier to legislate meaningful tax reform had been crushing failures. Old-line congressmen had opposed proposed reforms and even such progressives as Sen. Eugene McCarthy had not been willing to stand up to the strong pressure groups that mobilized in defense of existing privileges and inequities.

ELECTORATE APATHY

In truth, the lacking ingredient for tax change was public support. It is idle to expect sweeping reform from Congress itself. *Every last loophole in the law was put there deliberately by the House and the Senate* —whether it involves sweetheart deals for oil and cattle, or an absolution from all capital-gains tax for every man of property dying in the suburbs.

By my count, it is three decades since experts in public finance —people like the late Henry C. Simons of the conservative University of Chicago, Harold M. Groves of the progressive University of Wisconsin, Joseph Pechman of the neutral Brookings Institution—have presented a united front to Congressional committees in pointing out the glaring inequities in our present laws.

Were they heard? No. Was their message difficult to understand? No. Did the masses of voters in both parties, those in the heavily exploited middle-income ranges, respond mightily to proposals that were overwhelmingly *in their own best interests?* No.

On certain simple issues of enforcement—e.g., withholding at source of dividend and interest payments to cut down on known tax evasion—the mail of liberal senators would run 25,000 *against* to 133 *for!* Of course, that was sucker mail-mail drummed up by savings and loan associations and the like. (Why an S&L should ask people to write is clear in terms of *its* economic interests. Why lawabiding people should respond against *their* own dollar interests is a mystery. And why the executives of large corporations should have regarded such proposals for even-handed enforcement of existing law as the greatest infringement of liberty since King John signed the Magna Carta at Runnymede only cynics and satirists can understand.)

A MINIMUM PROGRAM

Sodom and Gomorrah cannot be unbuilt in a day. As a first install-ment, Congress should quickly pass at least the following:

1.   At the lower end of the income scale, *increase the levels of exemp-tions and standard deductions by enough to remove from the taxrolls millions of low-income taxpayers.*

Of course, it would be better ultimately to move to a full-fledged negative income tax. But until consensus for that has arrived, let us have a zero tax for those on the edge of poverty.

In the emergency days of World War II, when excess-profit tax rates were almost confiscatory and highest personal rates were 91 cents on the final dollar, each exemption was $500—far more in purchasing power than today's $600. Generosity at the lower end of the scale is long overdue.

2.   At the upper end of the income scale, *introduce a minimum tax rate on gross incomes that cannot be avoided by sheltered income.*

E.g.: You earn $100,000 of municipal-bond interest and realize $200,000 of long-term capital gains; your $30,000 of salary income was offset by deductions and research expenses to produce these capital gains.

Under present law, your twin with $300,000 ordinary income pays about $200,000 in taxes, almost four times your $55,000. Under a new minimum rate on gross income, you would at least be required to pay taxes on 50 per cent of your gross $300,000.

That wouldn't break you. It would make your twin feel better. Most important, your less lucky cousins will face lower tax rates once you are carrying your share of what Holmes called "the price of civilization."

PREJUDICE
March, 1970

As Mayor La Guardia once said after a gaffe, "When I make a mistake it's a beaut." I know what he meant. In the course of a recent inter-view for The New York Times I made some derogatory remarks about the caliber of students at Sweet Briar.

If I sinned, I have been made to pay for it. My mail has been full of denunciatory letters from female liberationists who are under no vow to be ladylike. What hurts more though are the well-merited reproaches from Sweet Briar, which happens to have a strong offering in economics and rightly resents being characterized as a frivolous finishing school.

I wish I could say that I was misquoted. But even though I was woefully ignorant about Sweet Briar and used its name as a surrogate for any girl's school, that did not keep me from opening my big mouth and slurring its good name.

So *mea culpa.* There is nought to do but make humble apology, both to the institution in particular and to the feminine sex in general.

IN JOCO NON VERITAS

The incident, however, has set me to pondering. Freud claimed that much is revealed by the jests we make, and I must ask myself why, in an unguarded moment, I found myself expressing a stereotype concerning the implied inferiority of women. Since I am an economist, that naturally raises the question of why women have an economic status so unfavorable relative to that of men.

That they do have such an inferior status there can be no doubt. On the occasion that my wife's class at Radcliffe celebrated its 25th anniversary, I was able to examine the range of their incomes and to compare them with the distribution of the same class at Harvard. Although I am an experienced man of the world, I must confess to shock when I saw the cold numbers before me. The top women's salaries literally ended about where the bottom men's began.

I know you will say that many college women become wives and mothers. That you must not compare part-time earnings with those from full-time work. That one must allow for the fact that many women return to the labor market after a hiatus of many years spent in the home, and that their loss of momentum explains their pauper-like wages.

But I reply that these explanations will not wash. A class at Radcliffe has long been, if anything, even more select in such qualities as IQ and erudition than the contemporaneous class at Harvard. And many Radcliffe graduates have pursued full-time careers. Why then do *they* turn out to have the incomes of librarians and of teachers rather than the incomes of corporation lawyers, NEWSWEEK editors, and machine-tool salesmen?

Confronted with these undoubted facts, a defender of the status quo will say, "Women get less because they are worth less." In its usual formulation this becomes little more than a tautology, deserving of the same reply that Hemingway gave to F. Scott Fitzgerald's remark, "The rich are different from us." "Yes," said Hemingway, "they have more money." (And exactly this reply is warranted to the assertion that the poor are different; experiments with the negative income tax in New Jersey show that the poor differ primarily in the fact that they are under the Biblical curse of poverty, and in not much else.)

Somebody has written an essay with the fascinating title: "The Student as Nigger." It makes the point that students are men with boys' incomes, who are expected to remove their hats and shuffle their feet in the presence of their superiors (if not their betters).

A woman would understand that essay. How many of them have climbed the executive ladder up to the rung marked assistant vice president only to be barred, Moses-like, from the Promised Land.

REDEMPTION

Tokenism has begun to rear its head. One or two blacks or females or French-Canadians look good on the organization chart. But do not knock it. Tokenism is the tribute that bigotry pays to conscience. If you feign a virtue, you may end up having it.

But I digress to philosophy from my task as an economist. What would be the effects of wiping out, or say for the sake of the argument, halving the earnings and productivity differentials between men and women?

Will the extra affluence of women have to come at the expense of the surplus value earned by men? Economics suggests that the removal of discriminations will pay its own way, adding to GNP about what it costs.

Chapter 9

ANY ROOM FOR LOVE?

There are but two selections here. A tiny chapter? Yes, but a tremendous topic—love.

We look at Professor Samuelson's definitional comments on love, and must agree with him that as "agape" it is precious among humans. Yet we must rely upon it, in another form, for the free lunch of life itself. God or nature do not "calculate cost or gain, or the merit of the receiver."

Does such quality of human love exist at all? Could it be increased in supply? The reading on "Blood" says yes to the first question, and also asserts its positive, practical utility; "the blood you get for a buck is simply not as good as that you get for love." For the second question, no answer is given here. Hope remains that we could learn from experience.

How best to allocate love's limited supply? Professor Samuelson says not to waste it within the competition of the marketplace. Where Adam Smith tells us, it is not from the benevolence of the baker that we should expect our bread but from the pursuit of his own self-interest—this is as it should be. We must instead direct this scarce "agape" toward the solution of those large social and environmental "prisoner dilemmas" which we face. Can we not add another small course to the free lunch?

LOVE
December, 1969

An economist writing on love? Next thing you know, plumbers will be penning sonnets on beauty.

Of course, I am speaking of love not in the Greek sense of *eros*, but rather of *agape* (which Webster's Third defines as "spontaneous self-giving love expressed freely without calculation of cost or gain to the giver or merit on the part of the receiver"). But I am not sure that these two can be completely—ahem—divorced: perhaps Soames Forsyte's troubles in bed were not unrelated to his overweening sense of property.

If the first seven editions of my introductory text on economics managed to omit "love" from the index, why cannot the eighth let well enough alone? It is not really that I have suddenly gone soft in the head. Rather it is a case of having, belatedly, come clear in the head: to explain the scientific facts that are out there to be explained, had love never existed we should have had to invent it.

Clearly I contradict what, at the University of Chicago, I was taught was the first and only law of economics: "There is no such thing as a free lunch."

MILK

No free lunch? What nonsense. That is a scientific law with only 4 billion exceptions. If it were true, no member of the human species would survive for even a week!

Freud claimed character is formed in the early years of life. (As father of six I digress to ask why, in that case, the world is not more clearly divided into the hard and easy teethers.) If Freud is right, we were all developed under communism.

For, as Prof. Lyle Owen of the University of Tulsa points out, family life itself is a form of communism with a small "c." In the home the doctrine prevails, "From each according to his abilities, to each according to his needs." The good parent does not say, "Because Tiny Tim is lame, he shall get the wing. The go-getters may compete for the drumstick."

It is only when we turn 10 that Freud's reality principle breaks in, and we are taught in school the parable of Capt. John Smith's Virginia colony—that he who does not work shall not eat. That simple lesson carries more weight with congressmen than all the proofs of another Smith on the optimality of competitive pricing.

And actually it was at Forsyte's London club that Samuel Butler was heard to say: "The world will always be governed by self-interest. We should not try to stop this; we should try to make the self-interest of cads a little more coincident with that of decent people."

The same point was made more professionally by the late Sir Dennis Robertson of Trinity College, Cambridge. At Columbia's 200th anniversary, he asked, "What is it that economists economize?" *Love,* was his surprising answer. Love is so precious because there is so little of it in the world. And that is why we must make what we do have go a long, long way.

MAMMON

The moral is to render unto the market that which the market can handle. Except in time of siege do not squander patriotism and agape on the allocating of beefsteak.

Hard-boiled game theory teaches that Macy's can serve as a check on Gimbels. If G quotes its price above the competitive margin, M will gain by undercutting. And vice versa. In the end of this special game, the consumer gains from the canceling avarice of market competitors.

But game theory also teaches "Prisoner's Dilemma." In this parable, the district attorney approaches each of two prisoners separately, saying: "Whether you confess, I have the evidence to send you both to jail for one year. If you *both* confess, I'll settle for a five-year sentence each. But if *you alone* confess, giving me the evidence to convict your pal, I'll get him a ten-year sentence and let you off with a three-month term."

Reflection yields the solution: "Universal selfishness would make each confess, giving both of them five-year terms. Only love can achieve the best common state of one year when neither tries to gain by telling on the other." *QED.*

Another Captain Smith fairy tale? No. Substitute "non-pollute" for "non-confess" and you realize why a 1970 economic treatise has need for love and for common rules of the road that we coercively enforce on ourselves.

The truths of economics cannot be captured in even a hundred laws. But somewhere on the sacred tablets this truth is written: do not render unto the market that which is not the market's.

BLOOD
September, 1971

Vilfredo Pareto, the great turn-of-the-century sociologist and mathematical economist, once attended a scientific congress. He listened with impatience to some spokesmen of the then popular "German historical school," which we today might think of as involving a blend between the economic iconoclasm of the young left and the humorless caution of middle age.

What left Pareto especially indignant was the claim, "There is no such thing as economic law." According to what may be apocryphal legend, Pareto later had his revenge.

Encountering his antagonist Gustav Schmoller on the street, Pareto raised his coat collar and shuffled forward to whine, "Where can I get a good dinner for 10 pfennigs?"

"For 10 pfennigs? No one can possibly get a good dinner anywhere for that."

"Aha," Pareto replied, "so there does exist economic law after all!"

What is the moral of this little tale? Does it demonstrate, for example, what I was brainwashed to believe in my innocent student days, that "there is no such thing as a free lunch"? Indeed, it was not until I had studied advanced economics that it even occurred to me to wonder what the no-free-lunch dogma was itself supposed to mean and be telling us about economic reality and feasible policy.

'ANGELS, NOT ANGLES'

I mention this because I have just been reading a remarkable, too-little-known book, "The Gift Relationship: From Human Blood to Social Policy," by Richard M. Titmuss of the London School of Economics.

The author compares our American system of providing blood with that of the British. Here the issue is something more vital than mere lunch. Blood to the dying or postoperative patient is the nutrient of life itself.

No Englishman pays even a shilling for all the blood his doctors prescribe for him. And blood is more plentiful there than in this most affluent country of the world.

Where's the catch? you will ask. We all know that medicine is "socialized" in Great Britain; so, although the patient does not pay directly for the blood that he receives, surely the long-suffering middle classes are bled white by the tax system so that paupers can live parasitically on the red cells and energies of their betters?

Wrong again. No one pays for the blood—not the state, not the patient, not the Red Cross.

Something for nothing? Yes, something for nothing and that something which poets have rightly symbolized as the most precious of all things.

No one pays for blood in England because no donor receives anything for his gift. That is, nothing except the "mere" satisfaction from giving. When I give blood in England that does not give me a surer claim on blood at a future date when I may need it. It does not give my child a preferred place in the queue for blood. All I get is the anonymous pleasure of knowing that I have helped my fellow man.

The next time you hear the expression "perfidious Albion," think of this remarkable example of social solidarity. When you read that British GNP is lagging, remind yourself of English courtesy in the bus queue and at the customs.

BLOOD AND MONEY

Meanwhile, what's the situation back here at home? The first thing to notice is that although we rely on monetary supply and demand to give us our daily bread, most of our blood and plasma is quite divorced from the market mechanism. More than two-thirds does come from donors who receive no cash in return.

To be sure, not all of this is completely voluntary. When a favorite teacher has a child dying of leukemia, all of his students and colleagues are urged to give blood. Often a consumer of blood, or his associates, are under specific compulsion to repay in kind for blood used. Not infrequently emotional blackmail is resorted to in this good cause.

But when all is said and done, the supply of voluntary blood in America falls increasingly behind the need for it. Recourse must be had to commercial donors.

We have in our everyday language the not very nice words "blood money." Today we should add the pejorative phrase "money blood." In terms of quality (red cells, hepatitis risk), the blood you get for a buck is simply not as good as that you get for love.

This should not surprise anyone. Wise people have always known that the love you get for love is better than the love you get for money.

Chapter 10

A LOOK BACK, A LOOK AHEAD,
A LOOK AROUND ...

It is enjoyable and refreshing to find our good friend and teacher, Professor Samuelson, reporting on the reactions he has received to some of these readings, and grading himself on the outcome of his predictions. He takes this kind of backward look in the first two selections of this chapter, "Keeping The Score," and "Report-Card Time," and also presents renewed analytical comments on the issues involved. While noting that he comes out moderately well in this review and self-appraisal, it should also be said that the expression "good friend and teacher" is used here advisedly, and with all due respect. To read this book is to become personally involved with the author.

Samuelson speaks as analyst and forecaster in the next four readings, starting with his 1969 forecast and carrying through the 1970 recession, ending up with analysis of "Springtime Euphoria" in 1971. For the record, the 1969 GNP of $930.3 billion was within his predicted range. As he notes in "Good Times Coming," he was off the mark in 1970, along with almost everybody else. GNP ended up at $976.4 billion, against his predicted $990 billion. He was back on the money with 1971s GNP of $1050.4 billion, which marked the first trillion-dollar calendar year for the economy, in terms of Gross National Product.

It is difficult to do justice in these brief remarks to the many analytical points made in these four readings. One isolated example is found in the observation that 4-½ per cent annual growth in real GNP is needed, just to maintain the status quo with respect to the rate of unemployment; greater than this if we hope to reduce it. Another is the desirability of a successful "incomes policy," which (let's face it) is the euphemism for wage and price controls of some type. Be that as it may, the promise of such a policy tool, if it can be made effective and equitable, is that of permitting us to move in closer to full employment and at the same time enjoy reasonable price stability.

In "GNP, *Non;* NEW, *Oui,"* the chapter concludes with discussion of this exciting, and only recently developed, concept of "Net Economic Welfare." True, the basic idea has been around for some time, in a qualitative sense. There is perhaps no teaching economist in America who does not bring into lectures the observation that the economic process results in the existence of some things with negative utility to society. Some have dubbed them "bads" to emphasize their contrast with the positive utility of "goods." People taking their first economics course forty years ago might have heard the word "illth" used in reference to "harmful goods." An awkward word at best, and perhaps tainted by value judgments as to what constitutes a harmful good, it is little or never used today. But it did bear a similarity to the serious concern of the present.

Although it can thus be established that the fundamental line of reasoning leading toward NEW has been within economics for a long time, and we are therefore exonerated of the charge of gross ignorance or complacency, the sense of urgency and more unique application to environmental considerations are developments of the more recent past. Newer still, and of greater analytical significance, are the serious efforts at quantification of Net Economic Welfare, referred to in the article.

As one of the social sciences, it might be argued that economics paid its lifetime dues when it made the tremendous contribution of national income accounting and analysis. But now it is noted by Samuelson that economics is, or should be, the calculus of the "quality" of life; not merely the "quantity" therof. By presenting published numerical values for NEW, standing alongside those of conventional GNP, economics can move toward such a calculus and revitalize its established accomplishments.

KEEPING THE SCORE
May, 1967

A sage once said: "Never look backward. Somebody may be gaining on you." Despite Satch Paige, after one has written a column in ecomonics for six months, it is a good time to call in the auditors. Even Charles Darwin, another sage, found it necessary to write down each argument against his theory of evolution, for, as he confessed, he always kept forgetting adverse criticisms.

Well, what went right? What wrong? As at Princeton, I shall use the honor system to grade myself.

PAUSE OR RECESSION?

The major economic question of our time is where we stand in the long Kennedy-Johnson expansion.

The days of our years are three score and ten. American economic expansions, according to the Old Farmer's Almanac, have a median age of scarce 30 months. Thus a 74-month rise since 1961 stands out as a veritable Methuselah of a peacetime boom. But is it now over?

There is one school of thought, mostly centered about Cook County, which says we are now in the Recession of 1967. Reason: last year's cruel cut in the money supply.

Indeed, a dean of the Chicago Business School is on the record that the 1967 money GNP will average less than the present rate. And some of the rasher members of this school think that last year's crimes by the Federal Reserve will provide us with a crucial experiment, in much the way that the 1919 eclipse provided a crucial experiment to test Einstein's Relativity Theory. "If we have a 1967 recession, then Keynesianism is wrong and the quality theory of money is the true faith.

Like many cute theories, this notion of a crucial experiment is balderdash. For some Keynesians think excessive inventories will bring recession; and some money bugs expect the recent rise in money supply to pull us out of the current pause.

Last fall I commented on the tightness of money and welcomed the turn by the Federal Reserve. At year's end, I sent an open letter to President Johnson, warning that the economy had become too soft to justify the kind of tax rise that should have come a year earlier.

Although my message must have ended in the dead-letter office, the budget turned out to be a wily one: new social-security benefits outweigh the deflationary effects of a tax surcharge whose passage is doubtful. So don't bet on a 1967 recession.

The mutual-fund industry did not like my view that their commissions be limited, which is understandable.

On the other hand, I lost few friends from expressing doubts about the scientific validity of stock-market forecasting by technical charts. It is indeed absurd to confront a philosopher with the ancient taunt: "If you are so smart, how come you ain't rich?" But, it was a fair ploy to bring up against those who claim ability to earn speculative profits the *ad hominem* argument that chartists usually have holes in their shoes.

Those who disapprove of our war activities in Vietnam were disappointed with my analysis which showed that America could "afford" an even larger war as far as the economics of the problem is concerned. But at least they could derive comfort from my conclusion that our prosperity would not necessarily be imperiled by peace.

SOCIAL-SECURITY PARADOX

Social security was by all odds the most controversial item touched on. Puzzled readers asked how to reconcile my assertion that everyone can draw more from the system than he has ever put into it with (1) common-sense arithmetic, and (2) published assertions that the young will pay more into the system than they will ever get out of it.

Instead of referring to the equations of compound interest given in my 1958 journal of Political Economy paper, let me explain.

So long as prices, real income, and population continue to grow at a compound rate of interest, each newly retired group can be paid benefits far exceeding what a private voluntary-insurance actuary could ever pay. Today's young get cheated only in the remote political event that tomorrow's more numerous young could opt out of the system. Q.E.D.

Where critics go wrong is in thinking that today's 20-year-old will retire in 2012 on benefits at 1967 levels. Only an ostrich could believe that.

REPORT-CARD TIME
April, 1968

When first deciding to write for NEWSWEEK, I wondered whether I might run out of topics to comment on. I need not have worried. The old Chinese curse, "May your children live in interesting times," has been visited on our own heads, and recently there has been an embarrassing excess of news.

Still, at intervals it is a good idea to take stock—to read over the mail, reconsider one's positions, and tally up the score. Since it is my custom to mete out grades to congressmen as well as classes, equity requires a severe self-examination.

TRIAL BALANCE

Taxes and inflation. My oft-expressed fears that the economy was going through an overexuberant phase have, alas, proved well-founded. Prices and wages are trotting faster than the creep we have learned to expect in any high-employment mixed economy. The open letter that I wrote last October to Congressman Wilbur Mills must apparently have ended up in the dead-letter office, and a tax increase is still not clearly in sight.

Even in the classroom there are no absolute grades: rankings must depend upon one's performance relative to others. So far, President Johnson—who before his announcement of retirement was being blamed for everything that happened, even week-end rain—has maintained the most prophetically correct economic policies, predicting too much ebulliency for the economy. What about the professed Presidential candidates?

Senator McCarthy has come out strongly against a tax hike. Prior to the decision to negotiate in Vietnam, this might have been justified as a tactical protest against the war and its escalation. But the reasons that he gave in repeated commercial TV announcements from New Hampshire amounted primarily to this: no one likes higher taxes and I am against their being imposed on you.

Sen. Robert Kennedy voted against the Senate amendment calling for a tax surcharge. The reason he gives for having done so is not one that I can criticize since it agrees with the argument that I employed in my November column. Kennedy repudiates any tax rise that is coupled with crippling expenditure cuts applied selectively, as in the Senate amendment, against the welfare programs of the Great Society.

As far as I can determine from research in the recent New York Times Index on the question of the tax surcharge, candidate Richard Nixon, like Br'er Rabbit, is saying nuffin'.

Gold and the dollar. While I was right to discern hope in last September's agreement, at the Rio meetings of the International

Monetary Fund and Bank, to institute "paper gold" in the form of Special Drawing Rights, no A+ was earned for prescience in sensing the imminent collapse of the pound. And I compounded my misdemeanor in expecting that the President's New Year message on the balance of payments, in which capital controls were made mandatory rather than voluntary, would fend off for a time the run on American gold.

On the whole, however, along with most academic economists, I have long been apprehensive that the dollar is not in fundamental equilibrium: because productivity in Europe and Japan performed such miracles in the 1950s in comparison with our productivity and costs, because our corporations have wanted to perform such large foreign investment in Europe, and because of our military and civilian aid programs (greatly compounded since 1965 by the Vietnam escalation)—for all these reasons, I deem the dollar to be an overvalued currency subject to large deficits.

DOLLAR OVERBALANCE

The gold run was thus no surprise. Nor were our capital controls, our tourist threats, our tying of foreign aid, and the innumerable *ad hoc* fiats equivalent to piecemeal depreciations of the dollar.

What can we do about this? Barring malignant quotas and tariffs, very little. Leaving Vietnam will help. Controlling inflation will also help. But international equilibrium achieved by creating unemployment at home is neither desirable nor feasible. Wishing for resumption of open inflation in Europe, and for a letup in the desire of our firms to invest abroad, might help a bit. But none of these, I fear, are substitutes for multilateral negotiation for an orderly change in the dollar exchange rate vis-à-vis the currencies of the surplus nations.

Of course, our luck might change. But Lady Luck, in my book, has always rated only a low pass.

THE NEW YEAR
January, 1969

For many years it has been my custom to publish for the readers of the Financial Times of London a general forecast of the business outlook in the new year. Forecasting is a dangerous game, and I sometimes wonder why I carry on this tradition.

For one thing, the editors are kind and do ask me very nicely for one more contribution. For another, old friends are thereby stimulated to write and one is loath in these days of uprooting to discourage any tradition.

Most important is the masochistic desire to make oneself climb out on a limb. How do I know what I really think until I read what my pen is writing?

THE FASHIONABLE FORECAST

One begins with the typical projections that begin, in October, to float around the banks, insurance companies and large corporations.

These tend to be remarkably alike—particularly if you take account of their date. No wonder all the October numbers cluster around common values—for after all, the economics profession is one cozy family and we are constantly on the telephone swapping surmises. Then, by December, we tend to shade our forecasts in pretty much the same way, as we react to the same general cumulative record of statistical information.

I have been speaking of a standard year. This year is hardly typical. At midyear, after the Johnson-Mills fiscal restraint, most analysts expected the economy to cool off: the last half year's growth in GNP was fashionably projected at an annual rate of 5 per cent, half of the first half's exuberant rate.

Early in 1969, after new social-security taxes began to bite into consumer's income, virtually no real growth was expected. It was believed that unemployment would rise enough to slow inflation down a bit. Profits were expected to be eroded away by stagnant growth.

NEW YEAR FORECAST

	1968	1969	% Growth in 1969
Gross National Product (billions)	$861	$924	7⅓*
Consumption expenditure	535	567	
Government expenditure	197	215	
Domestic investment	127	139	
Net exports	2	3	
Real Gross National Product (deflated for price changes)			4
Unemployment rate	3.6%	3.9%	
Profits (in billions, after taxes)	$ 51	$ 53	

*A range of 6½ to 9%

Then, according to that early forecast, the last half of 1969 was expected to be a period of renewed expansion, but on a healthier, more sustainable basis.

Such a forecast is now quite obsolete. Economists are shify characters who have the wisdom to cut their losses.

When this fall's retail sales zoomed and when spending on equipment and construction soared, the slide-rule boys moderated their bearishness.

Upward revision of estimates still goes on. But not to a large enough degree. Here are my hunches.

1.   The possibility of a 1969 recession brought about by fiscal overkill was never serious. Now the probability of recession is virtually nil.

2.   The probability of a significant slow-down in the first half of the year has become fractional. I suspect that the new Nixon team will be fighting inflation right through the Fourth of July.

3.   Money will get tighter. People say we cannot witness another 1966 money "crunch." I ask, why not? Won't the same causes tend to produce the same effects—higher interest yields, falling bond prices, tighter credit rationing, disproportional impact on savings-and-loan associations and on mortgage money for housing?

4.   Despite the indiscretions of the new Secretary of Commerce, Maurice Stans, I would hate to bet that the surtax rate will be cut in July.

Even the combination of Stansian horse-and-buggy finance with Friedmanian go-go monetarism will not convince the President and Congress that inflation is unaffected by lowering of tax rates. Only a Chicago Ph.D. could believe that, and there are few of this anointment in either house of Congress.

5.   Difficulties with our balance of current exports over imports we shall still have with us next year.

Admittedly the outlook that I have sketched is not the happiest that could be wished for. Generally it points to more of the same weather that has been plaguing the American economy since the Vietnam escalation of mid-1965.

Still there are many silver linings in the weather map depicted in the table below. Unemployment will remain low; real standards of life will rise. Wall Street will not fall out the window even if it does occasionally fall out of bed.

And, as readers of this column know well, there is one source of comfort. I could be quite wrong in my forecasts!

GOOD TIMES COMING
September, 1970

The recession turned out, after all, to be a mini-recession. Output stopped declining by spring, though the rise this summer will be slight.

Looking ahead to mid-1971, the experts expect no expansion vigorous enough to cut into the unemployment and capacity gap.

Nor do we expect much improvement on the inflation front: twelve months from now prices will be generally 4 per cent higher —a somewhat better performance than the 5-6 per cent rise in the twelve months past.

Housing starts should trend upward as interest rates continue to subside a little. Weak inventory rebuilding appears likely. The boom in fixed-investment spending on plant and equipment is finally over, but recent soundings on capital appropriations do not suggest any substantial decline in total dollar spending.

Whether or not stock prices will rise depends, as usual, on whether all this has been "discounted" already. The only opinion I hazard in this realm is that the usual lunatic fringe of technicians and chartists, who have been predicting an ultimte drop hundreds of points below the May Dow Jones trough of 631; will be sweating long before their forecast is realized.

POLICY LESSONS

All in all this is not a prospect that a Charles Dickens could describe as either the best of time or the worst of times. When we consider that the failure of Penn Central might have set off a liquidity crisis and that old-fashioned capitalism might well have generated a maxi-recession out of the 1969 situation, we naturally feel grateful to Congress for having over-ridden the puritanical budget-balancing of the original Nixon game plan. And, despite the desire of the president of the Federal Reserve Bank of St. Louis to prolong the decline in output for another year in order to break the back of inflation, most observers have applauded the Federal Reserve's restoration of growth in the money supply to a 4.5 per cent annual rate. Indeed, speaking for myself as an incorrigible New Frontiersman, I wish that chairman Burns and his colleagues would aim for even a somewhat higher growth rate in currency and bank deposits.

Recently I tried to comment for readers of The London Financial Times on what lessons we had learned from the experiences of this last year. There did not seem to be many.

Recent experience, I am afraid, rather tends to confirm the either-/or character of full employment and price stability. It points up how valuable it would be if only our mixed economy could somehow find a successful "incomes policy." With it we could aim at more expansionary fiscal and monetary policies, instead of having to rely upon the dead weight of unemployment and excess capacity to hold down inflation.

But to tell the sad truth, nothing in recent experience here or abroad has pointed the way toward a successful incomes policy. Reiteration of Galbraithian prose does not constitute scientific argument that wage and price controls could be made to work for any length of time in an effective and equitable manner. At the same time, one has to point out that the Nixon scheme for a national commission on productivity and an inflation alert by the Council of Economic Advisers is a blatant placebo.

HUMAN FAILINGS

If the past year has taught us little about the economy, it has taught us something about ourselves, something about our limitations as economic forecasters. In using the pronoun "us" I include myself, since the last nine months suggest that my prediction for 1970 of a money GNP of $990 billion was too high by more than $10 billion. And I also include monetarists who, like the First National City Bank, seem to have been strongly off-base in the overly pessimistic direction; and the Friedmanites, who warned that the 1970 recession had to be worse than the midi-recession of 1960–61.

Even the leading-indicator approach has had a disappointing year. Instead of correctly predicting in advance the contraction's trough, it was not until the June revisions that the leaders caught up with the crowd.

Since New Year's Day always brings forecasts that cover the whole spectrum of outcomes, a few analysts can claim 1970 to have been their successful year. Thus, although using diametrically opposed methods, both the Wharton school model and the monetary model of the Federal Reserve Bank of St. Louis came pretty near to the truth. Any model that can duplicate this accuracy year after year will deserve the respect of science.

STOCKTAKING
July, 1970

Now that 1970 is half over, where do we stand? Here are the questions I am asked most frequently in speeches before the public, and my best answers to them.

Q. How goes the inflation battle?
A. One begins to see signs that the peak of price rises is just behind us. This turning point has been long in coming. Certainly this does not mean stationary prices in the foreseeable future. But it does mean that our 6 per cent infaltion will probably be a 4 per cent inflation by next winter.

And the facts of last year confirmed what most non-Washington economists guessed—that you can't get much moderation in the pace of inflation without paying the price in terms of unemployment and even recession.

Q. Are we in a recession? Will it snowball into a depression?
A. Yes, we probably are in a recession, a mild one that falls between 1967's mini-recession and the 1960–61 recession. Such a recession is unlikely to become a maxi-recession, say like the Eisenhower recessions of the 1950s that saw production decline by more than 10 per cent and unemployment grow to 7 per cent.

I don't think there is any chance that this first Nixon recession will degenerate into a business slump like that of the 1930s. It is not that the human race is any smarter. It is simply the fact that every government and every political party knows and will use the rudiments of the New Economics that will suffice to prevent slumps from living on their own deflation and becoming chronic.

However, on the basis of the statistics available at midyear, I can't yet confirm the suspicion that the midi-recession will turn the corner in 1970's last half. That is why the first priority should not be given to keeping the post-Cambodian slide in business activity from gathering momentum.

CURRENT PRIORITIES

Q. Doesn't that mean giving up the fight against inflation just when it is beginning to show some fruits?

A. No. It means putting first things first. It means aiming for the right dosage in the trade-off between unemployment and inflation.

The fact that the Federal Reserve has let the money supply grow rapidly recently does not mean that it will be locked into an inflationary syndrome for the rest of the year. Nor is it the case that the Federal budget has now gone out of control.

Actually, the best-informed forecasters have recently been writing down their projections for the four quarters ahead rather than foreseeing an inflationary jag ahead. Both employers and union leaders must realize at the bargaining table that arriving at whopping wage increases will carry severe penalties on employment and profits in the less inflationary regime down the road.

THE PROSPECT AHEAD

Q. How bad will unemployment get?

A. The new Secretary of Labor now admits that it will probably go to 5.6 per cent. But one shouldn't be too surprised if it reaches 6 per cent, particularly since unemployment will continue to grow even after we have clearly turned the recession corner. Remember that ours is a growing population.

It is only cold comfort that black unemployment is doing a bit better than some of us had feared. Nonetheless, since last year, black unemployment has swelled more than white; when highly educated college students have trouble getting summer jobs, think how tough the search must be for ghetto youths.

Q. Mr. Nixon said many of our economic problems stem from the "transition" from peace to war. Does that mean we need war for prosperity?

A. It is true that engineers in the aerospace industry are out of jobs because of defense cutbacks. But I can't agree that our problem is caused by the windup of the Indochina war. Our unemployment comes primarily from Washington's desire to fight inflation. If there were no inherited inflation problem, monetary and fiscal policies could be shaped to offset reconversion unemployment.

Q. Will profits go to hell?

A. If the GNP turn is near, the worst is over for profit trends.

Q. Will interest rates come down?

A. Only slowly, unless the recession is allowed to toboggan downward. The liquidity squeeze is real, and new bond offerings will keep markets tight. Housing should pick up slowly as credit becomes more available and Federal agencies pump funds into construction. Plant and equipment spending has probably peaked out.

Q. Which way for stocks?

A. No comment.

SPRINGTIME EUPHORIA
May, 1971

It is said the ancient Turks used to be surprised every year by the coming of spring. Modern man does not seem to have made much progress since: each April along with the voice of the turtle and the scent of magnolia blossoms tends to come optimism about the GNP.

Where really do we now stand? Was the $28.5 billion rise in first-quarter GNP a remarkable jump? Does it indicate that, after all, the high Administration forecast of a $1,065 billion economy is on its way for 1971? Or as Walter Heller claimed in an interview, have we been experiencing only a lackluster performance?

I think I know the answers to these questions. The facts themselves are not much in doubt. Only their interpretations admit of controversy.

But do I dare express publicly the simply truths of economic life? Before the age of the atomic bomb, scholars nurtured the comfortable view that one told the truth and shamed the devil. (Gaetano Salvemini, that great European who heroically resisted Mussolini, was once asked by a colleague whether he should publish a finding that might give comfort to the enemies of humanity. Salvemini instantly replied: "Publish—though the heavens fall.")

Treasury Secretary Connally is no Salvemini. Recently he lashed at critics of the Administration's economic policy, not on the ground that they were wrong about the official forecast—it is public gossip that Connally himself would not have issued such inflated numbers had he been appointed to office earlier—but on the ground that cold-water criticism would hurt our chances of achieving business recovery and reducing the rate of unemployment.

HOW GOOD?

As an analyst of the business cycle, I cannot agree. Not all of NEWS-WEEK'S columnists together, with or without an assist from John Kenneth Galbraith and Leon Keyserling, can make or break an anointed prosperity. "Confidence" is an overrated ghost working within the economic machine; and, in any case, the only confidence that counts is not that made in Madison Avenue but that earned on Main Street.

Here then are the cold facts. Let them tell their own story.

- The first-quarter rise in GNP was a bit on the disappointing side. Two-thirds of it was attributed to the rebound from the auto strike. If it were not that retail sales picked up a bit in March and April and that inventory accumulation was especially modest early this year, one would really worry about the weakness of the economy and begin to consider whether the fashionable forecast of only $1,045 billion-$1,050 billion would be realized.

- The rate of price inflation has abated a little, particularly if we concentrate on the consumer price index. One is grateful for this, but one must also keep fingers crossed in view of the likelihood of higher food prices ahead, particularly of that overrated staple, meat.

- The administration's official forecast of vigorous real growth in 1971, which is to bring us by the middle of next year to 4½ per cent unemployment and a 3 per cent rate of inflation in over-all GNP prices, looks more doubtful today than it did when issued at the beginning of the year.

NOT GOOD ENOUGH

So much for fact. Now what about interpretation?

To say that 1971 will be better than 1970 is to say nothing. To say that we shall have economic growth between now and the November 1972 election is to say almost nothing. We could continue to grow for a dozen years without interruption; but if our rate of growth did not exceed the 4 per cent that we need just to keep up with the growth of the labor force and of industrial productivity, our rate of unemployment would soar far above its present 5 per cent level.

Par for the course, the level around which we reckon "birdies" and "eagles" and "bogies"—I am using words that our sports-minded President can understand—is not the point of zero real growth: it is the point of 4½ per cent growth; and at a time when unemployment is high and when there is a 5 per cent gap between actual product and full-employment product, par has to be moved upward to allow for a return to fuller utilization of capacity and manpower.

The official targets are good targets. I wish the Administration believed in them. Fortunately, Congress is responding to the nation's economic plight and is overriding the President's budget. For this Secretary Connally should thank the critics.

HITS AND MISSES

January, 1973

Once, after I had counseled an audience of experts always to study their past predictions in the hope of learning from experience, Britain's leading forecaster chided me: "Great mistake to look back. You'll lose your nerve."

I cannot agree. Lot's wife must be the model for the scientific analyst. So, here are some auditings.

Hit. The consensus forecast for 1972 was for a strong year. Broadly, I went along with this and am glad I did. If the same crowd is as lucky in 1973, it too will be a strong year of growth—over 6 per cent in real terms.

Miss. The wage-price controls have worked out better than my columns had suggested they would. The same logic would suggest that they will be with us all year. But I have a sneaking suspicion that logic is not the sole weapon to understand Nixonomics: perhaps once the Teamsters and Rubber Workers' wage agreements are buttoned down, the President will cut and run on wage-price controls—with the blessings of George Meany.

Hit. Alas, I was correct in my spring 1971 prediction that President Nixon would have plenty of time prior to the November 1972 election to defuse the economic issue by oxygen-tent Keynesianism. (I say alas as an opponent of Richard Nixon's re-election. By the doctrine of last-one-converted-first-one-to-renege, there is ground for concern that the President would prefer to have a recession early in his second term rather than late—so that his party could come up smelling like a rose for the 1976 election.)

In any case, I continue to believe that the next recession or stagnation will—like the last one—have written on its bottom "Made in Washington." This will not be because the Administration consists of spoilsports, but rather because any re-acceleration of inflation will be the signal for the Burnsian Federal Reserve and the Shultzian Treasury to take in sail hard.

THE NOT-SO-ALMIGHTY DOLLAR

Hit. For a dozen years prior to the financial crisis of August 1971, mine was one of the few voices crying out in the wilderness to warn against over-valuation of the dollar. That crisis and President Nixon's ending convertibility of dollars into gold have more than confirmed my pessimism.

All economists knew that it would take two or three years to learn whether the dollar depreciations agreed to at the Smithsonian in December 1971 would be adequate. But I must confess that last year's failure of our export surplus to respond appreciably to the medicine of depreciation makes me think that we are still not out of the woods.

Probably the Japanese should once again stop being stubborn and appreciate the yen still further beyond the 17 per cent appreciation of 1971. And no one need be surprised if more financial crises loom ahead.

For lasting reform of the international monetary mechanism, what we need most is agreement on more flexibility of exchange-rate parities. (For example, deficit countries should come to take it for granted that they depreciate their currency by 1 or 2 per cent each year; surplus countries, such as the Germans and Japanese, should come to take it for granted that they will appreciate their currencies 1 or 2 per cent each year.)

That way, over a decade, we can achieve the needed adjustments to different regional rates of productivity growth and of cost-push inflation. And that way we can end chronic one-way deficits and surpluses.

PRUDENCE IN PERSONAL FINANCE

Hit. For years I have been nagging that no-load mutual funds have essentially all the advantages of high-load funds for the investor canny enough to eschew salesmen. It is the no-load part of the industry that has been growing fastest in recent years. Interestingly, despite the penalty in redeeming load funds, it is the no-loads that have provided least redemptions and most market liquidity.

I am glad, too, that I jumped hard on the monstrous Martin report that tried to preserve—and extend by the strong arm of the government—monopolistic practices by the New York and other stock exchanges. Actually, under pressure from the antitrust division and civil suits, the financial establishment is at long last being made to shape up and become competitive in commission rates and other matters. But the Securities and Exchange Commission has a long way to go to meet its responsibilities.

Whenever I write about personal investment, I get letters from readers. I do my best but hope no one will consider it a *miss* if I duck the task of pinpointing next year's stock prices.

WHAT'S WRONG?

March, 1973

Economists say that 1973 will be a second year of vigorous real growth in employment, output and profits. Washington says that inflation will be kept below a 3 per cent annual rate. Yet there is a monetary crisis abroad. And the stock market has been hurting badly. No wonder that many people think the times are somehow out of joint. An old friend in Wall Street recently summarized for me some of the anxieties troubling men of finance. Here, in question-and-answer form, is my best appraisal of where we stand.

Q. What's wrong? On the surface everything seems fine. Yet I have the feeling that other people know something I don't know—something that lurks ominously below the surface.

A. Give names to your nameless dreads. Let's look them over.

Q. I keep a little index number of the average prices of commodity futures: soybeans on the Chicago Board of Trade, silver, copper, wool. In the last year my sample has gone up by 50 per cent! I keep asking myself: Are we in another 1919–20, when silk and staples soared sky-high—only to collapse in the grim 1920–21 recession that almost bankrupted such giants as Sears, Roebuck? More ominous, are we in the situation of Germany just prior to the 1921–23 galloping inflation that wiped out the middle classes? Don't laugh: you asked me to articulate my anxieties.

A. Volatile prices have indeed soared. So have wholesale prices. Undoubtedly there is bad news ahead for the cost-of-living index. It's not Washington's fault that there was a corn blight, bad snow cover in Russia and drought in Asia. Oil isn't scarce; but no one stands up to the new Mideast oil monopoly. And there's not really much that Washington can do about it all, except issue comforting public-relations bulletins that no one believes in.

Q. Let me break in. I forgot my worry about these dollar depreciations. The 1971 Smithsonian depreciation apparently didn't work. The speculators seem to think that the 1973 10 per cent dollar devaluation won't work either. Are we getting to be like a banana republic that depreciates, then has its prices and wages rise at home to undo all the good the depreciation could accomplish? With the result that chronic depreciation will become a way of life in the brave new world of floating currencies we seem to be moving into?

A. All these anxieties add up to the same concern—whether we are now in a vicious circle of inflation that will accelerate out of control.

I think the odds are against this. Remember that in Germany the central bank—their Federal Reserve—had been printing new money by the trillions in order to "catch up with" prices. There's nothing like this yet in sight here. Critics can fault the Fed for letting money grow by 7½ rather than 5 per cent. But remember that the economy needed real stimulus after 1970–71, and real GNP did grow by about 6½ per cent in 1972. The budget is definitely not out of control. Indeed, in terms of *real* goods and services bought by the government, the total called for in the new budget is down. Who expected that?

Q. Then inflation is no worry?

A. No. This spring's wage settlements are going to exceed the 5½ per cent standard. Instead of prices rising at year's end by 2½ to 3 per cent, I'd put my guess at 4 per cent. And this means continuing upward pressure on interest rates, short and long. But these are not banana-republic numbers. We can live with them. And so, I expect, will Wall Street be able to.

Q. What about the next recession? That's another of my worries.

A. Years ago we'd have called you neurotic if you worried about inflation and about recession at the same time. Now we know the world is schizoid. We've learned about "Stagflation"—inflation *cum* stagnation. There are respectable experts who think the present expansion will run out of steam by year's end. Their ranks are getting thinner as each week brings new evidence of strength in the economy. I'd even say the economy is overstrong. Better many quarters ahead of 6 per cent real growth, than to have the system blow off its top of steam with a few 8 per cent quarters that are unmaintainable. I'm a worrier, too. My fear is that, by 1974, Washington's fear of worsening inflation may cause them to put the brakes on too hard. But that's still a way off. And articulating rational, namable dangers may help to avert them.

GNP, *NON;* NEW, *OUI*
April, 1973

Thomas Carlyle complained that economics is the *dismal* science. That was last century.

Today the complaint is that economics is the *complacent* science. Supposedly, economics tells us, if we were to listen, how to grow, grow, grow.

But who is to say that more is necessarily better? Certainly no expert in the cells of malignant cancer would agree to that. To many thoughtful people, the prospect of "healthy" growth in the Gross National Product (GNP) is not unlike the spectacle of an arrogant young racer, barreling along in his Ferrari sport car down a dead-end country road. The smile on his healthy face is a measure of his ignorance that, at the end of the way, there lies an immovable brick object.

From this viewpoint the post-World War II miracle of GNP growth in Western Europe and Japan is *tragedy,* not progress. The human race occupies a spaceship with limited room and exhaustible resources. Like fruitflies in Professor Raymond Pearls' glass bottles at Johns Hopkins, the passengers multiply in number. And suddenly, with the help of Merlin the New Economist, those in first class on the spaceship have learned how to preempt on one last inglorious binge the dwindling rations that will be needed by all.

No wonder critics say, "Gross National Product" is too ... too gross. Economics is bankrupt if the only wares it can deal with are material wares, wares that despoil the habitat, and defraud the future."

As an economist, I have to agree that the accusation, if valid, would indeed be a serious one. But those who take the time to investigate economics seriously, I mean modern economics not that of your great-uncle Algernon, can satisfy themselves that the bill of indictment is a faulty one.

THE MOVING FINGER WRITES ON

As a textbook writer I would like to be able to believe that he who teaches a nation's youth its legends and tales is more important than legislators and kings. But this is vainglorious. Homer did not form the Greek spirit. He reflected it.

Therefore, the historian of the future, peering back to understand our age, could do worse than study carefully the successive editions of an economics textbook like mine. You will not find in the index of its first edition *Economics* (1948), "pollution" or "ecology." You will find back there the pressing concerns of the mid-century: eradication of mass unemployment, moderation of the business cycle, macroeconomic control of demand-pull inflation, ...

Then in successive editions, there appears on the horizon, at first no larger than a man's hand, the cloud of *cost-push* inflation. Dollar shortage comes and goes. Dollar overvaluation, alas, long tarries.

NEW IS WHAT'S NEW

Now that the ninth ediction is about to appear a quarter of a century later, what is new? Net Economic Welfare (or NEW) is a key motif, and high time.

Net Economic Welfare is the *corrected* version of GNP—corrected to subtract out from the conventional calculation those *non-material disamenities that have been accruing as costs to our economy* whether or not they have been recognized and charged against the industries and activities that cause them.

I refer to effluents that pollute our rivers and lakes: the mercury from industry and the phosphates from home washers. Included are the hydrocarbons that darken our skies: carbon monoxide, sulphur; nitrogen compounds. No need to enumerate further.

Included too are the disamenities of modern urban life. If you must pay a messenger to ride for two hours, then your trip to and from work is really a cost that must be subtracted from your cushy income that goes into the GNP.

To provide an estimate of all such subtractions from the GNP, I'd be able to benefit from the work of two Yale economists: Nordhaus and James Tobin, who prepared a 1972 monograph for the National Bureau of Economic Research entitled, "Is Growth Obsolete?"

THE SCORE

To go from GNP to NEW, you not only have to *subtract* items. You also have to *add in* items—items such as the value of work of housewives, which for no logical reason never got into the conventional GNP. But, when all's said and done, what does the record show about NEW?

NEW has been growing in America. But it has been growing at a considerably lower rate than GNP. What is more important, by my extrapolations of the Nordhaus-Tobin data, NEW will fall behind GNP's growth increasingly in the future.

But all this is not inevitable. Modern economics teaches us that we can trade off some GNP growth for more healthy NEW growth. It's up to the public.

Modern economics, in the age after Keynes, knows how to limit GNP's material growth in the good cause of healthier welfare growth. Grass need not grow in the streets in the process (as indeed might well have been true back in Calvin Coolidge's era of rugged individualism).

In short, modern political economy is the calculus of *quality* of life, and not merely that of national *quantity.*

Chapter 11
THE ECONOMICS OF POLITICS/ THE POLITICS OF ECONOMICS

At one point in this chapter, it is noted that national politics and elections generate the same kind of periodic interest as do the World Series or the Olympics. If this is so, and the assertion that "everyone" is interested in politics is permitted to go unchallenged, then these particular readings are a special treat to feed that interest. They bring together in one place the otherwise isolated and intermittent comments of Professor Samuelson on the relationships between politics, economics, and political candidates, over a four-year period of American economic and political life.

The chapter title is almost uniquely appropriate, in that it categorizes the articles into those that discuss how economic considerations influence the outcome of elections (the economics of politics), and those that indicate how political considerations influence economic policy actions (the politics of economics). Thus classified, it will be easy for the reader to discern that those written in even-numbered years of Presidential or Congressional elections are of the first type, while those of odd-numbered non-election years are of the second. This is entirely appropriate to the relative degree of readers' interest at a given time.

Samuelson is first and foremost an economic scientist. So if there is a third spirit afoot in these articles, it is that economics truly is an objective body of knowledge, the principles of which are agreed upon by economists of varying political persuasion. This is seen in such selections as "The Economics of Class," and "Economic Snake Oil."

Beyond this, it is almost impossible to discuss these selections without an excessively detailed commentary that would itself threaten to become political. Far better to let them speak for themselves.

CAMPAIGN ECONOMICS
August, 1968

"Hypocrisy is the tribute that vice pays to virtue." So said the Duc de La Rochefoucauld, a cheerful pessimist. He meant by this that men generally act worse than they speak.

In politics, the reverse is the case. One would have to be a despairing pessimist indeed to believe that public officials and political parties manage to behave as stupidly as their pronouncements read.

If statesmen performed in office the idiocies that they solemnly promised to perpetrate in order to gain office, the planet would long ago have perished—with a bang and a whimper, in both fire and ice.

BIG WHITE LIES

Let me illustrate with a dramatic instance. Franklin Delano Roosevelt campaigned for the Presidency in 1932 on a program of balancing the budget. Not only did he denounce Herbert Hoover as a reckless deficit spender; but, what most people have forgotten, he earlier broke with Alfred E. Smith because he could not stomach Smith's irresponsible advocacy of public-works relief programs to aid the unemployed.

All this is summarized in a story told about Judge Rosenman, FDR's faithful speechwriter and helper in the drafting of New Deal legislation. Some years after Roosevelt assumed office, he asked Rosenman to take some time off to determine how Roosevelt could rationalize the spending he and Ickes and Hopkins were doing with what Roosevelt had promised during the 1932 campaign. When next they met, the President asked the judge whether he had been able to solve the problem. Rosenman replied that after studying the matter carefully, he had only one bit of advice to give his chief: "Deny you ever made that speech!"

Is the moral that of Lord Acton, that power corrupts? That of Plato, that politics is the art of telling plausible lies? That of Macaulay, that while Charles I may privately have been a good father and husband, publicly he was a wicked King?

Let me not be misunderstood. It would have been utter folly for Roosevelt in the depths of the greatest depression the world has ever known to have tried to balance the budget. If Lord Acton had ever been a king or Pope, or even a Prime Minister, he might have learned the antidote to his much-quoted aphorism—namely, "Power sobers." Even Barry Goldwater, if he had somehow been elected in 1964, would have ended up doing most of the things that he bitterly criticized President Johnson for doing.

So be of good cheer when you read the platform of the Republican Party as it is solemnly enunciated at the convention. When it defends President Eisenhower for the fiscal lethargy of his second term, and castigates Presidents Kennedy and Johnson for getting the country moving again, despair not. And when the Democratic platform promises full employment with price stability and the dollar forever frozen at its present overvalued parity, laugh not. Nobody is listening. And nothing is being said.

It is not for a journeyman economist to try to fathom why the electorate seems generally to prefer liturgy to logic. If mousetraps pay, mousetraps will get built. If hot air and moonshine prevail, we must assume that supply is meeting a demand. Politics is the battle for survival: existentially, those who survive have to be the fittest.

THE DIFFERENCE IT MAKES

One would be wrong to infer from the fatuity of most campaign oratory that it does not matter who wins. Although a victorious Goldwater could not in 1964 have recreated the world of McKinley or Coolidge, he could most certainly have affected the rate at which our mixed economy departs further from *laissez faire*.

If, like me, you believe that governmental activism is desirable in order to sustain vigorous growth, increase equality of opportunity and of minimum living standards, and cope with worsening problems of environment and unrest, it is not all one whether you vote for Reagan or Nixon; for Nixon or Rockefeller; or for Nixon or Humphrey. This, extremists fail to see. From far out in Right or Left fields, all batters look alike. Extremists are blind to the vital, small differences that dominate the random walk of political evolution.

The count in November matters much. What matters is not simply whether a man has a majority of the votes, but also how large is the opposition. In our democracy we elect a team and not just a man. For this reason, party regularity, rather than being a substitute for careful thought, may instead be its consequence.

THE ECONOMICS OF CLASS
October, 1969

To a first approximation the Republican Party is the party of the affluent, and the Democratic Party is the party of the underdog. The same class orientation is true of the Conservative and the Labor parties in Britain. And as I contemplate in my mind's eye the various nations of the world—Norway, Germany, Chile . . .—I cannot think of an interesting exception to this broad generalization.

To a second approximation, money income cannot alone explain all the facts of political allegiance. Intellectuals, the world over, are the despair of their well-to-do uncles. (Even Moscow provides no exception once you substitute the coin of power for the coin of coin.)

Why is this? Is it because work long deferred maketh the mind sick? I hardly think so.

For one thing the major premise in such a syllogism is false to begin with. For the first sixteen years of life it is the intelligentsia, so called, who are the hardest workers of all. And at any age, just because a man is sitting down doesn't mean that he is not working.

No. Intellectuals tend to be liberal for the simple reason that *inequality*—if only you will *focus* on it *and think about it*— is at first blush abhorrent to most men. The strong burden of proof is against it.

GOLDEN SILENCE

No one knows this better than those who think with their pocketbooks. Take your wrist-watch tape recorder to any posh country club or uptown luncheon club. You will not hear disquisitions, in the manner of Edmund Burke or William Graham Sumner or Friedrich Hayek, on the legitimacy and functionalism of privilege. Such palaver would be thought only boring. Nor will a Geiger counter detect Freudian signs of suppressed guilt feeling. People are content to enjoy that which is theirs, and wise enough to let it go at that. (The same is true at beer picnics of $20,000-a-year journeymen plumbers. For them too it is not a matter of "Whatever is, is right." It is enough that "Whatever is, is.")

But an intellectual can be defined as one who will not let well enough alone. He must forever be examining things—and talking about them.

Ideologues of the right know this. To Edmund Burke in the eighteenth century half the battle was lost once that tiresome Jeremy Bentham got men to go around asking questions. "Why is that lass hung for theft of a handkerchief? And why is that duke not jailed for theft of a county?"

What was subversive was not Bentham's mumbo jumbo about pleasure and pain. It was his pragmatic assumption that *everything* about English life—from the usury laws to the design of prisons—was on the agenda for examination-*and reform.*

J'ACCUSE

Let me now, as they say in court, connect up with the current scene. At this moment, Richard Nixon is playing his historical role as Republican President, protecting—or trying to protect—the privileges of property. That, after all, as they say on Madison Avenue, is the name of the game.

How else can we understand President Nixon's recommendation that Congress drop its attempt to close the loophole of tax-exempt municipal-bond interest? And that the proposed one-year holding period for capital gains be dropped in favor of the old six-month period? And that the maximum 25 per cent tax on capital gains be retained?

Look not in the writings of Paul McCracken for a defense of tax-exempt municipal-bond interest. The same subsidy to local finance can be given cheaper by other devices. Nor will you find among Republican writers on laissez faire (e.g., Milton Friedman or the late Henry Simons) a brief for capital-gains loopholes. Look elsewhere for explanation. To the election returns. To the campaign contributors. To the lobbyists.

I am trying to be fair. I have said nothing about 27½ per cent depletion. Neither party can look itself in the mirror on that one. Nor have I attributed to election payoff the Nixon recommendation to lower the corporate tax; and to help the affluent business and professional classes by limiting the maximum rate on earned income to 50 per cent. On balance I oppose these measures, but recognize that disinterested authorities can make argument for them.

In defending tax loopholes that are indefensible, President Nixon has made a tactical class blunder. There is a taxpayers' revolt because the spectacle of more than 100 millionaires who pay no tax is, to the American people, revolting.

ELECTION ECONOMICS
October, 1970

Where elections are concerned, political science has few generalizations to offer, and the few it has become fewer with each new election.

What happened to the old law, according to which a senator cannot become President? Three of the last three Presidents testify to its repeal.

Or what about the finding of behavioral sciences that voters' opinions get set early and are unchangeable by exhortation, television or anything else? Harold Wilson, Tom Dewey and the pollsters in Princeton have learned to be skeptical of that alleged regularity.

If political science and sociology have still a long way to go in establishing a valid science of electoral behavior, history and historians are little better off. The late Arthur M. Schlesinger Sr., one of America's greatest historians, thought he could discern in our annals an approximate sixteen-year periodic cycle between conservatism and reform. This was applied to explain the coming 1948 victory of Dewey over Truman.

When cynical economists, who have spent their lives debunking the notion that the business cycle has a periodicity of 40 months, or eight and a half years, of whatever the latest astronomical findings declare to be the periodicity of sunspots, hooted their scorn, young Arthur Schlesinger, as he used to be called, declared the theory of cyclical political behavior to be an irrefutable tautology: what goes down must come up. This doctrine of the inevitable return to power of a vanquished party could be of comfort only to a Menshevik waiting on tables in Paris.

HOW MONEY TALKS

Political economy is only a little more useful. If simple-minded Marxism were right, only the rich should vote Republican. The blue-collared worker, whether he be black or white, Lithuanian, Irish or hillbilly, should vote Democratic to promote his economic interests. The small businessman and commercial farmer, ground down by the inevitable rise of large corporations, should oscillate between flirtations with Fascism and identification with the welfare state that provides social security, medicare and small-business credits.

This scenario is too simple by far. And yet . . . and yet. Once you allow for the historical one-party South, the special problems of blacks and Jews, this script does cover some of the facts—as you will learn if, on your way from the suburbs to the Union Club, you stop in the slums.

Still, economic determinism provides us with precious little to understand why, in a nicely balanced system of two parties, the Republicans can do so well in a year like 1956 and so badly in a year like 1964. In all years, their well-heeled business constituents can outspend on TV electioneering. On top of this, variations in business conditions affect the elections.

Bad times are bad for the ins. Had Herbert Hoover possessed twice the charms of Teddy Roosevelt, he could not have been re-elected in depressed 1932. (Losing a war is also hard on incumbents, as Wilhelm and Nicholas could attest. But what about the case of Nasser, whose popularity was untouched by *his* 1967 disaster?) A truth like this cannot be pushed too far: the fact that the country was truly prosperous in 1952, with employment full and prices steady, could not save the Democrats against General Eisenhower's Carlylean appeal.

THE HERE AND NOW

Bad times before the election are slightly more favorable to the Democrats, inflation slightly more favorable to the Republicans. The reason for this is that, despite the me-too protestations of both parties, the voters have a pretty shrewd suspicion that the Democrats tend to be readier with the public buck and the Republicans more tainted with financial orthodoxy.

As this November's election draws near, the economy is suffering both from unemployment and from continuing inflation. President Nixon, recalling how the 1960 recession helped John Kennedy defeat him, must feel that luck is rather against him.

The corner of possible recession may have been turned, as his advisers assure him. The turn, though, must be one of the least perceptible in our history. September's rise in unemployment to 5½ per cent may indeed be something of a statistical aberration produced by a late Labor Day, yet 5½ is the last number that the voter can know at the time of the election. The General Motors strike is another blow to Republican ambitions to gain Senatorial seats in Michigan and Ohio.

Still, economics is not all. How the people feel about the war, students, law and order will resolve the balance.

THE TWO NIXONS
February, 1971

To speak repeatedly of the "new" Nixon is as ridiculous as to talk of chronic seduction. Just as within every fat man there is a thin man struggling to get out, outside every thin man is a fat man struggling to get in.

What I am trying to say is that there has long been, there is still now, and there will continue to be an observable degree of schizophrenic inconsistency in the actions and utterances of the President.

In so saying, I definitely am not hinting at the "tricky Dicky" reputation that the President enjoys in some circles. Nor am I accusing him of Machiavellian hypocrisy or of cynical lack of convictions.

Quite the contrary, based upon long observation of his actions and utterances, I find the key to the puzzle is precisely the fact that *the President does have a definite ideology.* He does have convictions. And he would be only too eager to operate on the basis of these convictions if he could.

The root of his dilemma is that his true, inner convictions are not feasible and viable in the eighth decade of the twentieth century, as applicable to our version of populist democracy. Instead of likening Richard Nixon to William McKinley, it is more illuminating to think of him as John Adams, a Federalist deeply disturbed by the directions democracy is taking.

REPRESSED DESIRES

To learn what are the President's guiding convictions, I invite you to perform a thought experiment. Imagine that the United States had the British system of government, and that two years ago Richard Nixon was elected with an effective parliamentary majority that could be counted on for five years or more. What laws and programs would Prime Minister Nixon have enacted by now? Although history cannot be run over and over again, on the basis of his public and private utterances, the following actions seem plausible.

First, Mr. Nixon has always expressed concern lest government preempt too large a fraction of the GNP. Hence, a gradual program of tax cuts and limitation of functions of the Federal government would be the logical corollary of this *Weltanschauung.*

I submit that the actual growth of Federal expenditures and widening of programs has been in the face of initial executive opposition. An apparent exception to this generalization, such as the President's espousal of a family-assistance program, fits back into the pattern once you remember that the new program is being proposed in order to displace the present monstrous program of welfare.

A second major premise of the gentleman from southern California is the belief that government interferes unduly in the lives of the citizenry. An incomes policy, even in the form of jawboning or guideposts, was so alien to the philosophy of the new President in 1969 that even though they promised some reinforcement in the battle against inflation they had to be rejected. And let us make no mistake about it, the decision has cost the President political votes and popularity.

Coming right up to the recent State of the Union Message, one discerns the same ideological tensions at work. I pass over the issue of Cabinet reorganization as being of no interest and little significance except to students of bureaucratic administration. The issue of revenue sharing is central to my thesis.

In the mind of the President local initiatives are to be respected in comparison with acts of the Federal octopus in Washington. Therefore, a shift toward giving grants to the states without strings is desirable. Contrasting with this ideology is the sad truth that local and state government is *less* responsive and efficient than Federal. A program without strings invites competitive deterioration of standards.

THE REALITY PRINCIPLE

America is not Britain. Congress is not responsive to the executive. More fundamentally, in our present-day interdependent society, the scope of the public interest widens rather than narrows. John Adams must be turning over in his grave as every mixed economy moves increasingly toward redistributive welfare measures. The rights of property shrink as the rights of man expand.

President Nixon must therefore compromise with evil. What does it avail a man to please the shade of Herbert Spencer at the price of being a one-term President?

Richard Nixon did not recently board the Keynesian ship as a result of the open letters we professors have been sending out. A more powerful voice spoke—the voters', last November. And both Nixons were listening.

ECONOMIC SNAKE OIL
March, 1971

The economic report of the President has come out with a forecast for economic growth in 1971 that is $15 billion, or 1½ per cent, more than almost every forecast outside the government. Although economics is not an exact science, so that any forecast might turn out to be the true one, including this one, no jury of informed persons could possibly agree that the President's forecast of a $1,065 billion 1971 GNP—with all that it implies for improving unemployment and real growth by mid-1972—is warranted by the evidence now available.

Why this flagrant disregard for economic objectivity? Was it simply a case, as some old Washington reporters have claimed, that the President and his No. 2 man for domestic matters, Dr. George Shultz, merely overruled his experts on the Council of Economic Advisers and elsewhere, telling them that the warranted projection was simply unacceptable?

Such an explanation raises more questions than it answers. Why should the Administration wish to give an ostrich-like forecast? Why have we not had a rash of quiet or indignant resignations from scholars of impeccable probity?

A Talmudic exegesis of the wording of the economic report itself will suggest that its writers did not have their hearts in the rosy projections. The best that they can muster up is sentences like ". . . it seems more likely that with present policies the outcome [for GNP] would be higher than [$1,050 billion] and *could* be as high as $1,065 billion" (my italics).

SILLINESS

This is not the stuff out of which lasting stock-market booms can be made. All non-Administration witnesses before the Joint Economic Committee have been pillorying the new estimates. It is truly an exercise in overkill. Such unsound fellows as myself have been united with such admirers of the Nixon programs as business consultant Allen Greenspan in throwing to the wolves the flimsy arguments advanced in defense of the Administration's forecasts. The unkindest cut of all comes from Arthur Burns of the Federal Reserve, an old Nixonite, but no rubber stamp.

The Administration stalwarts are not even agreed on their defense. Shultz gives much of the credit for upping the ante to a new wonder equation cooked up by his 30-year-old assistant, Dr. Arthur Laffer. It is indeed a wonder model: in it a quarter's increase in the money supply instantaneously kicks up GNP by five times as much, and has no later effects. In it the pace of inflation is not directly affected by the amount of slack in the system.

It is a model that most enrages the true-blue monetarists by pushing their methodology to its logical absurdities. It is a model that, if true, would make it ridiculously easy for us to manage our economy with full-employment, inflation-less perfection. It is a model good for a laugh, and it might even turn out with the correct prediction. But why base policy for a great nation on such as this?

THE MIKADO'S WILL

Doctors Stein and McCracken of the CEA have testified that Laffer should not get the credit for the projections. Imagine clamoring over priority in a matter like this.

What case do Stein and McCracken put up for the estimates? They point out, correctly, that past first-year recoveries have had average growth rates in line with the government numbers. They point out, correctly, that most forecasters have a tendency to underestimate the strength of any movement in either direction.

But their major point is that these are official *targets* by the government. What the government *wills* it has policies to achieve. So believe, believe.

To have cogency, such an argument would have to be based upon the supposition that the fashionable forecast of $1,050 billion has been generally based on budget expenditures and deficits *lower* than those of the President and on unrealistically low estimates of the 1971 growth in the money supply to be expected from Dr. Burns and the Fed. This is contrary to fact.

So we are left with the Castro-like tactic of calling for 10 million tons of sugar, not because you can justify that as the likely figure but because to call for it may succeed in perpetrating a self-fulfilling prophecy.

We are in a Gilbert and Sullivan world in which Koko, the Lord High Executioner, loath to chop off a head, excuses himself with the syllogism:

"When Your Majesty says, 'Let a thing be done,' it's as good as done—practically it *is* done."

NIXON ECONOMICS
August, 1971

It is now official. What private economists of both political parties have been telling President Nixon since the beginning of the year— that there is no reasoned likelihood of a $1,065 billion GNP for 1971 and a 4½ per cent unemployment level by the middle of next year —has been conceded by the government.

The weakness of the GNP expansion in the second quarter surprised even the pessimists. Despite the stockpiling against a possible steel strike, real output grew at only a 3½ per cent annual rate.

What's the matter with that? Positive growth is better than the negative growth of last year, isn't it?

As the President's advisers know, with our population and productivity growing, it takes more than a 4 per cent rate of real growth just to hold unemployment constant at a high level. In order to get it down to even Secretary Connally's notion of the full-employment level, we need real growth rates of 5 and 6 per cent from now to November 1972.

No one can reasonably expect this third quarter of the year to be remotely that strong. A long steel strike would take its toll of income and jobs. If there should be no strike, or only a short one, working down the accumulated stockpiles of steel will depress production.

That puts it up to the last quarter of the year. Unless by that time we begin to see increases in GNP that come up to $25 billion per quarter, the President will go into the 1972 election campaign with unemployment above the 5 per cent level.

RATIONALIZATIONS

As they say in freshman philosophy courses, you can't make omelets without breaking eggshells. Isn't all this the cost that we must pay in order to end inflation? When Candidate Nixon tours Ohio and California for votes in 1972, can't he claim that he has stamped out the inflation bequeathed to him by the previous Democratic Administrations?

No economists have very good regression equations to estimate the future behavior of prices. For one cannot rule out a little good news on the inflation front sometime within the next fifteen months.

But the odds are that, by the next election, over-all and consumer prices will still be rising at the rate of almost 4 per cent per annum. To be sure, economic historians will judge this to be a significant improvement over the 6 per cent rates touched when the Vietnam-induced inflation was at its worst. Still, can you win many votes in a close election with such cold-comfort arguments?

Nothing that I have written is a secret, or even very confidiential. It is exactly what Paul McCracken of the CEA must have been telling the President at that fateful weekend meeting in Camp David. It is what I hear from officials of four out of five of the largest banks, Republicans to a man.

How can we account for the President's decision, enunciated through his new spokesman, Secretary Connally, that there is to be no change in the game plan? One can only speculate. Here are my thoughts.

WISHFUL THINKING

1.   There are monetarists advising the President who genuinely believe that the rapid growth in the money supply so far in 1971 is bound to lead to rapid rates of money and real growth, far beyond what the bulk of the forecasters expect. All the President needs is patience.

This raises the question as to why the President has confidence in such advisers. It is no secret that the forecasting ability of monetarism is selling at a huge discount on the markets of informed opinion.

2.   An alternative hypothesis is that the President has become despondent over the compatibility of U.S. high employment and stable prices. Faced with the choice of having to pay in later inflation for any engineered increase in present-day employment, Richard Nixon is taking the patriotic but politically unpopular choice of tolerating stagnation.

3. Finally, there is hope that so long as business is improving smartly in 1972, and even if unemployment is worse than what used to be called full employment, voters will be feeling so much better than they are now that they will vote the Republicans back in office.

This is a gamble that might work. But how sad that the nation must suffer from unemployment unduly prolonged. And what a pity that the government should be adding fuel to the economy next year, when we will be nearer to full employment, rather than now with slack at its worst.

ELECTION ECONOMICS
May, 1972

"There's no law west of the Pecos." I was reminded of these lines from bad Western movies when one of my colleagues in political science told me that all the cherished scientific laws of his discipline had been demolished by recent politics.

Here is a sample:

- No senator can be nominated for the Presidency in modern times. State governors fare better.
- If you come from an unimportant state and want to be President, forget it. You have no chance.

John F. Kennedy and Barry Goldwater killed off the curse against senators. With Senators McGovern, Humphrey and Muskie all from unimportant states, the second law bites the dust.

If political science is barren of political laws, what about history?

For example, what about the theory of the late Arthur M. Schlesinger Sr. that liberalism and conservatism follow sixteen-year cycles, longer than sunspot cycles but shorter than Kondratieff waves of the price level? Alas, its main finding—that Dewey would beat Truman in 1948—served to discredit it. The subsequent epoch of Eisenhower (who could have been elected as a Republican, Democrat or Rosicrucian), and the Kennedy-Johnson interregnum, do little to rekindle interest in the mumbo jumbo of historic epicycles.

CALCULUS OF VOTES

Well, what then about economics? Any laws of politics to be found in the dismal science? Or, at least, any leads about the odds? Let me inch my neck out.

1.   Prosperity favors the ins; depression favors the outs.

2.   Within the above pattern, other things being equal, the Democrats gain more from recession issues, the Republicans more from inflation issues. The independent voter has the sound instinct that the Democrats are looser with the public purse than the GOP. He doesn't need Keynes to know that spending makes jobs.

3.   Years divisible by four, regardless of party in power, tend to be years of greater GNP expansion. No mystery about this: every Administration wants to be re-elected; and it has some power to hypo business in the short run by advancing expenditures and postponing taxes. If you have a friend at the Fed in the shape of Arthur Burns, that doesn't hurt either. But it's a nonpartisan syndrome: just look at the conservative Wilbur Mills as he ups the ante on social-security benefits in the year he's running for the Presidency.

4.   Finally, you don't have to be a Marxist to realize that a dozen issues divide the Democrats: race, region, law and order, Vietnam, the Mideast, fear of Communism . . . But one great common denominator unifies the Republicans. It is the glue of *money.*

CHERCHEZ LE DOLLAR

Few businessmen I meet have much liking for Richard Nixon as a person. They find him a cold fish, uncomfortable in his skin, reserved and unpredictable. They have come to fear his Vietnam policy. But there is not one in ten of the business class who does not realize on which side his bread is buttered. Where profits are concerned, Washington is a pain in the neck. But less is to be feared from the Republican Nixon than from the opposition.

Auto pollution? Detroit knows this Administration will not force it into bankruptcy, or even austerity, just to achieve the perfectionist goals of us environmentalists.

The shift of Southern cities to the Republican ranks? The wonder is that the heritage of the Civil War could stave off economic determinism for a whole century.

Tax loopholes? President Nixon has lowered the top rate for the corporate presidents from 77 per cent down to 50. This is his value added, and it will be remembered at the suburban polls this fall.

Neither John Adams nor Alexander Hamilton would be the least surprised to learn that, given equal chances of winning office, the Republicans can count on far greater campaign contributions than the Democrats. Nor would they doubt that this pecuniary bias shifts the odds in favor of the party of property.

The Democrats have only one thing going for them: universal suffrage—one man, one vote.

CANDIDATES' ECONOMICS
May, 1972

You are an out-and-out conservative. The saddest day in your life was the day the Supreme Court was overruled in its rejection of progressive income taxation by the Sixteenth Amendment to the Constitution.

You look over the Presidential candidates. Which is for you?

Can the issue be in doubt? For all of President Nixon's flirtations with price-wage controls and family allowances, you have little choice but to vote Republican in 1972. A vote for Wallace, or a sit-down strike on Election Day, is to give half a vote toward the election of someone worse than second best.

Besides, the hope lives on in your bosom that the President doesn't really believe in controls and Federal spending on the down-and-out—that given half a chance politically, he will turn against them.

FRUSTRATED REVOLUTIONARIES

Alternatively, you are radical. The sickness of the current social order sickens you. Picking a candidate in 1972 is going to be an ordeal.

The incumbent can be cut off your list at once. President Nixon is your prime enemy.

Although Wallace is against some of the Establishment figures you hate, you know from history that Hitler's Fascism was helped to get into power by support from the lumpen bourgeoisie, whose status and economic base had been subject to erosion by modern trends. And, sadly, you realize that certain privileged sectors of the labor movement—the hard hats and high-paid union members who pack Wallace gatherings—have deserted the army of the proletariat in order to batten off the droppings of surplus value. No radical is going to be turned on by someone who is against proponents of busing and integration, welfare freeloaders, pinkos soft on Communism and pointy-headed and effete intellectuals.

So George Wallace is out.

For that matter, Hubert Humphrey you remember as President Johnson's sycophant at the time of the escalation of the Indochina war. Your real problem is whether there is any major candidate whose compromises you could tolerate: McGovern, Edward Kennedy . . . Perhaps you will fail to register, go fishing on Election Day, ostentatiously throw away your vote on the Prohibitionist candidate, or strike a symbolic blow for one of the splinter Socialist parties.

When we turn from the extremes toward the center, the economic differences between the candidates become more critical for choosing. What are the differences that will count between President Nixon, Humphrey and McGovern?

First, there are the characteristic differences in economic goals that differentiate the Republican and Democratic parties: the basic fact that the Democrats broadly represent those who are at the middle and bottom of the pyramid of wealth and economic power, while the Republicans represent those above the median-income levels. Although this fact cannot be overemphasized, there is no point in repeating it after my last column.

Among the Democrats, it usually is said that Humphrey is on the right and McGovern on the left, with Muskie in the excluded middle. But if the criterion of rightness and leftness were the degree of fiscal austerity versus fiscal expansiveness, Senator Humphrey need yield to no one out in left field. Has there ever been a bigger spender than Hubert Humphrey? I say this not by way of criticism, for I am no fanatical budget balancer or zealot for low expenditures.

WILD MAN FROM THE PLAINS?

The real *economic* issue in the struggle for the Democratic nomination is the question of whether George McGovern constitutes a genuine threat to existing realities in the distribution of income and privilege.

Here are some of McGovern's goals:

- Since Lloyd George's budget of 1911, it has been a commonplace to hold in check the concentration of wealth by means of inheritance taxation. To make this effective, loopholes have to be closed.

- The Nixon trends toward lowering business, rather than personal, taxes must be reversed.
- Priorities in spending are to be shifted from defense toward negative income taxes and other programs to provide minimum living standards.

This is not a populist, know-nothing program to bankrupt the country. But it is one to challenge the sincerity of liberals in advocating the just society. Will they put their tax monies where their mouths are? And are there enough such liberals to elect their man to the Presidency?

STATE OF THE ECONOMY
August, 1972

The recovery seems to be moving along the 1972 schedule forecast by the majority of the experts. The palm must go to Walter Heller, who, way back in April of 1971, predicted that the GNP would grow $100 billion in 1972 over 1971—i.e., by about 6 per cent in real terms and another 3 per cent in price-inflation terms.

This year the Nixon economists rejoined the club of fashionable forecasts. So both Republican and Democratic pundits can pride themselves on their accuracy and luck.

Now that the official GNP figures have been revised upward, we learn that output has been growing for the last three quarters—since last Columbus Day—at about a 7 per cent annual rate. Indeed, if one can believe that the second-quarter numbers will stand up under revision—which I doubt—this spring was a miraculous period in which price inflation was down almost to 2 per cent and output growth up almost to 9 per cent.

The recovery has been broad-based. Employment is up along with profits. At last unemployment has dropped to about 5½ per cent. Housing starts are holding up. Plant and equipment investment is living up to the advance official and unofficial surveys.

Interest rates, perhaps helped by renewed optimism that inflation will be under control, are remarkably steady for this phase of the business cycle. Even the stock market, which has been meandering downward during its hoped-for summer sunshine, has begun to look longingly at the hurdle of 1,000 on the Dow Jones index.

The one sour note to conflict with predicted patterns has been the continuing deterioration of our export-import balance. The Smithsonian medicine of dollar depreciation has yet to induce favorable response in our balance of payments.

POLITICAL ARITHMETIC

Does the fact that the economy is performing on schedule operate in favor of the Republican incumbent and against the Democratic aspirant? Has the President defused the "economic issue," so that he need now worry only about defusing the Vietnam war issue?

Let me explain why I think not.

Back last year—on April 22, 1971, to be exact—I was addressing the National Democratic Women's Club in Washington. I said many things they liked to hear—such as that the Democratic opposition in Congress was overcoming President Nixon's refusal to embark on an effective program to fight unemployment and make the recovery less anemic. The audience beamed over the chicken à la king.

But then I had to state a truth that the audience needed to hear. When asked how the economic issue would work against Mr. Nixon in the 1972 campaign, I said: "The present crew in Washington will have to be more incompetent bunglers than I think they are if they cannot keep this recovery going for the nineteen months until the November 1972 election. The job and production situation will inevitably be better in the fall of 1972 than it is now in the spring of 1971. That factor of improvement will be an element working in favor of Mr. Nixon, who would be in a sad strait if he had to go before the people today."

NOT GOOD ENOUGH?

I went on to add: "But all indications are that the President has waited too long in throwing away his old inactivistic game plan to produce anything like full employment by Election Day. Four years of dire memories will have accumulated by then: the doughnut will still have a big hole in it on election eve—even if the hole is not so gaping as it had been prior to the President's election-year conversion to Keynesianism.

"This factor of excess capacity and of unemployment well beyond that of the 4 per cent level will be an element working against Richard Nixon, and one that cannot be defused by last-minute im-

provements. Where the balance will fall between these two factors
—favorable to the opposition and unfavorable—must be predicted
by a political pundit and not a mere economist."

I have no reason to regret those words. George McGovern has
already been getting a resonant response to his charges that the
Administration has been derelict in its programs to fight unemployment. The tax-loop-hole issue cannot be talked down: not all the wit
and tears of assistant secretaries of the Treasury can convince people
that they do not have a grievance against their prosperous neighbors
who breathe through those loopholes. Added to this is one bit of bad
luck—soaring food prices.

Economics remains a '72 issue.

ECONOMIC ISSUES
October, 1972

The people I meet in the ordinary course of a year tend not to be a
random cross section of the American electorate. Professors generally
tend to be liberal Democrats. Editorial workers in the book-publish-
ing industry tend to be Democrats of the middle-of-the-road variety.
Sophisticated money managers in New York, uncharacteristically,
tend in economic matters to favor Keynesian expansionary fiscal and
monetary policies. A suburban neighborhood like the one I live in,
if it were in the Middle West or South or on the coast, would be
primarily populated by voters who favor Republican candidates. But
being on the East Coast, and in Massachusetts, my hometown is full
of registered Democrats.

Now, in 1972, things are different. What the public-opinion polls
show for the country—that George McGovern is trailing behind
Richard Nixon—shows itself in my biased circle of acquaintanceship,
too, but with various subtle modifications.

- Some people, who regard themselves as independents, this
  year say they will be voting for the incumbent President as the
  lesser of two evils. (That same group largely turned against
  Barry Goldwater in 1964.)
- Some say they won't vote at all this year. (I think they will, and
  I suspect that many will be voting for Richard Nixon.)

- Many assert their enthusiastic support for George McGovern, and for the McGovern programs.
- What may even be the largest group of all professes to be undecided. As I interpret what it is that they are saying, and what it is that they are not consciously articulating, they would (1) like to vote for George McGovern, (2) wish to vote against Richard Nixon and his Vietnam, civil-liberties and economic policies. But (3) they are genuinely scared that their comfortable middle-class standard of life may be jeopardized if George McGovern is elected President next month.

This is how I explain the unusual number of requests that I am receiving in these closing weeks of the campaign for explanations of the McGovern economic program and for reassurances that it would not cause grass to grow in Main Street and take away from the professional classes much of their superior incomes and earning opportunities. Of course, I have only myself to blame if, having spent a lifetime in cultivating the reputation for a cool head screwed onto a warm heart, I should now be deluged by invitations from groups with names like Lawyers For McGovern or Democratic Insurance Men of Connecticut.

Alas, the spirit is willing, but the flesh is weak, and the quantum of spare energy all too limited. Here, though, are the answers that I give to those genuinely seeking answers to their misgivings and doubts. They are as well answers that I have given to myself in deciding which candidate seems better for the country in the years ahead.

PROS AND CONS

To begin with, as an economist, I leave to others elaboration of the reasons why the Nixon-Kissinger policy in Vietnam has been a moral and political disaster. I happen to think that those abroad—in Europe and the Middle East—who feel they have to rely on the United States have been hurt rather that helped by the Administration's Indochina fiascos. If Cambodia was invaded to show the Russians that America is still a force to reckon with, the gambit badly misfired. The resulting effects on morale of the Army and isolationist sentiment of the American electorate would, if I were an Israeli, count heavily against Richard Nixon.

For those fearful of the McGovern tax program, I point out

exactly what it is in comparison with present law. I show that personal earnings at every income level—whether from work, dividends or interest—would be less heavily taxed if the McGovern proposals apply. (I freely admit that the tax loopholes of oil drilling, citrus groves and six-months-and-a-day capital gains would be harder hit.)

For those fearful of how employment, GNP, production and profits would fare under McGovern, I pull out a handful of different computer print-outs of forecasts made by nonpartisan university and banking groups. Two of these are neutral. Two show GNP higher under McGovern than Nixon. One shows GNP higher under Nixon. None shows an appreciable difference in the foreseeable degree of inflation.

I usually conclude with a quick review of the lower level of unemployment in peacetime Democratic as against Republican years. Then I leave it to the voter.

THE MORNING AFTER
November, 1972

Elections, like the World Series and the Olympics, provide us with periodic amusement. They also, occasionally, introduce marginal changes in the trends of basic economic policy. But it is astonishing how little the day-to-day business of the world is affected by the outcome of these bitterly fought struggles.

As a game, pick up the Federal Reserve chartbook and conceal the scale of datings under the charts. I defy you to name correctly, from any systematic changes in GNP data, stock market prices or anything else, which are the years divisible by four when elections have occurred.

Is this insensitivity of economic life to political events disillusioning? Perhaps to politicians it is. But to me it is reassuring. I would not like to see my family's well-being hang on how one candidate handles the illness of a running mate, or on how another's 5 o'clock shadow comes across on the TV screen.

Still, little differences accumulate over time into significant changes. It does, from the standpoint of history, make a real difference who gets elected. Moreover, the political process does not end on Election Day. Clausewitz said that war is merely diplomacy carried on by other means. The Presidential elections are similarly only the ordinary political struggle carried on at a high pitch. The task of a political party remains the same regardless of the outcome: all that is decided is whether it operates under the name of the opposition or of the Administration.

REGROUPING

Parties, like people, can have identity crises. In the face of the outcome, and considering the degree of disparity of voting strengths at the polls, it is the Democratic Party that must refind itself.

A few months ago, when I appeared on a panel of witnesses before the Joint Economic Committee, I heard an exchange between Rep. Barber B. Conable Jr. and John Kenneth Galbraith. It has stuck in my memory. Professor Galbraith had been pointing out the characteristic differences between the two parties, emphasizing that the Republican Party is the instrument of the business interests, particularly big business.

Congressman Conable objected and in the course of this said: "Professor Galbraith . . . I know that . . . you would rather have the Democratic Party liberal than to have it succeed." It was my distinct impression that the Republican congressman was delighted to have Galbraith succeed in getting the Democratic Party he had wanted.

Whether the shaft found its intended target I don't know. But I do know that it hit me hard as a McGovern supporter. And it sent me back to do my homework in rereading Galbraith's little 1970 book "Who Needs the Democrats?"

This is one of that witty author's wittier performances. And in two respects Galbraith was unquestionably right: first, he spoke out on the need to end the war in Indochina. Second, and this may shock those who patronizingly dismiss Galbraith as no economist but merely a left-of-center Bill Buckley, Galbraith urged the cause of a militant incomes policy in the form of direct wage-price controls— a message that President Nixon put into effect in August 1971, to the great advantage of the country and the President's re-election prospects.

PYRRHIC VICTORY

But in reviewing the book's major political thrust, I felt the congressman had a point. In effect, what Galbraith seems to be arguing is this:

The Democratic Party is the party of change. Anyone who does not shape up as a forward-looking liberal should get lost. Southerners, pols, old-line union leaders, wishy-washy worriers over their pocketbooks and comfortable way of life can all apply elsewhere.

Hindsight is easy. But this does seem to me to be a prescription for disaster. I would love it if all my fellow Democrats could be as enlightened as I am. But what Ike did to Adlai taught me that there is only one American people to work with. Great leaders like Franklin Roosevelt and John Kennedy lift people above themselves. Great parties thrive by holding together disparate interests.

The moral is clear. To let Richard Nixon capture the great middle in American political life is tantamount to abdication of the good cause. That high and mighty road is an easy and irresponsible road.

Now that the election is over, political fence. mending is the first order of the day.

Chapter 12

THE VIETNAM WAR

Stretching over more than a six-year period, the readings of this chapter present analysis and discussion, both economic and socio-political, of the Vietnam war. In addition, the chapter concludes with "Capitalism and War," an article not directly linked to Vietnam. This last article is an analysis of the questions and charges often made with regard to capitalism's alleged "propensity" to make war, or "need" to make war. The dialogism is balanced and objective. "Grains of truth" possessed by capitalism's critic are put in perspective and conceded, where that is appropriate. No easy answer is offered to the truly hard question of future war possibilities. But the traditional indictments against capitalism are rebutted and rejected, where that capitalism is in the form of the modern mixed economy.

As we continue to reflect on the Vietnam war experience, the selections presented here seem to read with undiminished significance. Certainly the reading on "U.S. Identity Crisis" can stand the test of just a few short years. The same will be true of the more recent "Economic Postmortem." Standing out in the postmortem is the indication that there was no economic basis for our involvement in the war. It was not in that sense American capitalism's war.

To say we are well out of it is to sound trite. But it is at least a comment that receives almost unanimous acceptance; not only from those who lived it, but also from your eight-year-old sister in the third grade, who for the first time in her life is spared that particular horror story on the evening television news.

THE ECONOMICS OF WAR
November, 1966

An army fights on its stomach, and even brave little David needed that stone to fell Goliath. So carrying on a war like the one in Vietnam is very much a matter of economics.

Whether or not we should do so, can we afford economically to carry on the present war, to escalate it, to prolong it? And can we afford to terminate it? Economists pretty much agree on the issues involved.

Will our "money" last?

For want of a nail a kingdom was lost, but no empire ever foundered because of a domestic shortage of legal tender. When you read in the financial press that our high interest rates have been due to "the money running out," that is not a canny description of fact so much as a proof that under the skin of every conservative wriggles a poet.

Is Vietnam depleting our economy of exhaustible natural resources?

Modern wars do involve using up metals and petroleum. The 1940 hope that Hitler would run out of petrol just before reaching Paris involved wishful, but not idiotic, thinking. (On the other hand, when young Maynard Keynes assured his Bloomsbury friends in 1914 that the war could not last more than a few months because modern wars were too costly for nations to afford, he was demonstrating the no-ninfallibility of economic science.)

THE NUMERICAL SCORE

A *quantitative* appraisal of real costs in terms of resources is needed. Louis XIV did bleed France white by his chronic warfare. When the dictator Lopez led his little country against most of Latin America, he left the women of Paraguay without husbands for a generation and the economy in ruins.

The Vietnam conflict uses but a small fraction of our gross national product. Full employment, the goal we strove for in the 1960s, is itself a greater drain on our mines and forests than Vietnam. (That is why it used to be said that you should buy U.S. Steel when you can't see your hand in front of your face in Pittsburgh, and sell it when you can.)

Will Vietnam put impossible inflationary strains on the economy?

Out of the mouths of elder statesmen come words: Herbert Hoover used to warn that "inflation is worse than Stalin." Not so.

Restrictive fiscal policy, along with tight money, can succeed in controlling an inflationary gap generated by a limited war—if there is a *will* to use these measures. When Schacht told Hitler, "If you spend one more pfennig, I will not answer for the consequences," he betrayed his ignorance of the sinews of war and his paranoia over inflation.

GENUINE PROBLEMS

Does the Vietnam war worsen our international balance of payments?

Yes, it definitely does. Even though much of our procurement is *tied* to domestic sources, offshore procurement is often a necessity. If peace broke out tomorrow, our drain of gold would be relieved and our freedom to pursue domestic goals would be much enhanced.

This brings us to the crucial question: suppose the cold war were suddenly to come to an end.

Can the American economy afford peace?

Last year when the Vietnam war heated up, I wrote that all fears of a 1966 slowdown had been dispelled. The rapid rise in our GNP since then showed this to be right. But was I right to have written so? *Pravda* was able to say that even American professors admit that the buoyancy of the economy depended on cold-war expenditures.

I had forgotten a lesson once learned. A businessman who had criticized my textbook singled out a typical sentence in it: "In this century government spending has grown faster than national income."

"Well, isn't that a fact?" I asked.

He squirmed, and then blurted out advice I thought never to forget: "Yes, but you ought never mention a fact like that without *deploring* it!"

Let me now be clear. *We do have the power to introduce expansionary fiscal and credit programs that will offset any decline in arms spending.* Whether the electorate will have the *political will* to ensure that we use these powers, with the decisiveness that war entails, is not so sure.

And in mentioning *that* fact, let me add that I do indeed deplore it.

ENDING THE WAR
June, 1970

The decision to invade Cambodia will prove to be one of the most costly in our history even if U.S. troops stay within a few miles of the border, depart by June 30, and destroy much of the enemy supplies. As a result of this decision, our society is being torn apart and President Nixon is less able to impress Russia in the Middle East or anywhere else with the power of the Presidency and of the American nation.

Those who are hawks, those who are non-isolationists, those who are interested only in profits, should themselves be massing before the White House to let President Nixon know that we should cut our losses in Southeast Asia. You should not have to send a boy from the college campus to do a man's work. And those who are interested in a Republican triumph at the next election should be begging the President to leash Mr. Agnew and be reminding him that it avails a politician little if he acquires the Wallace vote at the cost of not being able to govern as President.

What is needed is not communication between the university community and the President. When Mr. Nixon assures students that he too is in favor of saving lives and of programed withdrawals from Vietnam, he is not really agreeing with their recommendations and goals. For he speaks of withdrawal with victory; of successful Vietnamization of the war, and no scaling down of our aspirations for anti-Communists in Southeast Asia. The university community, after contemplation of the shortfall between the expectations of our military men and subsequent happenings, and after surveying the nature and likely viability of the South Vietnam regime, simply does not accept the major premise upon which both Presidents Johnson and Nixon based their policy—namely, that we have not already lost the war in Indochina.

WITHDRAWAL WITHOUT VICTORY

And the great American public—the silent majority—increasingly realizes this basic truth of a struggle already lost. Every analysis of opinion polls shows that the American people wish we had never got involved. And that, if victory requires the price of 50 to 100 American lives every week for years on end, our citizenry will not pay the price of victory or even of a stalemate.

Of course those same polls show that the majority are not ready to face with candor and equanimity the *admission* that our past efforts have been in vain and that we must leave Asia without victory. What the majority wants is to be faced with a *fait accompli*. There lies the challenge of leadership for Richard Nixon. If he will grasp the nettle for us, we, the great silent majority, will rise and call him blessed.

This does not mean that the President cannot on any one occasion alarm the majority into giving him momentary backing. But each such backing, wrung from the public under duress, will melt away in the subsequent months as the bill for continuation of the conflict is presented in terms of U.S. deaths and casualties.

THE FASCIST GAMBIT?

The only way that public support could be maintained for the current schedule of withdrawal and Vietnamization would be by a desperate attempt to polarize further an already split society. That would mean feeding Mr. Agnew pep pills and unleashing him with a vengeance. It would involve talk by the President himself of "a stab in the back at home." It would mean a Joseph McCarthy kind of attack upon the university community that would make Reagan's backlash look innocuous in comparison.

I cannot be sure that such a desperate ploy would not work. But the cool and calculating politician, which Mr. Nixon is believed to be by so many of his friends and enemies, will know that there is a terrible risk in such a strategy. American economic well-being and society as we have known it would certainly be casualties of such a policy, whether successful or not. And it is by no means certain that such a strategy would be successful in its goal of prolonging the war or keeping the middle-to-right Republican establishment in power.

Would Wall Street and the industrial complex back so rash a venture? I do not think so. For they sense that a society that is sick and divided will soon beget an economy that is sick and divided.

Corporate taxes dwarf private American investments in Asia. Business knows it can profit as much from peace goods as war goods, and has come to realize that peace need not bring mass unemployment.

U.S. IDENTITY CRISIS
June, 1971

Erik Erikson has taught us to look, in the lives of Martin Luther or Gandhi and in our own lives, for an identity crisis. Countries too pass through stages of uncertainty.

A few weeks ago, on the South Lawn of the White House, President Nixon told a group of Boy Scouts that this is a great time to be alive, and that America is in a great stage of its development.

Just because a statement is made in Washington does not necessarily mean that it is untrue. But a sampling of recent commencement speeches does not bear out the President's contention. And scrutiny of his face these days suggests that the present incumbent falls in the category of Presidents who have found the office something of an ordeal (Washington, Lincoln, Harding, Hoover, the latter-day Johnson) rather than in the category of the happy warriors who reveled in the job (both Roosevelts, Truman, Kennedy).

One has only to pick up an English weekly or pay a visit to the British Isles to realize that John Bull has suffered a failure of nerve. The Englishman can no longer deny that he is second-rate, and must suppress the gnawing doubt that even that scoring may be euphemistic.

Once before our own country went through a nervous breakdown. Prior to 1929 we were riding high. Sinclair Lewis's Babbitt and Sam Dodsworth, and even his Gopher Prairie Dr. Kennicott, felt genuinely sorry for the effete and unaffluent nations of Europe. H. L. Mencken might rail at our boobish bourgeoisie, but with Calvin Coolidge in the White House and Alfred Sloan at the wheel of General Motors we Americans knew that we were on the right track.

FAILURE OF NERVE

The Great Depression did not merely hit our pocketbooks. It shook our faith in the gods of the marketplace. Although Franklin Roosevelt could patch up our banking system, he could not—even if he had wanted to, which he didn't—restore our self-image as a capitalistic nation. It was not until after World War II and the Keynesian revolution that a new faith emerged: faith in the mixed economy, in which democratic government regulated the market economy and kept it prosperous.

By the time of John F. Kennedy's assassination in 1963, America had, so to speak, recovered her nerve. We proved that the economic system could be made to work at home. Through Marshall-plan and other foreign-aid programs and through private corporate investment, we proved to our own satisfaction that the ideology of the new mixed economy was worthy of export abroad.

Then along came the civil-rights movement and the realization that ours was an unconscionably divided house. Then along came the disastrous Indochina war and the disintegration of all national consensus.

ONCE AGAIN, SELF-DOUBT

Most important of all, along came the alienation of America's youth from our traditional comfortable morality. To think that quietness on the campus since the events of Kent State implies that this alienation is merely a transient phase—like swallowing of goldfish or other passing fads—is, I think, to misconstrue a malaise in our national life that goes very deep indeed.

Nor it is confined to the affluent young. The veteran returned from Vietnam brings his pot to the Detroit assembly line. Go to a working-class district of any American city and verify that there is no longer a measurable difference in length of hair between the sons of the hard hats and those of the attorney for the Civil Liberties Union.

Washington is worsening the situation by sticking to the game plan that keeps unemployment high. President Nixon's determination to try to end the war on his terms is, I fear, dealing irreversible blows to our nation's cohesion.

Most aghast at what is happening to American life are our erstwhile admirers abroad. The Japanese, for example, have been looking to America for their model. If your hero at school, the chap who is fair of mind and form, turns out to be not Galahad or even Lancelot, but rather a self-pitying and indecisive Hamlet, where does that leave you? It leaves you let down and looking for a new idol.

Most pleased by the disintegration that is going on during the term of President Nixon are the Soviets and the Chinese. They pinch themselves and whisper, "What went right?"

It is not too late for the President to exercise a little American pragmatism and flexibility. The stakes are high.

ECONOMIC POSTMORTEM
February, 1973

At long last we've managed to follow Senator Aiken's recipe: say we've won in Indochina, and pull American troops out of there.

Political science is a difficult subject. The jury of history will be out a long time on the question of how we got into the Vietnam war. And why we got out when we did, not sooner, not later.

One suspects that history, with its gift of hindsight, will judge differently than did Lyndon Johnson and his advisers the reality *at any time* of the "need to contain China." But in any case, once there was the Nixon rapprochement with Chou En-lai and with Brezhnev —these are obviously not independent developments—the domino-theory reason for American troops in Southeast Asia evaporated. This left us only with the Occidental desire to save face. Senator Goldwater tells us we still have it. Amen to that.

CERTITUDES

Economics is an easy subject. Let me analyze the Vietnam war in its relation to the American economy.

First, there was no *economic* basis for our involvement. By that I mean:

- There are negligible deposits of oil, copper, bauxite, uranium or other resources that could tempt an ITT or Exxon, in the pursuit of exploitative profit, to lean on Congress or propagandize the American public to start the war or to continue it.

- The Kennedy-Johnson mid-1960s prosperity had no need for a new war to keep the American GNP growing. On the contrary. As Johnson's economic advisers told him at the time, our 1965 escalation of defense spending jeopardized the smooth approach to full employment with reasonable price stability that was then taking place. The war brought, as the New Economists said it would, three years of demand-pull inflation—followed, as we feared it might be, by years of cost-push inflation whose end is still not in sight.

- The dollar as a key currency was a casualty of the Indochina war. In 1964, all the experts in international finance told me I was wrong to think the dollar was an overvalued currency at its pegged IMF parity. Maybe they were right. But *after* the Vietnam escalation, with its disastrous acceleration of our prices and imports, and its voracious squandering of offshore military spending, even the experts could see that the dollar was headed for depreciation.

- Did the war bleed us white economically? Like the South in the Civil War, was America forced by economic exhaustion to withdraw from Vietnam? Obviously not. No more than George III surrendered to George W. because England could no longer mount the needed war effort.

This fact is why my conscience would not let me, years ago, help the antiwar cause by certifying that here was a conflict we could not "afford." Plato advocated lies in a good cause. But surely he meant *plausible* lies.

DOUBTS

Finally, will war's end bring depression? Recession? Stagnation? Or, will it bring "a generation" of prosperity—with the Dow Jones index growing at 9 per cent a year till kingdom come?

Years ago, for a sheik's ransom, I agreed to write an article for Playboy on the economics of the Vietnam peace. However, as I told them, there was no hurry. Alas, I was right. And when peace finally came into sight, I could sense that the subject had become anticlimactic, not juicy enough for the palates of their readers.

The seismograph of economist George Shultz will scarcely record what diplomatist Henry Kissinger hath wrought. As they say in Wall Street, "It's already discounted."

During the first three Nixon years, defense expenditure, as a fraction of GNP, was slowly but steadily declining. In recent quarters it began to turn up. But this was not primarily because of stepped-up recent action in Southeast Asia. Rather it has been a case that Pentagon strategists have long felt that the Vietnam expense was keeping them from desired new hardware and manpower programs.

There will, apparently, be no peace dividend for labor, management, and the government to fight and dicker over. We do know how, in the age after Keynes, to convert swords into plowshares without chronic unemployment. But apparently we're not going to get the chance to use our newfound knowledge.

Sociology is no easy subject. But I take leave to doubt that the malaise affecting American society—racial strains, generation gaps, drugs and the counterculture, radical critiques and aspiration—will fade away now that peace is made.

CAPITALISM AND WAR
January 1973

Three questions deserve hard-headed and unflinching investigation:

1.   Are great, or little, wars inevitable because of the capitalist class's pursuit of profits? If not inevitable, are wars nevertheless more likely under noncapitalist regimes (socialism, feudalism, the modern mixed economy, . . .)?

2.   Are there *particular groups of capitalists* who profit from war— Merchants of Death in the form of munitions makers and, more generally, an entrenched and powerful military industrial complex? Are there imperialistic investors abroad, whose pecuniary interests are furthered or preserved by war? Is it the lobbying and political power of such interests that contribute importantly to the occurrence and duration of great and little wars?

3.   Leaving aside the parochial interests of the plutocratic or property-owning classes, is it the case that *all the citizens* of a market economy have a recognized or covert interest in war—for the reasons (a) that capitalism must break down in depression if it does not find imperialistic ventures that spend money, and destroy surplus goods, and (b) that the high living standards of the few advanced nations can be maintained only by the *exploitation* of the teeming billions who live in the impoverished underdeveloped nations.

Ideologists' Noise

To answer these questions, begin with the writings of ideologues: defenders of 19th century capitalism (Adam Smith's followers, Hayek, Milton Friedman, Barry Goldwater, your great-uncle . . .) revolutionary critics of Victorian capitalism (Karl Marx and Friedrich Engels, Rosa Luxemberg, and V. I. Lenin, Paul Sweezy and Paul Baran, Jack Gurley and Sam Bowles, your freshman brother at Yale . . .).

You find your work has just begun. One sweeping, monistic explanation cancels out another. Alas, there is no substitute for tedious analysis of historical experience, unsparing analysis of what makes the macroeconomics of the mixed economy tick, and sophisticated insight into the checks and balances of realistic power politics.

Plurality of Interest-Groups

Let's begin by answering a couple of the easy questions. Of course, *particular* groups benefit from war. Generals for one (and they both antedate the market system and postdate it). Sergeants for another. Assembly-line workers on bombers, their spouses, their unions, their congressmen . . . And let's not forget the corporations whose activities are specialized to the defense industry.

But little or nothing follows from this. *Somebody* stands to benefit from *every* dollar of the GNP. The plowshare industry stands to gain from peace, just as the sword industry gains from war. ITT has so well-hedged a portfolio that only God knows—certainly Harold Geneen doesn't—where its pocketbook interests lie.

The Age After Keynes

"Wait a minute," you will say." Aren't you forgetting, Professor Samuelson, that war expenditures may be an *add-on* to GNP—the something extra that permits under-consuming capitalism to get rid of its unemployment and its declining rate of profit?"

No, I am simply remembering that this is 1973, not 1903 or 1933. We are almost 40 years into the age of Keynes. I believe that Luxemburg and Lenin (and Hobson and Alvin Hansen) were right to worry about the sustainability of full employment in William McKinley's balanced-budget *laissez faire.* However, not a single mixed economy has had any problem these last 30 years with chronic insufficiency of purchasing power. (Go down the list: U.S.A., U.K., France, Japan, Germany, Little Belgium, . . .)

Nor in the century to come—1973-2073—will the ancient scourge of intermittent-shortage-of-purchasing power reoccur in the old form.

("What about recessions and stagflation, professor? Don't deny they still happen!") Of course they do. And in 1983 or 2013 they may still occur to plague the mixed economy. But Sweezy and Bowles know what Lenin and Luxemburg couldn't know—that the disease of cost-push which is involved in stagflation has *nought to do with insufficiency of domestic markets,* and cold- or hot-war escapades can do nothing to make it better.

Provisional Conclusions

After the few easy answers of somebody-gains-some body-loses-from-war-and-wars-no-longer-needed-top-prime-the-pump,   we are left with the hard questions. Space permits only a few tentative conclusions.

1.   A World War III between Russia and China, two non-capitalistic countries, is as likely as between any two market economies and as likely as a war between the U.S. and either Russia or China or both of them.

2.   The fact that the mixed economies of North America, Western Europe, and elsewhere will not *willingly* go through a communist revolution or takeover—coupled with the fact that the socialist societies of Eastern Europe and Asia will not *willingly* go through a counter-revolution or takeover—could produce acute or chronic warfare in the future. In this sense, "Capitalism-plus Communism" might be deemed potential causes of war.

3.   Revolution and insurrection cannot always be distinguished from war. The fact that wealth and power are unequally distributed, within nations and between nations, must be regarded as a potential cause of conflict and war.

4.   Adam Smith's "invisible hand of self-interest" leads you to pick the best growth stock, the best hi-fi, and to vote for Richard Nixon. That same hand will lead other people to take over in the future foreign copper mines and oil concessions. And who is to say that the invisible hand which leads people to the ballot box will not someday lead them also to the barricades and the front-line trenches?

Chapter 13

MARX, MARXISTS
AND SOME OTHERS

Why bother to read Karl Marx? In the opening selection of this chapter, marking the hundreth anniversary of the publication of Marx's *Das Kapital,* Professor Samuelson suggests that not even a great proportion of Marxists have read Marx's writings. But does this matter?

In the final selection of the chapter, on "New-Left Economics," Samuelson suggests that Ralph Nader might be elected President of the United States if college students could do the exclusive electing. That represents a lot of admirers. Yet doubtless only a fraction of them have felt obliged to read all of what Nader writings there are, or to carefully check his every speech for new insight. They know he is on the side of the angels, and that is enough.

Can it be the same for Marxists, it being enough to know that he was against the devils and evils of capitalism so that one thereby is spared the need to wade through even one, much less three, volumes of his gigantic work? Indeed it can, suggests Samuelson, at least for the revolutionary if not for the economist. Backed up by the sheer bulk of the book itself, the Marxist revolutionary can get by with little or no appreciation of Marxian economics.

Two notes of clarification or qualification should be made here. First, the reference to the straw-vote election of Ralph Nader is out of context to the total gist of the piece on New-Left economics. Samuelson says that only an "idiot of the right" could consider Nader a revolutionary, and he certainly is not the spiritual leader of the New-Left. This will probably come as no news to the readers of this book. Second, the parallel drawn between Marxism and Naderism was an easy one; but it was not meant to unfairly match Nader against the prodigious scholarship of Karl Marx which is referred to in the reading on *Das Kapital.* Ralph Nader's dedication to duty has already become almost legendary, but he has not yet had to cope with the unpleasant side effects of a "scholar's seat."

For a book that he says "changed the course of history," Samuelson's comments on *Das Kapital,* and on Marx the economist, are rather unflattering. He takes note of the book's obscurity and logical failures, perhaps even lack of ultimate theoretical conviction on the part of Marx himself. Technical shortcomings or other difficulties, however, did not stop the book from changing the world. Through the efforts of such a revolutionary leader as Lenin, it became the bible-like source of ultimate Communist truth, and Marx was nearly deified by much of the world's population.

Ideal complements to the discussion of *Das Kapital* and Karl Marx are the following two readings, on "Lenin," and "Rosa Luxemburg." In both, Samuelson writes to observe the hundreth anniversary of the births of these two contemporary revolutionists. In Lenin, "the father of his country," is found the driving managerial genius that could seize the Russian Revolution of 1917 and ultimately bring it to a secure conclusion in the name of Marxian Communism. This reading offers a fairly intensive analysis of him as revolutionary scholar and strategist, in which he comes out much better in the second role.

MARX'S 'DAS KAPITAL'
October, 1967

This year marks the hundredth anniversary of Karl Marx's great tome, "Das Kapital." Its first volume was published in 1867 during the hey-day of Victorian capitalism. Freidrich Engels, Marx's faithful friend and collaborator, had to edit the subsequent 1885 and 1894 volumes from the fragments Marx had left behind him at his death.

Like the Bible, the Koran, Newton's "Principia," and Darwin's "Origin of Species," "Kapital" is a book that has changed the course of history. More than a billion people today quote it as if it were the Scripture.

Yet "Kapital" is a book that few have read—I mean read *through.* For every thousand who have read the 1848 "Communist Manifesto" of Marx and Engels, scarcely five have read the Volume I of "Kapital," and scarcely one all three volumes. Yet those words also serve that only sit and go unread. For the sheer bulk of the book and its absolute self-confidence of expression serve to convince a third of the world that Karl Marx has proved scientifically not only the demise of capitalism, but also the inferiority of every rival brand of vulgar socialism to that espoused by Marx, Engels, Lenin and the latest local pretender to the apostolic succession.

CLARITY AND CLASSICS

Make no mistake. Even Marxists do not agree on the meaning of his key concepts—the labor theory of value, surplus value . . . But they do agree that it is all true. Obscurity in a bible is no defect: as Oscar Wilde said, ". . . to be understood is to be found out."

When I read a few years ago charming memoirs of what it was like for the young to be radical socialists and Communists in New York during the mid-1930s, I was struck by the fact that most of them had never pretended to do any serious studying of Marxian economics—and never felt the worse on that account! Apparently one had but to look around at the mass unemployment of the Great Depression to accept the wave of the future.

Perhaps it was always so. Bernard Shaw claimed that in his day he was the only Englishman to have read "Kapital," that not even H. M. Hyndman, the leader of the Marxian wing, had done so. But GBS was an inveterate boaster; and William Archer reports seeing Shaw in the British Museum simultaneously reading the French translation of "Kapital" and perusing the score of Wagner's "Tristan and Isolde." We can perhaps judge from Shaw's writings whose tunes stuck.

Marx was of a more determined cast of mind. He sat at the British Museum for literally decades. As the Germans say, Marx had the seat of a scholar. He loved Balzac and Beethoven but nothing could stand in the way of his plowing through the blue books in which were recorded the growing pains of bourgeois capitalism.

Marx read everything, the works of Adam Smith, Ricardo and even the vulgar apologist, Mill. (Decades later when there was a move to subsidize scientific research in Austria, the anti-Semitic mayor of Vienna was opposed, saying: "What is science? Merely what one Jew cribs from another." Still we perhaps must not judge other times by our own: though himself the son of a converted Jew, Marx in his letters to Engels could be grossly anti-Semitic, laughing at the socialist Lassalle for his swarthy complexion and curly hair in a manner that would do credit to a South Carolina Klansman.)

Despite the arrogant style of "Kapital," there is some evidence that Marx never quite convinced himself of his own theory. Like Coleridge, who conceived the poem "Kubla Khan" in an opium dream, Marx early glimpsed a breath-taking new theory of wage exploitation. But Marx could never put the pieces together logically, which perhaps explains why he put off finishing the book.

PROPHECY AND FACT

Why then do we remember the book's centennial? Undoubtedly because just 50 years ago, at its Golden Jubilee, Lenin achieved the Russian Revolution. William James referred to American worship of the bitch-goddess, Success. The whole world worships at this shrine: in China, Africa and the developing world, Karl Marx remains a force to reckon with.

For the advanced nations, Marx's timetable did not develop according to schedule. Why not?

In my interpretation it has been the development of the Mixed Economy which has forestalled the European drift toward Communism. The year Galileo died, Newton was born; 1883, the year Marx died, Keynes was born.

Marx was right that nothing stands still in the womb of history. But he bet on the wrong foal.

LENIN
December, 1970

Before the year goes out, notice must be taken of the hundredth anniversary of Lenin's birth. He is father of his country in the way that Washington is father of the United States, Ataturk is father of modern Turkey, and Nehru father of independent India.

But Lenin is more than that. To half the world's billions he is canonized, along with Marx. Although Stalin and Trotsky have been demoted as great thinkers, both the Soviet and Chinese leaders still lay claim to the legacy of Marxism-Leninism, as do Castroites, Guevarans and the New Left.

I am not interested here in the embalmed Russian father figure whose memory was celebrated all over the Soviet Union earlier this year. What about Lenin the thinker, the revolutionist who combines the sagacity of Adam Smith or de Tocqueville and the philosophical and scientific subtlety of Hegel with the pragmatism of Machiavelli and the bureaucratic effectiveness of Alfred P. Sloan Jr.?

Had that sealed railroad car been derailed on its 1917 journey from Zurich to Petrograd, we would know Lenin today as a minor writer in the Marxian vein—somewhere below Georges Sorel and Rosa Luxemburg, at perhaps the level of August Bebel or Karl Kautsky. Lenin's literary style is, to use the words of one far more expert than I, Adam Ulam, "turgid . . . tedious, repetitious, pedantical . . . [making] the original works of Marx and Engels shine like great literature in comparison."

MIND AT THE TOP

This is to blunt the point. We do not ask of great men—Alexander, Napoleon, Lenin—that they write with the precious elegance of Lytton Strachey, any more than we gauge the position in history of Winston Churchill by his Sunday painting or journalistic potboilers.

Strip Lenin of his role in history and you are left with his most popular, and perhaps most unoriginal, work, "Imperialism"—a pamphlet short enough to be read even by the New Left. But if you strip Lenin of history, you strip history of Lenin. The history of ideas is permanently different because a great leader thought what he thought.

Lenin's ideas on the role of the professional revolutionary, who is not a worker, in guiding and curbing the spontaneous class feelings of the workers; even his diatribes against rival socialists; and certainly his matchless opportunism in first utilizing the forces of anarchism and populism to crush capitalism, and then the forces of the centralized party to crush anarchism and the soviets—these are not garments removable from his person in the way that we can strip Frederick the Great of his flute playing or FDR of his stamp collecting. These are more truly flesh of his flesh than are those molecular remains on deposit in the Kremlin mausoleum.

TOWARD STALIN AND MAO

It is a pity Isaac Deutscher did not live to complete a life of Lenin comparable to his Trotsky and Stalin biographies. Still, as you review Lenin's works, and read the many commentaries on him, you cannot help being struck by his two most characteristic features: complete singlemindedness of purpose, combined with utmost flexibility of tactics.

There is an element of self-contradiction in this description, a bit like speaking of the world's thinnest fat man. Let me explain.

The one issue on which Lenin never wavered was the necessity —both in the sense of inevitability and desirability—of having a revolution. On this he never compromised; and, in October 1917, he realized his goal. Nor did he later, even for a moment, waver in taking actions needed to secure that revolution.

But in pursuit of this aim, Lenin could make the most amazing revisions of doctrine and strategy. Believing in the Marxian timetable of first a bourgeois revolution, Lenin expected a country like England to embrace socialism before a backward country like Russia. But as the disasters of World War I weakened the position of the Russian tsardom, Lenin dropped his opposition to the Trotsky view that the bourgeois stage could be skipped entirely by Russia. There are innumerable other examples of such creative zigzagging.

Finally, was Stalinism a perversion of Leninism? In its paranoiac stage, Stalinism was undoubtedly a perversion of Stalinism. Yet, despite Lenin's utopian utterances about the withering away of the state and his deathbed warnings against Stalin's ambitions, both Stalin and Mao have fair claim to be his heir.

ROSA LUXEMBURG
October, 1971

Eleanor Roosevelt conducted a radio interview some years back with Sissela Myrdal, then still a schoolgirl at Geneva's International School and yet to meet her future husband, Derek Bok, the new president of Harvard University.

In her refined manner, Eleanor began: "So, you are the daughter of Gunnar Myrdal."

Sissela corrected her, "Yes, and of Alva Myrdal too."

The reprimand was only proper. Alva Myrdal, besides being an eminent psychologist in her own right, has played a distinguished role in Swedish public life serving as an ambassador, Cabinet officer, and Member of Parliament.

It is right that any group coming out from repression—whether it be Protestants in Roman Catholic France, blacks in the United States, or women all over the world—should reject the self-hate and doubt implanted in them by their oppressors, seeking to find for themselves a distinguished history. When the brilliant young Disraeli incurred the jibes of "Jew boy" as he began his long climb to the top of the Victorian greasy pole, he consoled himself with the thought that when the Anglo-Saxons were cowering over fires in their primitive caves, his ancestors were princes of great realms in the Holy Land. So too do black students concern themselves with the African past.

So let us now sing the praises of famous women.

CHERCHEZ LES FEMMES

Where to begin? Any list of great women must contain the name of Joan of Arc. And surely the names of George Eliot and Jane Austen. (If Samuel Butler is to be believed, the Odyssey was written by a woman—our first great woman writer.)

I pass by such names as Catherine the Great, who enjoys a place in history only by virtue of her rank. I do so in the same way that I would exclude Louis XIV from the pantheon of great names: strip the Sun King of his royal robes, and who would pick him to run a bicycle shop or even serve as Assistant Secretary of State?

Each of us will have to make up her or his own list. And when they are compared, it will perhaps come as a slight shock to realize that it is by no means the case that women have had their best opportunities in modern times and in the nations of the West.

My purpose today is to call attention to Rosa Luxemburg, whose recent centennial was eclipsed by the simultaneous centennial of Lenin, her exact comtemporary. Rosa Luxemburg came by 1910 to occupy a leading role in both the German and Polish revolutionary parties. Indeed, an astute observer might have been forgiven for having formed at the time the judgment that Rosa had a greater future than Lenin, whom some considered slightly daft in his stubborn ultra-centrism.

Rosa Luxemburg was one of the few in the generation after Marx who improved upon his analysis. Until the age of Keynes made her theory of imperialism obsolete, she was right to emphasize the danger of unemployment and underconsumption to a self-contained affluent capitalism.

When the first trumpets sounded for war in 1914, her contemporaries in the Social Democratic Party doffed their pacifism and rallied to the Kaiser's colors. Not Luxemburg. As she once bitterly remarked: "There are only two *men* left in the party—Klara Zetkin and I." Although she agreed with Lenin that the war offered an opportunity for revolution, she had to regard it as a disaster to humanity.

MARTYRDOM AND FREEDOM

In the aftermath of the Kaiser's defeat, her Spartacus Party attempted a rash and unpopular *Putsch.* Despite her warnings of its folly, she went along with this disastrous move. While being taken to jail, Rosa Luxemburg was murdered by rightist Prussian officers, whom the Weimar Republic never brought to justice.

Although no conventional woman—lame from birth, she was not pretty-pretty; her marriage was an arranged one, so that she could participate in German politics; her lover was her lifelong revolutionary colleague—still Rosa Luxemburg was no ersatz man. Artistic and musical, with a passion for botany and ornithology, she spoke out against tyranny, whether in 1900 Berlin, 1918 Moscow or, she would say, 1971 Washington.

"Freedom is always and exclusively freedom for the one who thinks differently." That was the legacy from prison of this remarkable human being.

NEW-LEFT ECONOMICS
December, 1971

Maugham was right. To know your own country, you must know other countries. And if Mohammed will not go to the mountain, the mountain can come to Mohammed. Through the eyes of the visitor to America, we see ourselves with new light.

Our most recent de Tocqueville is Assar Lindbeck, a Stockholm professor who had the good luck to visit Columbia and other American universities when the New Left was formulating its ideology. Lindbeck is himself a rarity, a professor of economics generally sympathic to the social-democratic movement, a man young enough to burn with un-Swedish neutrality in opposition to our Vietnam war but just old enough to remember the flirtations with Hitler's doctrines of the super race to which some of his countrymen succumbed in the days of the successful blitzkrieg.

I have been reading his new book, just published in paperback by Harper & Row, "The Political Economy of the New Left: An Outsider's View." In a shorter version, it has already made a stir in its Swedish, Danish and Finnish versions, and I was glad after reading it to write a foreword. My prediction there was that it would draw blood from both the radical right and the radical left. That prediction is beginning to come true. The book's greatest interest, though, will be to the more numerous readers who fall in between.

HO HUM?

But, we keep telling ourselves, the campus is quiet these days, now that Kent State is past, and the troops are coming home from Indochina. Once we bribe poor whites and blacks to serve in a volunteer Army and release our college boys to hold down the well-paying jobs that create so much value-added for our GNP, all this New Left nonsense will wither away.

How naïve can you be? If straw votes on college campuses could elect the next President of the United States, without doubt one candidate would win in a landslide. And it wouldn't be Nixon. Or Muskie. Or McCarthy. Or McGovern. Or Bill Buckley. Or Kennedy. It would undoubtedly be Ralph Nader. And John Kenneth Galbraith would be, not his Agnew, but his John Adams or André Malraux.

Only an idiot of the right could think of Nader as a revolutionary. Galbraith is neither of the old left nor the new: he is as innocent as Keynes was of any knowledge of Marx, Kautsky, Luxemburg, Hilferding, Sorel, Gramsci, and not much more guilty in his knowledge of Veblen, Tawney and Burnham.

A closed society like Czarist Russia was vulnerable to change only from the extremes—from a Lenin. Change comes to our open society from just off center.

Most of the world never changes its consciousness, merely proceeds in the way of its fathers and grandfathers. With rare exceptions, those Dartmouth men who wear a Nader button today will be wearing a David Rockefeller button—not a Reagan button!—at the five-year reunion.

All the more important then are the 5 or 10 per cent of the population who do change their consciousness of the world; and who, as opinion pacesetters, help to form the new Establishment ideology. As Lindbeck has discerned, what the New Left believes in caricature—that both bureaucracy and the market are anathema and must be replaced by . . . by the kibbutz and commune—most young people take for granted in a watered-down version.

LOST CAMELOT

To those who had lost faith in rugged individualism, Franklin Roosevelt restored the vision of the mixed economy in which periodic voting at the ballot box would rectify the evils and inefficiencies that resulted from dollar voting by consumers in the stores and by the employers in the labor mart. Since the death of John F. Kennedy, simple faith in New Dealism has ebbed away among the young.

Lindbeck throws light on this. He points out that *if* you cannot believe in the legitimacy of consumers' sovereignty (consumers being allegedly brainwashed by advertisers), you can likewise not believe in the legitimacy of voters' sovereignty (voters being allegedly brainwashed by the military-industrual complex and the patriotism establishment). The result is, to coin a word, *alienation*.

To use Lenin's scathing phrase, is this merely an infantile disorder that, like acne, will wither away with age? Among intellectuals in Britain, Japan, France and Italy, it has not. Lindbeck's readers will ask, "Why should the U.S. be different in this respect?"

Chapter 14

SOME ADVANCED ECONOMIES

As the title of this chapter indicates, and the limited number of readings confirms, there is no pretense here of a comprehensive survey of the world's "advanced economies." It might be fair to assert that their relevance goes beyond the countries specifically discussed, but the reader can be the judge of this.

The first selection, "True Income," is aimed at pollution in the United States, and is a 1969 call for action. A key point made is that all of us have society as a partner. We have to face up to paying the full costs incurred in this partnership; not just the visible costs of traditional social functions, but also the hidden social costs resulting from the damage we inflict upon our environment. Hopefully, we can thereby eliminate some of the harm done and in all instances at least minimize it. Further, the invisible hand of self-interest cannot be relied upon as a solution. In its quest for profits, if Giant Corporation X is a pollution culprit, it accomplishes little to wring our hands and blame the corporation for doing what comes naturally. As the reading says, "It is society's job to set the rules of the road."

The article on "Japan Revisited" was occasioned by a 1971 trip. Coming as it did soon after President Nixon's August 15th suspension of international convertibility of the dollar into gold, plus the imposition of a ten per cent surcharge on dutiable imports, Samuelson found the Japanese talking about "Nixon shock," and he responds to this. There is much appreciation of Japan's tremendous growth in output and real incomes, but also criticism of the neglect evident in not keeping up in the area of needed social overhead capital. In this regard, he says Tokyo is "a mess."

The article titled "A Good Life" discusses specific features and the general character of the Swedish economy, and draws some comparisons with the United States. Based on his recurring visits to Sweden, one has to place an authoritative value on these perceptions from the sensitive antennae of Samuelson the economist. He indeed finds Sweden's accomplishments impressive, and we come out second-best in more than one comparison. Most reassuring to a liberal advocate of a progressive mixed economy is Sweden's demonstration that a government can be strongly interventionist, in the interest of income redistribution and other aspects of economic welfare, and yet be highly sensitive to the "protection of personal rights and civil liberties."

In the only other article of this chapter, "What's Happening to the Affluent State?" we find Samuelson somewhat uncertain about the continuing, long-run ability of Sweden to maintain the "Scandinavian pattern." The English-language magazine, "Sweden Now," asked Professor Samuelson for his views on the future of advanced states such as Sweden. This particular reading is his response. It makes no hard predictions but does mention the ugly possibility that, thanks to the "acids of modern life" or "the Berkeley disease," they and we could become "politically overdeveloped" but economically impotent.

TRUE INCOME
October, 1969

I once heard the treasurer of the MIT faculty club explain in his annual report that we had really broken even that year were it not for the item "depreciation." He was an eminent acoustical engineer, who obviously regarded depreciation as some artifact dreamed up by impractical accountants.

Now it is true that little had to be spent on furnishings while the club was new. But it is also true that the clock is ticking all the time for matter animal, vegetable or mineral. And he should have known that whenever our faculty are not earning Nobel prizes, they are shuffling their feet and spilling cocktails on the rugs.

My point is that most of us are poorer than we realize. Hidden costs are accruing all the time; and because we tend to ignore them, we overstate our incomes.

I don't mean the other fellow. I mean you, the suburban reader of NEWSWEEK with your alleged $20,000-a-year income.

WHAT'S MINE

First, there is the obvious point that *your* income is not the $20,000 gross figure. Yours is what is left over after you've paid taxes. (I almost wrote "your" taxes.)

Henry Moore, the great English sculptor, is said to earn $600,000 a year but to be able to keep $25,000 of it. Of $8 million, the Beatles could keep but $2 million.

It will make for greater happiness if Moore thinks of himself as a $25,000-a-year man. Of course, if taxes were less . . . But then wouldn't it be nice if the second law of thermodynamics were repealed so that perpetual motion were possible? (And if my Aunt Sally had wheels, she'd be a stagecoach. But she doesn't.)

Society is Henry Moore's partner. Without society we would not have Moore the noble savage piling pretty stones on the beach. Without society, we have wolf boy—unkempt, speechless, and dead at 11.

Less commonplace is the fact that costs are accruing in our advanced economy that no traditional accounting methods can measure. Thomas Hobbes said that in the state of nature the life of man was nasty, brutish and short. In the state of modern civilization it has become nasty, brutish and long.

Sulphur dioxide is seeping into the atmosphere as I write. A $20,000-a-year man cannot afford to eat salt pork. No more can he afford to breathe noxious air. Each day at the stores, he chooses to pass up salt pork in favor of beef roast. Each year at the polls he will find himself voting for expensive programs to fight pollution—air pollution, water pollution, noise pollution, even heat pollution.

American ingenuity raises incomes about 3 per cent a year in real (price-corrected) terms. On $20,000, that's $600 a year—or a doubling of real income about every 25 years.

But don't you believe it. Much of that increase is already preempted. Look at the fuel picture alone.

- Higher stacks for power stations are expensive.

- To remove sulphur from coal is uneconomic. To remove it from oil is feasible but expensive, and "sweet" oils are both rare and costly.

- Though nuclear fuels burn clean, a large fraction of their heat is wasted and serves to pollute even our bigger rivers. Cooling towers add to the cost of power, yet disturbance of the ecological balance of nature is the only alternative.

- Strip mining, coal's most economical source, despoils the countryside.

The citizen cannot have it both ways. If we make Con Ed mend its ways, we must not complain when the postman brings around the monthly utility bill.

THE PUBLIC INTEREST

When TV showed recently the rape of Lake Erie and no public outcry followed, I felt as outraged as at that Kew Gardens murder before half a hundred spectators.

And of the auto, one hardly dares speak. As Los Angeles proves, it is the ultimate despoiler. Expecting Detroit to tame the unspeakable internal-combustion engine out of the profit motive is like expecting the American Tobacco Co.—oops, I mean American Brands, Inc.—to commit economic suicide, or like turning venereal-disease control over to the expert attention of ponces and madams.

It is society's job to set the rules of the road. If we don't do so, we must not blame the corporations for doing what comes naturally to them. For our unnatural behavior it is we who deserve to be hanged—or, more appropriately, to be stewed in our own juices.

A GOOD LIFE

January, 1971

Americans make good tourists but poor settlers. There are few countries in the world that the average American would consider moving to. I of course exclude artists who spend a few years on the Left Bank, or businessmen and diplomats whose livelihood depends on their living abroad.

At five-year intervals I have been visiting Sweden since the end of the second world war. On a recent trip to Stockholm I came away with the distinct impression that at last the standard of living there has pretty much achieved parity with that in this country.

I say this fully realizing that, if you look up numbers in the almanac, you will find real per capita GNP in America still a few per cent higher than in Sweden. But it is hard to believe that the average level of living in Greater Boston—I do not speak of affluent New York City or Los Angeles—exceeds that of the average resident of Stockholm. If I should be wrong about this comparison, replace Boston by Greater Baltimore.

To be sure, the cost of living is high in Sweden today. Eggs cost more than a dollar a dozen; a luxurious dinner will be dear in either place. Still public transportation is far better there than here. Life is less crowded. Life expectancy significantly exceeds that in the States: not only is infant mortality lower, but at every age the advantage is to the Scandinavians. In all candor, I ought to make the observation, unpopular in the present age of sensitivity to claims of racial differences, that the northern stocks may possess some genetic advantage in longevity. The labor party Prime Minister perhaps does not deserve all the credit.

QUALITY

It is the quality of life, and not simply its economic affluence, that one finds appealing in Scandinavia. Quality? you will say. What about the notorious sexual immorality there? What about the flagrant drunkenness in the land of short winter days? And, to quote one of our most astute Presidents, what about the high suicide rate in Sweden's welfare state?

Well, what about them? If Scandinavia pioneered ahead of the rest of the Western world in the secularization of everyday life, we have caught up with a vengeance. Not too long ago the U.S. wrested the title for most drunkenness away from France. On one of his bad days, a present-day psychiatrist might be willing on a U.S. college campus to trade some of our drug problems for old-fashioned addiction to John Barleycorn.

Few demographers will accept the statistics which show significantly lower suicide rates in Switzerland, Canada, Japan, the U.K., and the U.S. than in Scandinavia. Thus, in many cultures—not all Catholic—care is taken to avoid recording suicides for what they are. And, I would like to add, there is a world of difference between a suicide by a 79-year-old scientist suffering from terminal cancer and the suicide of a young Japanese couple because they were refused use of the family automobile.

EQUALITY AND FREEDOM

It is fruitless to try to compare the incommensurable: is a Strindberg hero happier than a Verdi heroine? What is exciting about the Swedish experience is how they have taught the world the feasibility of combining moderation and justice.

For 40 years Scandinavia has been successfully tackling poverty. Rich and poor alike have access to modern medicine, while the level of the profession is maintained. In those countries people do obey the traffic lights: they are taught to do so in school! And besides you can be fined on the spot for jaywalking.

What is remarkable is not that Sweden is a welfare state, but that the redistribution of wealth and the government interventions into business life have been done in an environment of jealous protection of personal rights and civil liberties.

Progressive reforms are the first step down the road to serfdom. So once proclaimed Dr. Hayek, seeing in the social-security innovations of Bismarck and Gladstone the seeds of dictatorial Hitler and Stalin.

What nonsense! The argument was never very convincing in terms of its logic—which indeed consisted of little but reassertion. Experience in the years since 1945 has not been kind to the Hayekian prophecies. Whatever Britain has become, it has not become Orwell's 1984.

Had it not existed, the world would have had to invent Sweden —where government plays a major role, yet remains handmaiden of the people.

WHAT'S HAPPENING TO THE AFFLUENT STATE?

September, 1971

Thirty years ago, when the Carnegie Foundation wished to commission a study on the race problem in America, it picked Gunnar Myrdal from Sweden precisely for the reason that he was unencumbered by previous knowledge of the subject. By this criterion, I am well qualified to speculate on the future of Scandinavian society, for mine is only a superficial acquaintance with the deep currents of modern life in those countries.

A knowledge of current trends in American society may, per- haps, make up in part for this deficiency. For I have long insisted that much of what is called the "Americanization of Europe" is merely a reflection of the fact that we reached affluence earliest, and what one nation will want to do at a high level of income turns out to be very much like what another nation will come to want to do in the same circumstance. Finally, it was an advantage to de Tocqueville that he came to America with the eye of a stranger. By contrast with his European preconceptions, he could discern the new features of the developing American society.

In 1950, Sweden was a middle-class society. That old and some- what misleading expression, "the middle way," was intended to de- scribe the Scandivanian blend between capitalism and socialism, but the pun on the word "middle" is suggestive in its class connotation. Not only had the aristocracy come to count for nothing, except on the shrinking society pages, but in addition most of the working class had, in effect, moved up into the middle classes. In this, Sweden was approaching the state that had long prevailed in America, where almost everyone tells Dr. Gallup that he belongs to the middle class. This pattern contrasts, I think, with that in England, where Disraeli's "two nations" still has a reality today. Accent and school background combine with a genuine feeling on the part of the working classes that it is unamiable for an able young chap to go to night school and better himself and be upwardly mobile, in a way that seems odd to any American observer.

Although both America and Sweden were until recently middle class. I think it fair to say that in Sweden to be middle class meant to be a member of the bourgeoisie. To be bourgeois, perhaps, means more than to be in a certain income bracket and percentile of the income distribution. It means to have the customs and unconscious preconceptions of the kind of family written about in Thomas Mann's autobiographical novel *Buddenbrooks.* The characters one views on the stage of Ibsen and Strindberg represent that class in its tensions, guilts and hypocrisies; in a larger sense, the great age of the 19th-century novel outside of Russia, from Jane Austen to George Eliot, Stendahl to Balzac and Flaubert, reflect the *mores* of that society. To understand the distinction between the bourgeoisie and the mere middle classes, the American example is instructive. Ours has long been a plutocracy. Where money counts, entrance into the elite is quick and turnover is high. The example, which I take from my wife's family, of a genteel spinster who lives frugally on an inheritance so that it can be passed on intact, would be a commonplace in Europe, but within America a rarity outside New England or the Old South.

Acids of modern life

When I describe Sweden as having been a bourgeoisie in 1950, this dating is emphasized to pinpoint the fact that the acids of modern life have been undermining the bone and cartilage of the bourgeois *weltanschauung.* A visitor to Stockholm is struck by this process. More than in any other Scandinavian country, he expects to encounter in Sweden formality of manners—the bow, the handshake, the *skal,* the speech of welcome and of thanks for the food, the flowers and candy and thanks for the hostess. Only in Japan does he meet so elaborate an etiquette. But, and this is my point, at each five-year interval the visitor notes a further decay in the protocol, or at least in the seriousness with which it is obeyed. During the last Nobel week in Stockholm, I heard not a single speech of welcome in which my host did not excuse himself in words such as these: "Earlier at this point it would have been customary for me to make a speech, but that is no longer necessary." Nevertheless, plainly contradicting himself, he would proceed to extend a cordial welcome.

This decline of the bourgeoisie, which one sees going on all over the world, seems to me to be ultimately traceable to two related causes. First, there is affluence itself. When a Belgian of my acquaintance came out of a Nazi occupational prison and vowed to have 10 children, his father was aghast: "You are dissipating the thrift of more than a century in one generation." In an affluent society thrift is no longer a necessity to keep from falling into the abyss of poverty.

The second cause contributing to the erosion of middle-class values seems to be higher education. The song after World War I went, "How're yer gonna keep 'em down on the farm, after they've seen Paree?" And how, I ask, can you keep them happy making and selling soap in Cincinnati or Gothenburg after they've been to Yale or Uppsala?

Take only the ancient questions of Swedish neutrality. Twenty years ago that had a clear and palpable meaning. A country which last saw war in the Napoleonic epoch was reluctant to become embroiled even in good causes. How different things are now. Nor, I believe, is this merely a reflection of the revulsion occasioned by the Vietnam war, bad as that war is. In an earlier age, sensitive consciences would also have disapproved strongly of the British campaigns against the Boers or Hitler's acts against minorities. But disapproval would have been a matter of private conscience and not been permitted to become an issue of national politics.

The generation gap highlights these changes. Youth culture tends to foreshadow general culture, not merely because young people grow up, but also because people when young have less of a vested interest in previous patterns of society. Let me illustrate the changes that seem to be going on by a personal anecdote. Last December, the publisher of the Swedish translation of my economics textbook gave a nice lunch for me. I asked him, "Why did you bother to prepare a Swedish translation? All educated Swedes know English." He replied, "Our students are losing their English. They are better than early generations when it comes to the speaking vocabulary needed to travel abroad. But where grammar and subtler vocabulary are involved, there is a falling off in their mastery of the language because they are no longer drilled at school in the way they used to be."

I found this incredible, yet when I asked around for corroboration, I was assured that this was indeed so and that the very translation of a basic text like mine would contribute further to the process. Still, I could not feel satisfied with the answers until one person gave me the clue to the puzzle. "Actually, no one likes to study for exams in a text outside his native language. I didn't like it in my time, nor did my father before me. But, today, what students don't want to do, they don't have to do."

The Berkeley disease

The Berkeley disease, which is the Cambridge or Paris or Buenos Aires disease, travels everywhere. Anyone who remembers the respectful, but silent, members of a Scandinavian economics seminar must welcome the change. But without question, all this is undermining to the established way of doing things. Nor is the end in sight. Although many of those who participate in the new forms of youth culture when they are 23 will, by the time they are 33, fit into the suburban mold of business and professional life, it is naive to think that the next generation of middle-aged people can ever be the same as their fathers and grandfathers.

When acid eats in, where will the process end? What will remain? I do not think there is any way of predicting the answers. As the Russians are learning, once you permit a loosening of the structure of society, there is no telling how far it will go. The post-Victorians long since learned this same lesson.

The present age, it seems to me, is quite comparable to that of the early 19th century. Edmund Burke deplored the passing of the feudal order. To Jeremy Bentham and the other utilitarians, no custom in England was sacrosanct. Why, they asked, does yon woman hang for stealing a handkerchief when this Countess can with impunity enclose the common lands of a whole region? The established modes of law and life could not stand up under such a scrutiny.

Today, the same fundamental questioning is under way. It is not merely that people ask, why is US Steel permitted to pollute the Great Lakes? External effects that go beyond the corporation itself have always been open to regulation and zoning. Now, the *Yale Law Review* can seriously propose that General Motors no longer be permitted to introduce annual style changes in its automobiles, even though such practices are conducive to its long-run profit and similar policies are available to its few large rivals. Literally nothing is sacrosanct. Any day Ralph Nader may come knocking at your door. Not only does he bring the force of public opinion to bear against the corporation for doing what corporations have traditionally felt was at their own discretion. The force of law follows hard upon the heels of public opinion. The public needs the protection of an *ombudsman;* the harried chairman of the board is learning that he needs on his personal staff a representative of the new culture to give him advance warning of the direction from which the next tornado may blow.

Special significance

If I am at all near the mark in these speculations, they may have a special significance for Scandinavian society. The United States is so affluent, so endowed with varied natural resources, that our rate of material progress can taper off without revolutionary consequences. We shall merely advance a little slower toward even greater affluence.

Perhaps the same will be true of Sweden. Continuing to grow no less slowly than her peer, the United States, she may find her lead being reduced in comparison with Japan or Italy or West Germany.

She can comfort herself with the consideration that they, too, in their turn, will begin to succumb to the blandishments of affluence. But perhaps this complacent prospect does not truly apply to a small country, not blessed with a wide spectrum of natural resources, whose material pre-eminence was attributable to her ingenuity and puritan-ethic diligence.

After my last visit to Sweden, I wrote in *Newsweek* and elsewhere that there was something of a miracle involved in the Swedish welfare state. It was almost too good to be true to find a society in which egalitarianism in legislation coexisted with zealous productivity, piece rates and other incentive mechanisms. Minute regulation of business life by a strong state coexisted with jealous preservation of personal liberties, civil rights and democratic checks and balances on government by an alert electorate.

Events since then, such as the strikes and revolts of the professional and white-collar classes, suggest that it may indeed have been too good to be true, and that in the future the Scandinavian consensus will wear thin. Whether that will be good or bad for Sweden I am unable to say. But I know it will be a sad thing for the world which looks toward the Scandinavian pattern. I think of a sensitive critic of the present order like Prof. Joan Robinson of Cambridge University. Alienated from her own society, too-long hopeful that the Stalinist bureaucracies of Eastern Europe would soften, Mrs. Robinson has turned her eyes toward China and North Korea. In all of her many writings, I do not recall any evaluation of the Scandinavian alternative, an alternative that is ever-present in the minds of American economists of my generation.

The word socialism means nothing to them. Nasser and Nkrumah labeled socialism on their banners; but good intentions concerning planning do not bring chickens into every pot. If the balancing act by which Sweden is able to generate rapid technological advance within a framework of social redistribution gives out, what abyss lies below? The shadow on the wall for all of us, I fear, is not the totalitarian revolution of a Lenin or Mao. It is not a relapse into the *laissez faire* of Queen Victoria or President Coolidge. Argentina, I dare to suggest, is the pattern which no modern man may face without crossing himself and saying, "There but for the Grace of God . . ."

In 1945, no competent economist could have predicted that countries like Argentina or Chile would fail to grow mightily in the next quarter of a century. With temperate climates, they stood at the take-off point for rapid advance. Yet, even before correction for burgeoning population numbers, their rate of real GNP growth has been almost negligible. How was this miracle contrived? The time has long passed when we can continue to blame Argentinian stagnation on Perón. Uruguay, the one-time Switzerland of Latin America, had no dictator. Yet it managed to escape economic growth.

Why? I suspect the answer has to be found in populist democracy. If in the time of England's industrial revolution men had had the political power to try to rectify within a generation the unconscionable inequities of life, in which a privileged few live well off the sweat of the multitude, it is doubtful that the industrial revolution could ever have continued. The outcome would not have been a rational, planned economy with a Professor Tinbergen or Frisch at the helm. The outcome would have been legislated increases in money wages of as much as 40% per year. The outcome might well have been pretty much like that we have seen in those Latin American countries which have reached the brink of economic development while, so to speak, fully or overly developed in the political sphere.

The Schumpeter prophecy

Rome was not built in a day. Rome did not decline in a day. I see no realistic danger that Sweden or Canada or the United States will this year, or in the next decade, revert to the stagnation of Latin America. But it may well be that the wise social observer, 30 years from now looking back toward our time, will have discerned the beginning of the process I describe. Thirty years ago, my old teacher Joseph Schumpeter, in his *Socialism, Capitalism and Democracy,* predicted that the very successes of the mixed economy would produce alienation in its young. He was wrong in his timing, so very wrong. But who can walk the streets of Princeton or Stockholm or Toronto and deny his prescience?

JAPAN REVISITED
November, 1971.

Visiting Japan for the first time in a dozen years is an overpowering experience, particularly at this time of crisis in Japanese-American relations.

To paraphrase Lincoln Steffens, "I have seen the *past*. And it worked!" The miracle of Japan's growth needs no retelling. The mills of the gods grind exceeding fast when they grind at 10 per cent interest.

Japan is now the No. 3 economy of the world. Undoubtedly she will pass the Soviet Union in this century. By 2000 her per capita GNP may outstrip ours just as we outstripped Britain, the 1800 champ.

What we call the NEP, the Japanese call the "Nixon shock." Business surveys show a swing to fear of recession more violent than I have ever seen before.

Such despair, I think excessive. Once the yen has been appreciated 15 per cent vis-à-vis the dollar, Japan's more efficient exporters will be able to hold their share of world markets. That is, they'll be able to compete *if* given a fair chance and not made special targets of import quotas.

A COOLIDGE WORLD

Being in Japan led me back to my childhood world of the 1920s. Here is a democracy where the trains run on time; a society where *the people* run on time—run, not walk.

Japanese and German citizens, led to disastrous military defeats by leaders seeking glory, came out of the war sick of the state and politics. An able young Japanese no longer dreams of going into the foreign service or army. Like the Yale graduates of 1925 he wants to culitvate his garden, that is, make his pile. His wife wants the three C's—car, color TV, air conditioning. And she is getting them. Even the peasants are prosperous. It shows what providence and 10 per cent growth can do for a poor country!

Perhaps Keynes was right when he said that it is better for a man to tyrannize over his pocketbook than tyrannize over his neighbor. A man from Mars—make it Venus—who knew no history of wars or bigotry, might well rank Germany and Japan as the two most *decent* societies of the postwar world.

The question is, can the rest of the world afford Japanese growth? And can the Japanese afford to grow in this next decade according to the pattern they have maintained in the past?

Let me begin with Japan's problem.

> *Ill fares the land,*
> *to hastening ills a prey*
> *Where wealth accumulates,*
> *and men decay.*

Tokyo is a mess. Only the Japanese could live in it. New Yorkers would bring it to a big bang in a month. The world's largest city, it may be the most polluted and congested.

And this is only typical of the neglect in social overhead capital that has been going on for a generation. Man does not live by transistor radios alone. A government more interested in roads for trucks than sidewalks for people is not meeting its accruing social costs.

I must not exaggerate. Life expectancy—a test of whether prosperity reaches down to all strata of society—has improved dramatically and soon will surpass our mediocre record.

THE WHITE PERIL

Still, Japan is no longer a poor Asian country. She can afford the housing she has neglected. The Nixon shock can prove a blessing if it makes her now turn inward.

Actually, Japan has little choice. According to the OECD, she is slated to grow 160 per cent in the 1970s, as against less than 60 per cent for us and the Europeans. To keep to an export-oriented boom, in which she maintains her exports at 9 per cent of the GNP, Japan's exports would have to grow three times as fast as those of the rest of us.

Is it really feasible for her to aspire to so great a further penetration of world markets, now that she is already such a significant fraction of total trade?

There is the further factor that Japanese are not given the fair share they deserve. We veer from contempt of Japanese as capable only of making shoddy Christmas-tree ornaments, to thinking of them as supermen whose costs and precision Americans and Europeans could never compete with. Ugly racism has to be fought, in the economic as well as political and social spheres.

Another time I must return to the unspeakable voluntary and mandatory quotas that President Nixon's team—notably Secretary Stans and his Assistant Secretary—are trying to impose on textiles, steel, autos and TV's. Aimed at the Japanese, the knife cuts our own throats too.

Chapter 15

THE LIBERATED CORPORATION?

That the business community is no longer held to be a hero in the aggregate is not a surprise to most, least of all to the business community itself. "Business in a Doghouse" tells us what we might suspect —the members of that community are eager to alter this state of affairs for the better.

This diminished esteem is partly explained by the disparity between what society now expects of the corporation, for example, and the reality of its performance. In turn, much of this disparity derives from the notion of the social responsibility of the corporation. In "Love That Corporation" we learn that its desire to recapture lost glory leads the corporation to undertake what might be called charitable acts which benefit purposes applauded by society. In this way the corporation shows itself to be the good citizen, aware of the problems which are part of the social setting within which it prospers.

Not all are cheered by this development. Beyond certain disgruntled stockholders, some, including economist Milton Friedman, argue that these contributions are in effect a tax on the corporation's customers, its employees and, of course, its stockholders. What is the legitimacy of this tax? It appears to violate that time-honored precept of "no taxation without representation." Is this not inconsistent with democracy?

The specific obligations which society perceives as falling within the corporation's social responsibility include more than charitable acts. Society now asks—Does this firm take account of *all* of the costs of producing its product (e.g., the effects of its effluent)? Does it take account of the costs to society which follow from the very existence of its product (e.g., product safety)?

Corporations are not without ears, and they sometimes respond by altering their behavior so as to conform more closely to society's expectations. "Love That Corporation" sagely cautions us, however, that in order to ensure that the good corporation is not victimized by the laggard one or does not itself backslide, society should judiciously reinforce its expectations with legislation.

Does this apparent social conscience of the corporation reflect a liberation of those who control it from slavery to the interests of those who own it, the shareholders? The separation of control from ownership was examined several decades ago by Berle and Means. Out of this Berle-Means thesis have come the theories of corporate behavior which cite the passing of the goal of profit maximization. "Corporate Giants" asserts, however, that there has never been a form of business organization better equipped and more inclined to maximize the firm's profits than the modern corporation.

Whether it seeks only to maximize profits or whether it strives to achieve other goals, one might conjecture that the giant corporation is at least able to do what it will to fulfill itself. The closing circle of social responsibility suggests, however, that the actuality is that of "The Businessman's Shrinking Prerogatives."

BUSINESS IN A DOGHOUSE
January, 1969

Passing of The Saturday Evening Post brings home how much America has changed from the days of Calvin Coolidge when businessmen came first in the social pecking order. It drove poor Henry Mencken almost to sobriety that the boobs who ruled over our pocketbooks should also rule over our hearts.

When Henry Ford said, "History is bunk," he meant that historians and professors generally were a bunch of sissies, not worth their derisory pittances and not worthy of setting out on a camping trip with real men like Harvey Firestone, Thomas Edison and Ford himself. The editors of the Post agreed with Ford and pleased their readers with articles and fiction—it was hard to draw the line!—glorifying what James Truslow Adams called America's true business, The Business Civilization.

In a sense, Karl Marx would have agreed with Ford. To Marx,

businessmen were the exploiters of labor. But they were the crew who counted. It was in the library of J. Pierpont Morgan that the Executive Committee of Capitalism fell into session. College deans, like the *castrati* sopranos or wrist falcons of an earlier century, were mere lackeys and parasites living off "surplus value" rather than contributing to it.

That is why, during World War II, Averell Harriman was such an effective ambassador to Russia. Stalin could feel that in dealing with the heir of the great railroad tycoon, E. H. Harriman, he was in touch with the control center of the United States. John D. Rockefeller being unavailable, Harriman was the next best thing.

Here we have once again a demonstration that Marxism is indeed the opiate of the Marxians. Like LSD, it makes one feel full of insight while diverting attention from the laws of motion of society.

TURNOVER OF THE ELITE

Though the Post was buried in 1969, it really died with the 1929 crash. Since then, the mighty have been humbled. Business has become the whipping boy of American public opinion.

Our folk heroes are no longer the Horatio Alger characters who luck out their way to business success by rescuing and marrying the boss's daughter. Actually, in the meritocracy of the corporate jungle, a Harvard M.B.A. is worth more today than blood relationship with the constitutional monarch who chairs the board from age 60 to 65. If you don't believe it, listen in at the country club.

The declining fraction of the graduating classes at the Ivy League and prestige colleges who now head for a business career testifies to the reduced prestige of business as a profession. Postgraduate study is all the rage. The professions of law, medicine and teaching seem to carry more appeal to college graduates than the most princely offers of the corporate recruiters who swarm to the campuses.

In accordance with an old prediction of Joseph Schumpeter, the children of capitalists become alienated from the system in very consequence of its unlovable effectiveness. They are like soaring birds who come to despise the wings that give them flight.

No one feels this change in social status more than business itself. Like any minority group, executives have become sensitive to public disapprobation. How to be more loved has become a major preoccupation of the business establishment.

A NEW MANDARIN CLASS?

History never moves in one-way trends. From the depths of un-popularity produced by the Great Depression and the Liberty League idiocies of the Roosevelt haters, the stock of business made a wartime recovery, but not to anything like the pre-1929 levels. Oppenheimer and Fermi—not General Grove or du Pont's Greenewalt—are folk heroes of the atom bomb.

Eisenhower, like most Republican Presidents, did invite managers back into the temple. Still, times had changed. Perhaps George Humphrey was no more incompetent a Secretary of the Treasury than Andrew Mellon had been in the 1920s; yet he seemed less competent, and the capricious history books will register him as a liability in the balance sheet of business prestige.

An uncritical reader of Burnham and Galbraith may think I have missed the point that business, itself, is being taken over by a new set of technicians out of Washington. According to this naïve view, the Executive Committee still meets, but it now meets in the Washington Cosmos Club.

Because it takes a myth to kill a myth, this quarter-truth is well told. But it won't sell a million magazines.

LOVE THAT CORPORATION
December, 1970

Cambridge, Mass.—Last Christmas I wrote a column on economics and love. Under the mistaken preconception that these, like oil and water, cannot mix, several people applauded either my innovation or my recantation.

Illustrative of this widespread misconception is the following typical query:

"Professor Samuelson, is it really a finding of economics that corporations should *solely* maximize their profits, disregarding any special obligation to the public interest or to the humanitarian needs of their workers and consumers?"

I was glad to be able to reply, "Yes, Virginia, a large corporation these days not only may engage in social responsibility, it had damn well better try to do so."

Let me tell the ways.

First, let's forget the sterile problem of semantics as to whether the corporation is a person distinct from its employes and owners. As Descartes would say, the corporation holds committee meetings— therefore it exists. It pays taxes. It hires new people and after they are dead it continues to operate.

Second, we can dismiss the legal argument that the Board of Directors has no right to squander the shareowners' assets in Galahad causes. The stamp of legitimacy is on the other side.

The whole issue is what *are* the shareowners' assets? For decades the courts have upheld charitable giving by corporations. Today you'd be in more trouble with the authorities—the Stock Exchange, the S. E. C., the boys at the downtown eating club, to say nothing of the bailiff—if you tried to run a business along old-fashioned Sewall Avery lines of immediate profit than if you took account of the public interest.

Let me not overstate the case. It is true that Henry Ford 2d cannot operate today like Henry Ford, his grandfather. But neither can he operate like St. Francis of Assisi. The several hundred large corporations react to, and set, an evolving code of social conduct. So long as anyone does not depart too markedly from the ruling norm, it will not be penalized out of existence by market competition.

Thus, if International Harvester attempted by itself to solve the problem of general inflation, or even inflation in farm equipment prices—or if its board set out, by wage and price policy, to rectify the inequitable distribution of incomes in the United States—after a very few years International Harvester would be eliminated from the roster of Galbraithian giants. The elimination process would be a bit slower, but not less inexorable, if Allis Chalmers, Deere, Caterpillar, Dodge Trucks, and General Motors joined it in this unilateral crusade for social justice.

To advance the good cause, one must not expect too much of altruism. It is nonsense to look to General Motors, or even the Big Three, for voluntary solution of the problem of air pollution. It is only good sense to impose by the force of law—by regulation and taxation—an obligation for the auto makers to produce exhaust systems that lessen pollution of the environment.

Corporations, I am afraid, are persons, born like the rest of us imperfect and subject to sin. Thus, the small man is no better than the General Electric board. When I drove into a Los Angeles service station recently, I noted that the lead-free gas pump was neglected. I soon found out why: good people, men who love their wives and never fail to contribute to the collection plate, are not willing to pay more for gasoline which, if they alone use it, will only imperceptibly purify the atmosphere for the rest of the community. (Although not an admirer of Nixon economics, I must ask in this connection: why did Congress so cavalierly dismiss the President's suggestion of a penalty tax on leaded gasoline?)

I quote a final example from the recent book by William F. Buckley Jr. Lapsing for once into good sense, Buckley is arguing that coercive limitations can in such good causes as quarantine against plague add to total welfare and the algebraic total of human freedom:

"I asked Professor [Milton] Friedman, 'Is it your position that, assuming the community decided to license the whores, it would be wrong to insist that they check in at regular intervals for health certificates?' Yes, he thought that would be wrong—'After all, if the customer contracts a venereal disease, the prostitute having warranted that she was clean, he has available a tort action against her.' "

In response to a number of letters using this *reductio ad absurdum* as a reason for indicting economics, my reply is simply to demur. There is nothing in economics that leads to such a conclusion. Economics cannot tell us what to believe; it can help us to sort out the costs and benefits of various arrangements, as those costs and benefits are defined by the ethical value systems that we bring to economics.

Using civil suits to penalize undesired behavior *after* it takes place is indeed often a better social device than expensive and unpleasant inspection prior to behavior. But I cannot imagine a worse case to illustrate this purely tactical precept.

Thus, in principle, a veneral disease could be of irreversible type. Second, the courts would undoubtedly come to apply the doctrine of *caveat emptor,* let the buyer beware, to transactions such as these—what does it mean for a prostitute to warrant that she is "clean"? Finally, what are the assets against which the victorious plaintiff can levy? The mind boggles.

Hard cases are said to make bad law. Paradoxes cannot be counted on to define good economics—not on Christmas or any other day of the year.

CORPORATE GIANTS
March, 1971

A. A. Berle Jr. is dead. His passing provokes memories of the golden years before World War I when, reportedly, great scholars were great undergraduate teachers. When William James, Josiah Royce and George Santayana walked Harvard Yard, no man knew the language of Fortran and few lisped in differentials. But, I have it on high authority, every schoolboy savored the varieties of religious experience and to have heard Kittredge was to know Shakespeare.

More than Dutch elm disease has changed the face of college life. A feature of that bygone age was the presence of the prodigy: pygmies as well as giants strode the earth of Cambridge then. One would give much to witness the sight of precocious, knickerbockered undergraduates mingling with the Stovers and Merriwells in that gothic age of academe.

Berle was one such prodigy, at pretty much the same time that the mathematician-to-be Norbert Wiener and the musician Roger Sessions matriculated prior to the onset of puberty Wiener wrote an autobiography entitled "Ex-Prodigy"; but those who knew him, or have read the book, will realize that he never outgrew the scars of genius.

It is easier to pass from the ranks of precocity to the realms of generalized harmonic analysis and cybernetics than it is to mature into a man of affairs. Yet Berle, graduating from law school, practicing and teaching law, went on to become a New Dealer, an expert on Latin America and a successful force in the La Guardia reform movement and the formation of the Liberal Party in New York.

A NEW GENUS

It is not for any of these, though, that A. A. Berle Jr. will be remembered in the history of thought. It is for something that he discovered and analyzed as far back as 1933 that merits his fame.

I refer of course to the Berle-Means thesis that the large corporation in American life represents a new genus of life, a unit in which there is *separation of ownership and control.* As we go back to read the brief book by Gardner Means and Adolph Berle, "The Modern Corporation and Private Property," its contents seem so familiar and true as to appear almost trite. To accept such an evaluation is to fall victim to the optical illusion of hindsight, like the boy who said, "Of course, Columbus discovered America—how could he have missed it?"

Fewer and fewer hairsplitters are left to claim that the corporation has no identity separate from its owners, workers and consumers. With the same lame logic, such reductionists regard Greta Garbo as simply a collection of DNA, and the solar system as merely nine something-or-others moving around the sun. The tax collector knows better. The corporation exists. (And, I may add, constitutes a good pooler of risks and therefore provides an excellent object for income taxation.)

The statistical evidence for separation of ownership and control —i.e., the evidence for the fact that in every democracy involving tens and hundreds of thousands of individuals, whether it be a trade union or a religious denomination, collusions of effective minorities exercise decision making—has become firmer with each passing decade. What follows from this unchallengeable fact?

TRACKS OF THE BEAST

Is it the case that the pre-Berle-Means unit of business, in which the owner of capital was all-powerful, adhered to the laws of profit maximization prated of in the economic textbooks? But that the modern corporate giant answers to a different drumbeat from the pursuit of cost reduction and profit (now and in the longer future)?

I used to go along with this fashionable myth. Study of the facts of life will show, however, that the old tycoon of industry was a capricious bird, with behavior to be understood as much from Freud (if not Krafft-Ebing) as from the handbooks of operational analysis and managerial economics. If anyone in the universe minimizes costs and calculates present discounted values, it is committees in the large-scale corporation. To be sure some inside managers, with minimal ownership, perpetrate hanky-panky and minor mayhem. But cheating on the boss did not begin yesterday, as the cuneiform tablets of babylonia will confirm.

The boss they cheat we now know, thanks to Berle, is (1) the government, (2) the employees, (3) the consumers and, let's not forget, (4) those proxy-controlling owners. Our task is to insure that the giants remain responsive to the public interest.

THE BUSINESSMAN'S SHRINKING PREROGATIVES

Spring 1972

It is obvious that in the years ahead, the so-called private corporation will find itself increasingly subjected to external constraints never dreamed of at the Harvard Business School. Not only will the corporation president find he cannot follow policies that will pollute the atmosphere; he will also discover that hundreds of traditional ways of making business decisions will simply no longer be available to him. Society will expand business's responsibilities and take increasing part in deciding how they are to be met.

What will be the new framework within which business decision-making will have to operate? How will the new way of life affect growth in national product and distribution of incomes among the social classes?

Confident and detailed forecasting is quite impossible in so cosmic an area as this. The economist who has studied the econometric patterns of past GNP growth can often predict with some assurance that a particular region is on the brink of a vigorous expansion or is nearing an epoch of relative stagnation. The general laws of technology, despite what you read in the Sunday supplements, are conservative and regular and fairly predictable in their unfoldings. Not so the social environment. It takes a seer and a prophet to pinpoint the changes in this sphere. Alas, even a child's re-reading of history will show the seers and prophets of the past lacked genuine sorcerer's hats. Neither Karl Marx nor Henry Adams nor Oswald Spengler have been at all near the mark in their prognostications.

Although I shall not rush in where they were brave to tread, I think it is useful to speculate, to let hypotheses well up freely, unrestrained by inhibitory criticisms. The critical testings of experience and analysis will reject and elect among the many possibilities.

PROPHET OF DOOM

Almost thirty years ago, Joseph Schumpeter, in his *Capitalism, Socialism and Democracy,* predicted the shape of things to come after the second world war. "Capitalism in an oxygen tent"—that, in a nutshell, was his vision of the timid new world. Such a capitalism, he thought, could linger on for quite a while. But he did not really expect the hospital invalid to perform with the vigor that the youthful capitalism had, in his view, prior to the first world war.

Schumpeter was dead wrong. In the two decades since his death, the modern mixed economy has surpassed in performance classical capitalism at its finest hour. The miracle is not that Japan's economy has been growing for two decades at better than 9 percent per annum in real terms—remarkable as that performance has been. The miracle is that all over the Western world, whether in cynical Austria, effete France, mercurial Italy, or complacent America, real growth rates and average living standards have strongly and steadily outperformed the most daring predictions that could have been made by any objective observer of the years between the two world wars.

The developing countries—once called "backward countries" but which can in plain truth, be called poor countries—have generally speaking not grown as rapidly economically as the more technologically advanced nations. The widening gap is sad to observe and ominous to contemplate. But it is insufficiently realized that the divergence is not the result of poor performance by the developing nations as compared to either their own pasts or the pasts of the affluent nations at earlier stages of development. Rather it is the mushrooming affluence of the technologically advanced nations that is placing them further out front. Actually, the 1960s saw most of the world's low-income regions grow at rates more rapid than those which generally prevailed in the years of high capitalism, when Queen Victoria reigned in Balmoral Castle and Calvin Coolidge dozed in the White House.

PREMATURE TIMING

Was, however, Schumpeter's error merely a case of premature timing? For there are unquestionably parts of the world where material progress has been slow. Witness the miracle of almost negligible economic growth in Latin America. And not even those most sympathetic to the ideals of socialism can find much to cheer about in the lack of economic progress in societies newly freed from colonial rule. What Nkrumah or Nasser or Nehru were able to accomplish under the banner of rational social planning has, in the short run, been disappointing. To the satirist, it is not a case of business in an oxygen tent as much as business in bedlam.

Although I am not an expert on Latin America, I cannot reject the suggestion that the slow growth of Argentina or of Uruguay (the one-time "Switzerland of South America") or of pre-Allende Chile is related to the fact that these societies are neither fish nor fowl, nor good red herring. They place social demands on industry that industry simply cannot effectively meet. Antipathy toward the corporation and the bourgeois way of life has served to hamstring performance. It is nonsense to continue to blame the dictator Peron for a stagnation in the Argentinian economy which has prevailed in the decades since he lost office. But it is not nonsense to infer that the populist imperatives upon which Peron so skillfully played have a pivotal role in explaining the miracle of Argentinian stagnation. There is a dictum attributed to Lenin to the effect that we will ruin the capitalist system by debauching its currency. That is not a very intelligent way to hurt an economic system and advance the day of successful revolution. By contrast, there are few better ways to ruin a modern mixed economy than to insist on 40 to 70 percent increases in money wage rates within a brief period of time. This, to a degree, has happened time and time again in the unhappy economic history of Latin America.

SHRINKING BUSINESS PREROGATIVES

It is thus interesting to note some new forces developing in the wealthier nations. New demands for greater social responsibility are being made of business. At the same time, the principal old demands —ever greater productivity and higher living standards for all—continue to be strongly pressed, perhaps even more so than at any time in the past.

In the face of the rising tide of social concern, some business strengths may be lost. Of course, there will always be sacrifices that are well worth making if on balance the common good is advanced. I am not concerned with the fact that zoning ordinances and taxes on effluence will undoubtedly prevent the corporation of the future from polluting the environment. Of course that will happen. But when it does, it will not be so much a case of losing old legitimate corporate freedoms as being required for the first time to follow good practices. Society and the Promethean business giants will be the better for such fetters.

I am interested, however, in contemplating the restrictions which may be placed on the exercise of previously accepted prerogatives.

For example, in the United States, management cannot always shut down an unprofitable textile plant and throw its labor force out of work so that the firm can move to a more congenial environment where net labor costs are lower. In Northern Italy, corporations are not always free to trim their labor forces as their efficiency experts would desire. Collective bargaining takes place over the numbers to be employed as well as wage rates, fringe benefits, and severance pay. There may be a problem here. It is not that my heart bleeds for the corporation, but that one realizes that consumers and the earners of real wages also have a stake in the avoidance of dead-weight-loss practices.

SOCIETY'S POWER

At any rate, the line between rational concern and paranoia is a fine one. I have no wish to conjure up hobgoblins to terrify the denizens of the executive suite. I shall content myself with one last example of new pressures on corporations.

Ralph Nader is a social force of primary significance. The movement with which his name is associated represents much more than "mere consumerism," although that movement will itself be of increasing importance in the years to come. Naderism involves participatory democracy on the part of the workers and the public interest. You are naive if you look only at the number of proxy votes the Nader movement is able to mobilize against management. Even if foundations and universities are increasingly persuaded to cast their votes against management, it will be scores of years before opposition votes now 3 and 5 percent become majority votes of 51 percent.

The leverage of such movements is not to be found inside the corporate ballot box, but in the minds of men. Once the public comes to believe that what is deemed good by General Motors is no longer good for the public, they will not wait for victory in the voting of shares and proxies. *They will strike directly by legislation.*

Let me illustrate. A group at the Yale Law School recently came up with the ingenious suggestion presented in an article in the *Yale Law Journal,* that the antitrust division of the Justice Department prevent by legal action the large auto companies from introducing substantial annual or semiannual model changes. This pattern of contrived obsolescence, which Alfred P. Sloane Jr. innovated to help bring General Motors to its present size and prominence, is said by the Yale reformers to constitute unfair competition and to promote monopolistic imperfection of markets.

At first glance, one might tend to dismiss such proposals as utopian and no real threat to existing corporate hegemony. But often, quite often, criticism prompts some governmental response which can lead to change—even if only through the reaction of an industry to such attention.

I can recall that years of criticism by economists like myself of the monopolistically imposed minimum brokerage rates of the New York Stock Exchange got absolutely nowhere. Yet when the Department of Justice entered the fray with an announcement that it intended to bring antitrust suits against this anomalous practice, it was only a short time until the New York Stock Exchange and the Securities and Exchange Commission drastically modified the industry's practices.

We must resolve many competing demands. Business is being challenged and society shapes business's ability to respond. Can we tread a path that will avoid the excesses of private greed and narrow-minded management on the one hand and the debilitating destruction of all business prerogatives on the other? We have within our grasp a system that can meet the legitimate demands made upon it now and in the future.

Chapter 16

SOME TWENTIETH CENTURY ECONOMISTS

Anyone reading these chapters in the order they appear doesn't need to be told that there is much personal enjoyment, as well as professional fulfillment, in being an economist or a student of the subject. Professor Samuelson's enthusiasm and enjoyment, with life itself and with economics in particular, emanate from every reading. That spirit is nowhere more evident than in the selections of this last chapter, where he has the opportunity to comment on some of his fellow economists and on economics itself.

Samuelson is not individually guilty of academic provincialism, but economists as a group probably are. We are no different in this respect than the members of any other academic field or profession. We bask in esoteric camaraderie at our professional meetings. We relish the contributions made by great economists of the past, and even their personal idiosyncrasies. We take pride in the accomplishments of our modern, living superstars, and the influence that economics has in shaping rational public policy. And why not? One turns on the television to see how the political conventions are going, and finds Professor Galbraith debating William Buckley. On "Issues and Answers," Professor Milton Friedman might be explaining the virtues of flexible exchange rates. Who is meeting the press, on "Meet the Press?" Professor Walter Heller. And coming on the "Face the Nation" is Chairman Herbert Stein of the Council of Economic Advisers. If the intrepid viewer persists until the six o'clock news, he might find himself still confronted by the faces or comments of Drs. Shultz and Burns, speaking for the Treasury and Federal Reserve. Economics is amply endowed with able people, so the cast may change over time. But the point is made, and the point persists, that economics is what's happening.

Commenting on the first-time award of a Nobel Prize in Economic Science, Samuelson says, "Economics stands between physics and literature. That is its peculiar charm. At the same time that it offers analytical problems difficult enough to tax the finest brain, economics deals with the pressing policy issues that concern man and society." Suppose this is seized upon to argue that the pressing policy issues call for drastic restructuring of the economic system, that "radicalism is what's happening," and that economics is not aware or "relevant." The economic consensus can respond negatively to the first claim, noting also on the last claim the effective contributions made, to the other side of the debate, by our growing band of professionally trained radical economists. They have the ability and knowledge to frame properly the appropriate tough questions and challenges, bringing reality and order to what otherwise might never rise above the level of economic babble. The concluding comments of this chapter's "Who's Who in Economics" are in this area.

As a final note on academic pride, we do find Professor Samuelson kidding himself and the rest of us, at the end of the selection on "Joseph Schumpeter." He comes on with amused and feigned frustration that no economist was included in a particular series of paperback books, dealing with masters who have made the modern mind. To avoid coining a phrase, we can say you can't win 'em all.

The first co-recipients of a Nobel Prize in economics, as noted by Samuelson, were Ragnar Frisch of Norway and Jan Tinbergen of The Netherlands. In the following year, 1970, the award went to Professor Samuelson himself. It was an honor richly deserved for his ability and contributions in the forefront of mathematical economics, in positions of professional leadership and responsibility, and as a gifted teacher-writer. His introductory economics textbook is the most successful college book of all time. Fortunately, we are under no oath of silence here, and the publication of these remarks are not subject to his prior censorship. Therefore such accolades are possible.

GALBRAITH
July, 1967

In his journal, Ralph Waldo Emerson speaks of a departed neighbor for whom the minister found eulogy so difficult that he had to confine himself to the remark: "He was good at laying fires."

The arrival of John Kenneth Galbraith's latest book, "The New Industrial State," puts me in a quite different frame of mind. If it were not open to misunderstanding, I would be tempted to say of Galbraith: "Now there's a man for whom it would be a pleasure to deliver a eulogy."

Indeed, why wait? Just as you can't take it with you, so you cannot hear the nice words that posterity will be saying about you. Which is a shame. Tom Sawyer had the great pleasure of attending his own funeral. And why should not Kenneth Galbraith, while now in the prime of life and at the top of the greasy flagpole, be given the tributes that are his due?

As Dr. Samuel Johnson said, on commemorative occasions, one is not under oath. On such occasion praise should be fulsome praise. For this *inter vivos* tribute, let my motto be *nihil nisi bonum.*

THE SCHOLAR AS ARTIST

It is given to few scholars to leave their mark on the language. Galbraith has bequeathed at least two expressions that will survive: the "affluent society" and the "conventional wisdom." I suppose that in England Tawney had a similar impact with his "acquisitive society." But in this country you will have to go back two-thirds of a century to Thorstein Veblen's "Theory of the Leisure Class" for such lasting idioms as "conspicuous consumption," "the higher learning" and the "instinct of craftsmanship."

I know a professor at Yale who thinks that—in scholarly matters —fine writing is a crime. His is a position like that of James Mill, who told his son John that poetry was vastly overrated (but who added that since it is overrated John ought to try his hand at it). My austere friend thinks that ideas and arguments should stand or fall on their bare merits, without, so to speak, the benefit of irrelevant fig leaves.

Certainly if good writing is a crime, it is a crime of which most social scientists are quite innocent. But Galbraith is an exception. He does not write for his brethren within the guild. He is, par excellence, a noneconomist's economist.

Indeed, Galbraith is the philosopher of the younger generation. This spring I participated in a panel before college newspaper editors convened in Washington. For a textbook writer it was a chastening experience. It was not of supply and demand or even of saving and investment that these youths came to talk, but of "private opulence and public squalor." As one Midwest editor put it crudely: "Why is it that business can make profits putting flowers on toilet paper rather than devote its creative energies to reviving our decaying cities?" I had to use fire to fight fire, and reply in Galbraithian terms that it is the business of the citizenry, and not of business, to make it profitable for resources to go into urban redevelopment.

THE SCHOLAR AS BOGEYMAN

If J. K. Galbraith is the Pied Piper of the new generation, he is the bête noire of the corporate world. When the Gallup polls in 1960 veered away from Nixon and toward John Kennedy, rumors swept the money markets of Europe that Galbraith was to replace William McChesney Martin Jr. at the Federal Reserve. And that alone contributed to the panic of October 1960 when hoarders bid up the price of gold to $40 an ounce. An unguarded remark by Galbraith can send the Dow Jones average down $2; his guarded utterance can send it down $5.

According to my old master, the late E. B. Wilson, the Harvard Board of Overseers forgets its place every 37 years on the average and tries to interfere in academic appointments. The last time was when Galbraith was appointed; but good sense and good manners broke through. (The time before the time before that was in President Eliot's day when a historian was barred for religious reasons: there were getting to be "too damned many Unitarians around.")

Now Galbraith is the brightest jewel in the Harvard crown. To get my morning coffee I have to fight my way through the crowds of foreign visitors to Cambridge, bent on seeing the glass flowers and having their picture taken with J. Kenneth Galbraith.

But for his humor, Sydney Smith might have become a bishop. Galbraith, like Lincoln, has managed to live down his native wit. Sage of the Mixed Economy, he is part of our affluence.

MEMORIES
June, 1969

When Diaghilev revived his ballet company he had the original Bakst sets redone in even more vivid colors, explaining, "so that they would be as brilliant as people remember them." Recent events on college campuses have recalled to my inward eye one of the great happenings in my own lifetime.

It took place at Harvard back in the days when giants walked the earth and Harvard Yard. Joseph Schumpeter, Harvard's brilliant economist and social prophet, was to debate Paul Sweezy on "The Future of Capitalism." Wassily Leontief was in the chair as moderator and the Littauer Auditorium could not accomodate the packed house.

Let me set the stage. Schumpeter was a scion of the aristocracy of Franz Josef's Austria. It was Schumpeter who had confessed to three wishes in life: to be the greatest lover in Vienna, the best horseman in Europe, and the greatest economist in the world. "But, unfortunately," as he used to say modestly, "the seat I inherited was never of the topmost caliber."

Half mountebank, half sage, Schumpeter had been the *enfant terrible* of the Austrian school of economists. Steward to an Egyptian princess, owner of a stable of race horses, onetime Finance Minister of Austria, Schumpeter could look at the prospects for bourgeois society with the objectivity of one whose feudal world had come to an end in 1914. His message and vision an be read in his classical work of a quarter century ago, "Capitalism, Socialism, and Democracy."

WHOM THE GODS ENVY

Opposed to the foxy Merlin was young Sir Galahad. Son of an executive of J. P. Morgan's bank, Paul Sweezy was the best that Exeter and Harvard can produce. Tiring of the "gentlemen's C" and of the good life at Locke-Ober's with Lucius Beebe, Sweezy had early established himself as among the most promising of the economists of his generation. But tiring of the conventional wisdom of his age, and spurred on by the events of the Great Depression, Sweezy became one of America's few Marxists. (As he used to say, you could count the noses of American academic economists who were Marxists on the thumbs of your two hands: the late Paul Baran of Stanford; and, in an occasional summer school of unwonted tolerance, Paul Sweezy.)

Unfairly, the gods had given Paul Sweezy, along with a brilliant mind, a beautiful face and wit. With what William Buckley would desperately wish to see in his mirror, Sweezy faced the world. If lightning had struck him that night, people would truly have said that he had incurred the envy of the gods.

So much for the cast. I would have to be a William Hazlitt to recall for you the interchange of wit, the neat parrying and thrust, and all made the more pleasurable by the obvious affection that the two men had for each other despite the polar opposition of their views.

MEETING OF OPPOSITES

Great debaters deserve great moderators, and that night Leontief was in fine form. At the end he fairly summarized the viewpoints expressed.

"The patient is capitalism. What is to be his fate? Our speakers are in fact agreed that the patient is inevitably dying. But the bases of their diagnoses could not be more different.

"On the one hand there is Sweezy, who utilizes the analysis of Marx and of Lenin to deduce that the patient is dying of a malignant cancer. Absolutely no operation can help. The end is foreordained.

"On the other hand, there is Schumpeter. He, too, and rather cheerfully, admits that the patient is dying. (His sweetheart already died in 1914 and his bank of tears has long since run dry.) But to Schumpeter, the patient is dying of a psychosomatic ailment. Not cancer but neurosis is his complaint. Filled with self-hate, he has lost the will to live.

"In this view capitalism is an unlovable system, and what is unlovable will not be loved. Paul Sweezy himself is a talisman and omen of that alienation which will seal the system's doom."

All this I had long forgotten. And a few years ago when I reread Schumpeter's book, I graded him down for his gloomy views on the progress that would be made by the mixed economy—capitalism in an oxygen tent, as Schumpeter put it. His failure to predict the miraculous progress of the postwar years earned Schumpeter a C in my eyes.

However, university happenings reveal an alienation of privileged youth entitling Schumpeter to recount.

TWO REMARKABLE MEN
November, 1969

Nobel Prizes have been given annually since 1901 in the fields of physics, chemistry, medicine and physiology, literature, and peace. But this year, thanks to a fund contributed in honor of its 300th anniversary by the Bank of Sweden (a central bank like our Federal

Reserve), a Nobel Prize in Economic Science has been awarded for the first time.

In choosing Ragnar Frisch of the University of Oslo and Jan Tinbergen of the Netherlands School of Economics, the Swedish Academy of Sciences has started the new annual award off in fine style. Economists all over the world have applauded their choice of these two men of genius.

I use the word genius in its eighteenth-century sense—not to imply a transcendental scholar who is beyond human capability, but rather to designate men of the highest originality and versatility. In honoring these two econometricians, we are calling attention to what everybody within the profession of economics has known for three decades now—namely, that the scholarly subject of economics has become a highly mathematical and statistical discipline. Frisch and Tinbergen have each been pioneers in the development of modern economics.

REWARDS AND RECOGNITIONS

In the areas of the hard sciences, the Nobel Prizes have generally been deemed fairly chosen. All the great names are there: Einstein, Planck, Rutherford, Bohr, Schrödinger and Heisenberg, Dirac, Fermi, Woodward Watson and Crick.

When it comes to Peace, the Norwegian awarders have a more difficult assignment; and indeed in some years the authorities have felt obliged to pass out no awards. Literature too offers some real problems. If memory serves, some great writers—such as Tolstoi and Proust—were passed over in their lifetimes whereas some obscure Scandinavian and Latin American writers have been honored.

In medicine, Sigmund Freud never quite made the grade: could he not at least have received a consolation prize for his skill in literature? And since I am passing judgment on the universe, may I suggest that there must be one of my readers with a paltry $2 million to contribute in order to set up a Nobel Prize in mathematics. It is a shame that Poincaré, Hilbert, Birkhoff, Littlewood, Wiener, Kolmogorof and von Neumann have not been accorded the distinction that they so richly merited.

Of course it can be argued that all distinctions are invidious; that they subtract from rather than add to the sum total of human happiness. According to this view one man's triumph is another man's disappointment. I took little stock in this notion until I was brought up short in reading about the life of Lindemann—Lord Cherwell,

Churchill's scientific brain-truster. Once, upon receiving a certain prize, he was heard to say in an Oxford Senior Common Room: "What would be the point of getting an honor like this if one couldn't picture the discomfiture of particular rivals who were hoping they'd be the lucky ones?" Imagine thinking in those terms. And if one did so, imagine confessing to it.

SCIENCE AND ART

Economics stands between physics and literature. That is its peculiar charm. At the same time that it offers analytical problems difficult enough to tax the finest brain, economics deals with the pressing policy issues that concern man and society.

Although primarily scholars' scholars, these men have been passionately interested in public policy. Independently of Keynes, Frisch developed many of the modern models used to tame the business cycle. Tinbergen was one of the first macromodel builders who attempted to measure statistically the dynamic relations that drive our economic system forward through time, an endeavor that is still very much alive today.

What is the personality required for genius? Who can say? Each was splendidly endowed by nature with brain and drive. But where Frisch is the dashing prima donna, Tinbergen is a gentle soul with an abhorrence for power—truly a "humanist saint." Yet Tinbergen was long the chief government economist in Holland—their Walter Heller, so to speak.

By American standards I guess that both men might be called socialists. Yet their political views had nothing to do with their being chosen. And by helping to give us the knowledge to make the mixed economy work, these men, in my opinion, have done more for the preservation of freedom in the world than all the ideologues of laissez faire.

WHO'S WHO IN ECONOMICS
January, 1970

They say you can't follow the game without a program. But it is the hardest thing in the world for someone who is outside a profession to get an informed view about its pecking order.

This was brought home to me a few years ago when a colleague found he had to have a new and delicate operation. He was given his choice between two well-known surgeons, X and Y. But how was he to decide? He had never gone beyond a sixth-grade hygiene course and even then, he asserts, he lacked talent for the subject.

By chance he learned that Dr. Y was a dashing fellow. Since my colleague is anything but that by temperament, he chose Dr. X by elimination. The story has a happy ending, which is why I am telling it. But when I happened to recall it in a lockerroom colloquy with some topflight surgeons, they slapped their thighs with amusement at the notion that anyone could regard the two men in question as remotely comparable. They all agreed that Dr. X was unquestionably better than Dr. Y.

Now, it is the same in economics, and I suppose for that matter in plumbing or tiddlywinks. *Within* the profession we know exactly how people and places are to be rated. True, there is not 100 per cent agreement, but the thing that is surprising is how close rather than how discordant are these guild valuations.

WHERE CAMELOT IS

First, until recently the best economics scholars have tended to be in the universities. To mention this may seem to be a banality. For where else, you might ask, could they be? Actually, however, in countries like the Soviet Union, the best economists would not dream of being simply professors. The professors there tend to be mere ideologues, useful only to indoctrinate the young into the pieties of Marxism. The real scholars are found in the government institutes or academies, where genuine research can be done. Moreover, even in our own culture, the university as the preferred site for the exploration of scholarly knowledge may be a transitory thing. Harvard, before president Eliot's day, was only a finishing school for the elite. Under the pressures of student activism today—and I am reporting, not complaining about, a trend—universities may revert once again to that status.

A second fact about professional life is that, in recent years, high-quality work has been maintained in numerous universities. Again, this is not necessarily a normal pattern. In France, a young academic commutes from Paris to his provincial university and dreams of the day when he will be called back to a chair in the metropolis. And as recently as World War II, the only really proper old school tie in economics was that of Harvard, just as in mathematics it was that of Princeton. And as the famous Flexner Report greatly reduced the differential in quality between the first and the 50th medical schools, so academic competition has in recent years created strong centers in economics on both coasts and at many places in between.

THE NEW ESTABLISHMENT

Indeed, it might be argued that there is too great a uniformity economics today, too little variety. After a recent lecture at a Southern university, a senior came up to me, saying, "Sir, I want to do graduate work in economics, but I don't go for this new mathematical and statistical lingo. Where should I apply?"

I was truly stumped. In the old days, there was always the University of Wisconsin with its institutionalist orientation. Or there was Berkeley, Calif., where Leo Rogin and Robert Brady preached a radical populism. But today there seems to be no hole to hide in—everywhere you go, you encounter three-stage least-squares correlation or worse.

However homogeneous modern economics might appear to an outsider, an insider can always point to the schismatic University of Chicago (with its Rochester business school, UCLA and Virginia farm clubs) for a refreshing departure from the new orthodoxy of the "mixed economy." Also there is Kenneth Galbraith, though his constituency is the world, not the groves of academe. And we can look forward to the day when the question-raising by the new radical economists, who now number some hundreds, will have produced a vigorous tree of research and knowledge.

Science is an open club whose kings reign on short leases. As I write, some young worker is killing off a king, to which we say, "The king is dead, long live the king."

JOSEPH SCHUMPETER
April, 1970

Just as there is a stock exchange on which stocks and bonds are quoted, so too there is the bourse of intellectual opinion on which literary and scientific reputations are evaluated.

For a long time Henry James was quoted at a severe discount. Canny investors could have taken a flyer in him for fabulous capital gains. But beware! Even T. S. Eliot could not revive Rudyard Kipling, and the long-awaited George Meredith comeback never got off the ground.

Just because prices fluctuate, do not think the process is a random walk, lacking all rhyme and reason and subject only to dart-board strategy. For one thing, after a writer dies he tends for a time to go into a decline. If not at once, after a few old scores can be risklessly paid off.

It is just twenty years since Joseph Schumpeter died. Although it is not my practice to tout profitable speculations, today I'd like to suggest that Schumpeter's diagnosis of the probable decay of capitalism deserves a new reading in our own time. The general reader cannot do better then begin with his 1942 "Capitalism, Socialism, and Democracy."

SOUR SMELL OF SUCCESS

Nothing that has happened in recent years at Berkeley or Harvard would have come as a surprise to those who have absorbed this work. And if there are good clubs in the great beyond, one can picture Schumpeter—a spry 87-year-old by this time, Martini glass in hand —reading The New York Review of Books and chuckling with clinical amusement. Only his Viennese veneer keeps him from saying, "I told you so. The successes and rationalism of bourgeois capitalism will breed a swarm of discontented intellectuals—to fan the flames of hostility toward an efficient but unlovable system with no mystique to protect it."

George Bernard Shaw wisecracked, "He who can, does. He who cannot, teaches." Schumpeter, also something of a believer in the superman thesis, gave this canard an extra twist, asserting in effect: And he who cannot teach, agitates.

For all his tone of objectivity, Schumpeter was a reactionary. But as Holmes said of Spengler, he is the kind of rascal who gives you a run for your money. His pages are larded with insights, as for example:

- Monopoly pricing and restrictions on output "are often unavoidable incidents of a long-term process of [innovational] expansion, which they protect rather than impede. There is no more of paradox in this than there is in saying that motorcars are traveling faster than they otherwise would *because* they are provided with brakes."

- "... Precisely because of the fundamental stability of the social structure ... the intellectuals were driven into a desperate radicalism and ... criminal violence. Theirs was the kind of radicalism whose intensity is in inverse proportion to its practical possibilities, the radicalism of impotence."

Schumpeter is referring here, not to Weathermen or black militants, but to life under the Russian czars. This cool conservative goes on to say: "Marx's glowing phrases and chiliastic prophecy were exactly what they needed to get out of the dreary desert of nihilism."

MIND SHRINKERS

I was reminded of all this on a recent trip to England. All the Sunday papers there carried favorable reviews of a new series of Fontana paperbacks, each devoted to a "master" who had "made" the modern mind.

What a crew the first five were! No one begrudges a pivotal role to Camus. But surely it is a libel on any age to claim Marcuse, Fanon, Lévi-Strauss, and Guevara for its gurus.

Herbert Marcus: now there's a great short sale for you. And as for Guevara: nobody could be as spoiled, incompetent, and mindless as his admiring biographer makes him out to be. Obviously, here is a case where the CIA has commissioned a *reductio ad absurdum.* But it will never work. We do not remember Robin Hood for his efficiency, and Guevara, like Roland, will live forever precisely *by virtue of* his incompetence.

Fanon, like de Sade, radiates to a wave length in the human soul —not to be confounded with *mind.* The few weeks that Lévi-Strauss spent in the bush were quite enough for his prepared Cartesian mind. Since Stephen Leacock died, I have encountered nothing so ... so rare as his new algebra cookery. One doubts his vogue will outlast the midi.

But there I go. A disgruntled intellectual, with tongue out of joint because no economist was included in the series. No Keynes. No Schumpeter. No, not even a Galbraith.

FRANK KNIGHT, 1885–1972

July, 1972

One of America's most influential intellectuals died recently. But few people would recognize his name.

Frank Knight was professor of economics at the University of Chicago for half a century. He never retired; when he died in his 80s his fountain pen was still full. Knight was the founder of the Chicago School in economics: if he was Abraham, Henry Simons was Isaac and Milton Freidman is Jacob.

Although, as far as I know, Knight was never invited to the White House, you can see his influence on Washington in the decisions that Secretary George Schultz will be making on foreign-exchange rates and in the mordant wit of Herbert Stein, chairman of the Council of Economic Advisers. But this is only the visible peak of the iceberg. Even radical economists, as I shall argue, bear the stamp of Frank Knight's thought.

CRACKER-BARREL SOCRATES

How did The New Yorker miss doing a profile on so singular a personality? A profound philsopher and superb economic technician, he was also the village atheist and a sage of the Will Rogers vintage. These days professors tend to come from Exeter Academy or the Bronx High School of Science. Knight was of that turn-of-the-century generation who—like Karl and Arthur Compton and Wesley Mitchell—came off the farm.

He used to say in his squeaky voice that he became an economist because his feet hurt him following the plow. Perhaps nearer the truth was the fact that when he was a graduate student in philosophy at Cornell, he was given an ultimatum: "Stop talking so much, or leave the philosophy department." This gave Knight no choice but to gravitate down into economics. (It also made him an authority on the laws of talk, as in his dictum: "Sociology is the science of talk, and there is only one law in sociology. Bad talk drives out good.")

Frank Knight was a skeptic who doubted the ability of man through government to better his condition. Capitalism—alas!—is the best we can settle for. Thus, if Doctor Friedman is one of those optimists who thinks that capitalism is the best of all possible worlds, Dr. Knight was one of those pessimists who is afraid that this is indeed the case.

I shall not argue here the issue of determinism vs. free will. But if you believe that man can hurry forward the clock of evolution—that a Marx or Lenin can advance the date of the inevitable revolution—then you must concede man can retard that clock. From 1932–1945, faith in the market-pricing mechanism as the organizer of the economy sold at a discount.

THE COUNTER-ROVOLUTION

It was the priceless contribution of Frank Knight and the Chicago School to remind us of the market's merits. This is a message that falls on deaf ears in the common rooms of Britain's ancient universities. But it is one whose relevance a Russian, Yugoslav or Czech can understand.

And make no mistake about it. Rumors of the death of the market, like those of Twain's death, are greatly exaggerated. In Britain and Scandinavia, Socialist governments have in the last quarter of a century often been displaced from office. In America, too, the pendulum swings. The role of Frank Knight in this counter-revolution is pivotal.

A central feature of Knight's thought is his antipathy toward the mixed economy. As he put it, a planned economy is simply a well-managed penitentiary. It was this simplistic element that came to disillusion me with my boyhood idol. And I fear it made Knight a poor prophet of events that were to come after 1932, as when in a moment of despair, he declared that the only choice was between Communism and Fascism and he for one preferred Communism.

Knight's antipathy toward the prevalent post-New Deal world is not unlike that of a Herbert Marcuse. Many of the New Left are Knight without the market.

As a sage has said: "The ideas of economists and political philosophers, both when they are right and when they are wrong, are more powerful than is commonly understood. Indeed, the world is ruled by little else. Practical men, who believe themselves to be quite exempt from any intellectual influences, are usually the slave of some defunct economist . . . I am sure that the power of vested interests is vastly exaggerated, compared with the gradual encroachment of ideas."

Although, as J. M. Keynes also said, "in the long run we are all dead," Frank Knight lives on.